SPOI
THE

With clim
inent, any
concerns
how to in
Managemer
tal theory
how sport
the import
munities.
occupies i
related to

- facilitie:
- finance
- leadersł
- marketi
- operatic
- stakeholder relations;
- strategic planning.

Including contributions from leading academics and practitioners, *Sport Management and the Natural Environment* is the perfect foundation text for any course touching on environmental issues or social responsibility in sport, and essential reading for any sport manager looking to improve their professional practice.

Jonathan M. Casper is an Associate Professor and Sport Management Program Coordinator in the Department of Parks, Recreation, and Tourism Management in the College of Natural Resources at North Carolina State University, USA. His research program focuses on enhancing quality of life through sport. His research in this field relates to informing sport organizations about better integrating sustainability efforts into organizational operations, marketing, and fan/participant engagement. Dr Casper has published in leading peer-reviewed academic journals specific to sport and sustainability and presented his findings at international conferences. He also serves as a consultant for collegiate athletics departments and sport sponsors on sustainability initiatives.

Michael E. Pfahl is an Associate Professor and Undergraduate Program Coordinator in the Department of Sports Administration in the College of Business at Ohio University, USA. His current research interests are primarily conducted from a qualitative perspective and include the convergence of media, technology, and sport, environmentalism and sport, and human resource issues in sport organizations. Dr Pfahl has conducted consulting activities for several different sport and non-sport organizations around the world. These activities include consulting related to environmental efforts for the Cleveland Cavaliers and sponsorship for the Lamphun Warrior Football Club (Thailand), among others. He has published his research in top academic journals and presented at conferences and events around the world.

SPORT MANAGEMENT AND THE NATURAL ENVIRONMENT

Theory and practice

*Edited by Jonathan M. Casper
and Michael E. Pfahl*

Routledge
Taylor & Francis Group

LONDON AND NEW YORK

First published 2015
by Routledge
2 Park Square, Milton Park, Abingdon, Oxon OX14 4RN

and by Routledge
711 Third Avenue, New York, NY 10017

Routledge is an imprint of the Taylor & Francis Group, an informa business

© 2015 J. Casper & M. Pfahl

British Library Cataloguing-in-Publication Data
A catalogue record for this book is available from the British Library

Library of Congress Cataloging in Publication Data
Casper, Jonathan M.
Sport management and the natural environment : theory and practice /
Jonathan M. Casper & Michael E. Pfahl.
pages cm
Includes bibliographical references and index.
1. Sports administration. 2. Sports--Environmental aspects. 3. Social
responsibility of business. I. Pfahl, Michael E. II. Title.
GV713.C37 2015
796.06'9--dc23
2014043130

ISBN: 978-0-415-71540-9 (hbk)
ISBN: 978-0-415-71542-3 (pbk)
ISBN: 978-1-315-88183-6 (ebk)

Typeset in Bembo
by GreenGate Publishing Services, Tonbridge, Ken

MIX
Paper from
responsible sources
FSC   FSC® C013056
www.fsc.org

Printed and bound in Great Britain by
TJ International Ltd, Padstow, Cornwall

CONTENTS

FIGURES

TABLES

CASE STUDIES

BIOGRAPHIES

Editors

Jonathan M. Casper is an Associate Professor and Sport Management Program Coordinator in the Department of Parks, Recreation, and Tourism Management in the College of Natural Resources at North Carolina State University. His research program focuses on enhancing quality of life through sport. His research in this field relates to informing sport organizations about better integrating sustainability efforts into organizational operations, marketing, and fan/participant engagement. Dr Casper has published in leading peer-reviewed academic journals specific to sport and sustainability and presented his findings at international conferences. He also serves as a consultant for collegiate athletics departments and sport sponsors on sustainability initiatives.

Michael E. Pfahl is an Associate Professor and Undergraduate Program Coordinator in the Department of Sports Administration in the College of Business at Ohio University. His current research interests are primarily conducted from a qualitative perspective and include the convergence of media, technology, and sport, environmentalism and sport, and human resource issues in sport organizations. Dr Pfahl has conducted consulting activities for several different sport and non-sport organizations around the world. These activities include consulting related to environmental efforts for the Cleveland Cavaliers and sponsorship for the Lamphun Warrior Football Club (Thailand), among others. He has published his research in top academic journals and presented in conferences and events around the world.

Authors

Kyle Bunds is an Assistant Professor of Sport and Sustainable Community Development in the Department of Parks, Recreation, and Tourism Management in the College of Natural Resources at North Carolina State University. His research focuses primarily on the intersections of sport, development, and the environment. Particularly germane to this project is his focus on the development and policy evaluation of environmentally focused organizations. Dr Bunds has published in top academic journals and presented at international conferences on research specific to sport, development, and environmental evaluation.

Ryan Cabinte (JD, MBA) is an Associate Dean at the Presidio Graduate School. He serves as counsel to numerous social enterprises and mission-driven organizations, particularly in the areas of strategy and law.

Chris Chard is an Associate Professor at Brock University. His research interests focus on the business of sport (sport finance), with an interest in understanding how sport organizations can increase operational capacity. Specifically, he has focused recent research on the sustainability of sport enterprises using Triple Bottom Line (TBL) theory to advance understandings on how to maximize capacity and make sport organizations sustainable from a financial, environmental, and social perspective.

Lynn Crowe is a Professor of Environmental Management at Sheffield Hallam University. An ecologist and planner by training, Lynn has a particular interest in enabling more people to enjoy their natural environment more often, and the public benefits to be gained from recreation in green spaces. She has been involved with many different public agencies in the UK. She has just completed two terms as a Board Member of Natural England. Previously she was a Member of the Peak District National Park Authority, and has also worked closely with the Forestry Commission's social science research team. At SHU, Lynn was responsible for the management of the Countryside Recreation Network—a network of 28 government agencies and other organizations involved in research collaboration and the dissemination of good practice throughout the UK and Ireland (www.countrysiderecreation.org.uk) between 2003 and 2011.

Yuhei Inoue is an Assistant Professor of Sport Management in the School of Kinesiology at the University of Minnesota. His primary research interest is to understand the ability of sport to serve as a means of community development and a solution to social and environmental issues. Dr Inoue's work has been published in peer-reviewed journals, such as the *Journal of Sport Management*, *Sport Management Review*, *Tourism Management*, and the *Journal of Business Ethics*. He has also made several presentations at international academic conferences, such as the annual meetings of the North American Society for Sport Management, the Sport Marketing Association, and the Strategic Management Society. Dr Inoue received his Ph.D. in Business Administration from Temple University, his M.A.

in Sport and Exercise Management from the Ohio State University, and his B.A. in Sociology from the University of Tsukuba.

Timothy B. Kellison is an Assistant Professor in the Department of Tourism, Recreation and Sport Management at the University of Florida. His primary research interests are organizational theory and public policy. Within these fields, his research has focused on the politics of sport facility financing, urban and regional planning, environmentally sustainable design, and human resources management. The unifying theme of his scholarship is the study of the ways in which sport organizations act as community leaders with respect to various sociopolitical issues. Kellison's work on sport and the environment has been published in peer-reviewed journals including the *Journal of Sport Management*, *Sport Management Review*, and *European Sport Management Quarterly*.

Courtney Keogh is a graduate of the Bachelor of Sport Management and the M.A. (Sport Management) from Brock University in St Catharines, Ontario, Canada. Her research focuses on environmental sustainability, particularly the advances in Canada's top golf courses.

Izabel Loinaz (MBA) is the CEO and principal consultant of Spring Partners Inc, operating in the fields of sports, recreation, health, and sustainability. Ms Loinaz is a member of the teaching team of the Business of Sports and Sustainability certificate course and Research Affiliate at the Presidio Graduate School.

Cheryl Mallen is an Associate Professor at Brock University. Her research focuses on sport facility and event management with a specific focus on environmental sustainability performance—including tools to measure performance, developing understandings concerning barriers to performance, and strategies to enhance an evolving level of environmental performance, including best practices, challenges, trends, and required competencies. Also, her research interests extend to knowledge transfer processes and sport ethics.

Adel Mansurov holds a Bachelor of Sport Management from Brock University, St. Catharines, Ontario, Canada. He went on to the Master's program in Sport Management and is currently completing law school at the University of Ottawa, Canada.

Brian P. McCullough is an Assistant Professor and Coordinator of the Sport Sustainability Leadership specialization in the Master in Sport Administration and Leadership graduate program at Seattle University. His research focuses on environmental sustainability within the sport industry with particular interest in understanding the decision-making processes of upper management in sport organizations to implement environmental sustainability initiatives, how those programs are deployed within a sport context, and to further understand how sport can be used as a vehicle to influence spectators' everyday environmental behaviors.

Lisa Delpy Neirotti founded the sport management program at the George Washington University in 1991. Since then she has established a strong curriculum in the Business School at both the undergraduate and graduate level. Based on her work with sport mega-events, specifically the Olympic Games, Dr Neirotti co-developed the Green Sport Scorecard to help educate sport teams, organizations, venues, and events on actions that could reduce their environmental impact and to measure achievements over time. She is also the co-author of the *Ultimate Guide to Sports Marketing* and oversees the GW Sport Philanthropy Certificate.

Sheila Nguyen is the Director of the #3 globally ranked Sport Management Postgraduate Program at Deakin University (Melbourne, Australia). Sheila has a Ph.D. in Sport Management from Florida State University (USA), specializing in corporate social orientation and stakeholder management, with ongoing research interests including corporate social responsibility, environmental stewardship, measurement, and research design. She has had experience working with licensing/marketing (PGA Tour, USA) and corporate consulting (William Morris Agency, Beverly Hills, USA), and she worked as part of the broadcasting team at the 2010 Asian Games (Guangzhou, China) with clients such as NHK, Al-Jazeera, KBS, and CCTV. Sheila is a member of Baseball Victoria's Board of Directors and is part of the Committee for Melbourne business leadership program. She passionately advocates for environmental leadership within the sport industry and its communities, is Leadership in Energy and Environmental Design (LEED) Green Associate certified (since 2011), and recently passed her National Australian Built Environment Rating System (NABERS) assessor exam.

Larissa Prevett joined CLT envirolaw as a Junior Associate in 2013 and assists clients in the development and implementation of strategic sustainability solutions, including the sustainable management system for the events sector, ISO20121. She holds an LLB in English Law with Hispanic Law and an LLM specializing in Competition Law, both from University College London. Previously, Larissa gained experience in procurement operations at the multinational Tata Consultancy Services based in Latin America, and she has also worked in London at BASIS (the British Association for Sustainable Sport).

Austin Stahl is a recent graduate of Journalism in the Honors Tutorial College (HTC) at Ohio University with certificates in Entrepreneurship and Environmental Studies. He is also the founder of Archer Technologies, a semifinalist for the 2014 Ohio Student Clean Energy Challenge, one of 10 teams selected in the state and the first ever from Ohio University. He was nominated for a Green Innovation Award at the Ohio University Innovation Awards Gala for his efforts. Austin is currently researching best practices in the B2B marketing space and assisting Ecolibrium Solar in the creation and implementation of a strategic marketing plan.

Colleen Theron is qualified as a solicitor in England, Wales, Scotland, and South Africa, and holds an LLM in environmental law from the University of Aberdeen (with distinction). Colleen is also the founder and director of CLT envirolaw, a niche sustainability company providing specialist advice to companies and directors on sustainability issues. She lectures at Birkbeck University and is a director of Finance against Trafficking. Colleen is the co-author of *Strategic Sustainable Procurement: Law and Best Practice* and has published broadly on CSR issues. She is currently working on a research project of return on investment on sustainability in the sports sector.

Sylvia Trendafilova is an Assistant Professor in the Department of Kinesiology, Recreation and Sport Studies at the University of Tennessee (Knoxville, TN, USA). Professor Trendafilova's research focuses on the sustainable management of sport and explores corporate social responsibility and the benefits these activities have on different sport organizations. Her work is informed by theories from political economy, sociology, and behavioral analysis. She has presented at national and international conferences. Dr Trendafilova has published in peer-reviewed journals, and has contributed to M. Parent and T. Slack's book *International Perspectives on the Management of Sport* and to J. L. Paramio, K. Babiak, and G. Walters's book *The Routledge Handbook of Sport and Corporate Social Responsibility*.

FOREWORD

The intersection of the sports industry and environmental stewardship provides a unique opportunity for creating added business value while at the same time holding the potential to persuade millions of people to make the kind of cultural shifts that are urgently needed to mitigate the risks associated with climate change and other ecological challenges.

How do sports teams, venues, and leagues create added value through sustainability? First, they are collectively saving millions of dollars in operating expenses by lowering their energy, water, and waste management costs through conservation, recycling, and composting programs. They are also creating and enhancing corporate sponsorship programs through sustainability-focused partnerships. Not only does this generate sponsorship revenue, it drives authentic greening initiatives at sports venues while encouraging the global supply chain of sports to respond to new market demands for ecologically preferable products. It also enhances a team's brand by exposing their fans to socially responsible environmental messaging. All of these benefits generate a win for business as well as a win for the environment.

The sustainability journey for professional sports teams got off to a quiet start over 20 years ago. The NFL was the first league to get into the game when it started greening its jewel event, the Super Bowl. One of the first venue recycling programs was implemented at Super Bowl XXVIII in 1994 at the Georgia Dome. The Philadelphia Eagles created the first comprehensive professional sports team sustainability program called Go Green in 2004. One year later, in 2005, MLB Commissioner, Bud Selig, quietly launched a league-wide sustainability initiative in collaboration with the Natural Resources Defense Council (NRDC), which was not publicly announced until 2007. In 2008 and 2009 NRDC launched greening programs with the NBA, the NHL, MLS, and the USTA, and in 2010, in collaboration with Paul Allen's Vulcan Corporation, NRDC co-founded the Green

Sports Alliance, which made its public debut in 2011. The GSA was launched with six professional sports teams from six leagues all based in the Pacific Northwest. Since then, the Alliance has grown to over 300 teams and venues representing 20 leagues, and it is now branching out internationally as well. Even NASCAR has developed a robust sustainability program, which includes recycling, renewable energy, and alternative fuels, and a new, environmentally oriented electric vehicle race series called Formula E was launched in 2014. In July 2014, the NHL released the first sustainability report ever produced by a professional sports league. Clearly, professional sports is embracing sustainability and making it a part of a new way of doing business. And so are colleges: solar panels, recycling and composting programs, energy efficiency, fan education, and water conservation have been embraced at colleges throughout the United States, growing the sports greening movement more broadly.

Sports is big business and a huge cultural influence, whether at the professional, collegiate, or youth level. While only 13 percent of Americans say they follow science, 71 percent of adult Americans say they follow sports. Scientists and environment advocates have been trying for years to get our attention from government and business elites about the impending dangers we face due to our insatiable appetite for all types of material goods and our reliance on fossil fuels. Now is the time for professional and collegiate sports to step up to the plate and start using its influence to show that there's a better way to play, one that makes sound business sense while encouraging millions of fans to take practical steps to take better care of the planet.

Professional sports has historically played an important role in helping us face many of society's big challenges. This influence goes well beyond helping us define our sense of community or providing a weekend escape from our daily reality. Sports has led us through some tough issues and times. Think of the influence that Jackie Robinson had on the civil rights movement, the role sports played in helping us move beyond the September 11th attacks, or the role that Title IX has played for women in our society. Most recently, sports is being drawn into the issues surrounding marriage equality and domestic violence. Clearly, the sports industry is in a position to use its influence to shape our future. Sustainability provides another opportunity for sport to lead and for the people teaching and studying this material to help develop a winning game plan to fight for our economic and physical wellbeing. The stakes have never been higher and the need to act more urgent.

The days of denying climate change have passed. We cannot stick our heads in the sand and ignore the problem, doing little to nothing about it, continuing business as usual. Finally, the world is waking up to the fact that things need to change and sports is helping to raise that awareness. Indeed, sports may hold our best opportunity to do what the political, scientific, and environmental communities haven't been able to do for the past 30 years.

This book covers a broad range of topics that will provide a strong foundation on sports and the environment. The future belongs to you and the future generations more than to those currently in positions of power and influence today. The intersection of sport and the environment will play a large role in your future. You can stay on the sidelines and watch it unfold or you can get in the game.

Scott Jenkins
Stadium General Manager, Atlanta Falcons /
AMB Sports & Entertainment Group
Chairman, Green Sports Alliance

PREFACE

This book is guided by mainstream natural environment research in sport and business. Its central departure point is the recognized need to address environmental issues in the world of sport and the unique social, economic, and political spaces sport occupies in society. This has resulted in the identification of key managerial issues related to sport and the natural environment. The book examines the impact of the natural environment across the primary functions of a sport organization. These issues include the strategic need to incorporate the natural environment into sport organization operations, the operational needs of a sport organization in relation to natural environment issues (e.g., facility design and management), the related accounting and financial challenges related to environmental issues, and the marketing and communication of environmental issues including the relationships between and among stakeholders (e.g., fans, suppliers, local community, local government).

The first section of the book focuses on the foundational aspects of sport and the environment. Chapter 1 provides a summary of the key reasons why sport managers are becoming increasingly aware of the environmental impact of their operations. It highlights the need to take action in this area and the rationale for why sport managers need to address environmental issues as part of their overall strategic planning. Chapter 2 outlines theoretical foundations for understanding pro-environmental behavior within sport originations and how this understanding can be used for influencing behavior. Chapter 3 is a unique and important chapter for sport management educators as it focuses on the integration of environmental issues into sport management education, an underserved area of emphasis in the field.

The second section of the book contains several chapters dedicated to strategic sport and the natural environment issues. Chapter 4 explores three broad management implications: awareness, knowledge, and action. These issues are explored from the sport manager perspective and focus on their direct impact on environmental actions and planning. Chapter 5 provides a foundation on the origins of sport environmental initiatives and the thought leaders that follow. Chapter 6 explores how environmental policies fit within larger strategic processes relevant to sport management and development. Chapter 7 brings together various aspects of corporate social responsibility in relation to the environment, mostly because this is a common area for sport managers to take public action related to environmental issues. In Chapter 8, the web of a sport organization's stakeholders are linked to their role in the process of addressing environmental issues because they play a significant role in determining a sport organization's actions. Chapter 9 explores the process sport managers undertake in identifying, addressing, and evaluating environmental actions through metrics.

The third section begins with Chapter 10, where marketing efforts and strategies are examined in relation to environmental efforts. Chapter 11 focuses on the ways in which sport managers can communicate with stakeholders as they develop and implement environmental strategies. Chapter 12 explores current and future ways that environmental efforts can be communicated, emphasizing the growing use of digital space.

The fourth section of the book focuses on financial operations focusing on budgeting and the *bottom line*. Chapter 13 focuses on the key development questions about the financial aspects of incorporating the natural environment into sport organizations' operations. Chapter 14 outlines how revenue generation can occur in environmental activities through sponsorship efforts.

The final section focuses on facility management in relation to the environment. Chapter 15 looks at strategic environmental planning efforts related to the environment and how different types and levels of events can incorporate environmental actions into them. Chapter 16 focuses on how current facility design, planning, construction, and maintenance are taking environmental issues into account.

The main purpose of the book is to accomplish the following goals:

- Produce a high quality introductory text dedicated to the study of the natural environment and its relation to managing sport organizations.
- Present theory, concepts, and principles from sport, environmental studies, and management and apply them within sport management contexts.
- Be the market leader text on sport and the natural environment and serve as a reference for the subject within library texts.
- Stimulate new empirical and theoretical work in the area.

The goals of this book are to:

- provide a broad view of the ways in which the environmental issue touches all aspects of a sport organization;
- illustrate ways in which organizational units can work to create area-level and organizational-level goals, objectives, strategies, and tactics related to environmental issues;

- illustrate examples of how sport organization personnel dealt with environmental issues;
- provide a departure point or foundation for scholars, practitioners, and students to further explore environmental issues in sport.

ACKNOWLEDGEMENTS

Dr Casper would like to thank his sister, Kristin, for inspiring him to take on this world of research and his children (Kali and Bryce) whose environment we are trying to protect. He would also like to thank his colleagues at the College of Natural Resources for fostering a culture that makes this topic so relevant.

Dr Pfahl would like to thank his family (Nichakorn, Natalie, and Amelia) for supporting him each and every day. Additionally, he would like to thank all of his family, friends, and colleagues who work in the environmental space in an effort to improve our existence with(in) nature.

SECTION I

Theoretical foundations

Sport and the natural environment

1

INTRODUCTION

Sport and the natural environment

Jonathan M. Casper and Michael E. Pfahl

Why sport and the environment?

Sport, in all its forms, creates an environmental footprint like everything else in life. Additionally, sport is also interwoven in culture and society and the sport industry can use its unique influence to provide much-needed business leadership in ecology and sustainable practices (Natural Resources Defense Council (NRDC) 2013). The tangible effects of sport organization environmental actions can help in supporting public health, reducing pollution, protecting habitats, saving energy and water, environmental behavior change in sport fans' lives, and far beyond. These effects have initiated a sport environmental movement with two broad goals: to reduce the ecological footprint of sports activities and to exploit the popularity of sports to raise environmental awareness in general (Schmidt 2006).

The sport ecological footprint is resultant of sport origination functions (e.g., general operation, hosting events, and maintaining facilities) and spectator impact (attendance and viewing). For example, millions of fans attend sporting events, meaning millions of people travel to and from games, most of them in cars or by other public transport. Upon arrival numerous non-food items are purchased requiring production, packaging, transport, storage, etc. (e.g., foam fingers, hats, magazines). Fans at sport facilities produce varying levels of waste after each sporting event (e.g., paper wrappers, cups, food waste both in and outside the stadium). While fan-produced waste often gets the majority of attention, even the athletes themselves generate waste when they play. Water bottles, game notes, wrappers, etc. are produced by the athletes and add to the overall waste footprint at an event.

At the same time, sport provides a visible platform from which to speak and educate about environmental issues. Sport is a significant part of many cultures (Horne 2006), and the constant attention it receives means that it is a useful platform to address and to publicize environmental efforts in a general way (e.g., benefits of recycling) as well as specific measures (e.g., how you can recycle at our stadium). Sport fans have an affinity for sport organizations both psycho- logically and consumptively (e.g., their mood after a big win; their willingness to support sponsor products). Therefore, sporting organizations and events can serve as environmental platforms to not only educate fans but also to influ- ence sustainable behaviors within their everyday lives (e.g., Seattle Mariners' Sustainable Saturdays).

Taking environmental action through sport is a significant step towards improv- ing the impact of sport on the environment. Although academic literature on sport and the natural environment has grown significantly over the last decade, most of the research to date regarding sport and the natural environment is published in a variety of academic journals related to the areas of tourism, recreation, and sport management (e.g., Casper et al. 2012; Elliot and Delpy Neirotti 2008; Hums et al. 1999; Inoue and Kent 2012; Jin et al. 2011; Lenskyj 1998; Pfahl 2010, 2011, 2013). The scope of environmental issues in relation to sport is like those in many other businesses and organizations (e.g., energy, water, waste, carbon/GHG, trans- portation, supply chain footprints (Sharma 2000; Sharma and Vrendenburg 1998; Shrivastava 1995)). Given the complexity of the issues involved, scholars have used the traditional business press to study and to theorize about strategic issues related to the environment (Esty and Winston 2006; Fineman 1997). In the business litera- ture, the natural environment is studied based on strategic implications (Hart 1995; Hart and Milstein 2003), changes in organizational culture (Govindarajulu and Daily 2004; Harris and Crane 2002), and operational and systemic issues (Kitazawa and Sarkis 2000).

The challenge facing sport scholars and sport professionals alike is similar to that of other organizational personnel where the sheer scope, depth, and breadth of environmental issues need to be understood and addressed. To date, there has not been a comprehensive effort to tie together all the threads within the discus- sion of sport and the natural environment. Some studies are focused on particular aspects of this area (Inoue and Kent 2012; Jin et al. 2011; Mallen et al. 2010; Mallen and Chard 2011; Pfahl 2011; Schmidt 2006), but do not take into account the multiperspectival, holistic, and multi-functional nature of sport, the environ- ment, organizational management, and stakeholder engagement. In sport, given the relatively new interest in the topic, little research has focused on synthesizing the broad aspects of natural environment issues in relation to organizational oper- ations. Additionally, since most sport organizations function as service-oriented organizations, the operations and stakeholders involved can be very different than most business operations. There is a need to examine the natural environment and sport from a broad and holistic perspective. It is imperative to outline the intercon- nected environmental elements within sport organizations (e.g., marketing, facility management) in order to better focus strategic planning for environmental issues (e.g., goals, objectives) as well as the resulting tactics (e.g., energy audits).

Sport and the natural environment: perspectives

A myriad number of ways to address environmental issues exist and are dependent upon the situation or context at hand (e.g., energy use, water use, paper use, waste generation) and the stakeholders involved. Moving the environmental issue from only a political, social, economic, or technological one and into the realm of inter-connected *ands* versus *eithers* or *ors* makes it a strategic one. Strategy is grounded in awareness, knowledge, behavior, cognition, and action, and each of these aspects is linked to strategic elements within an organization of any kind.

Each day, sport brings entertainment and enjoyment to millions of people around the world. The demand for sport means that it must be available for fans when they want it. In the nineteenth century and in the early part of the twentieth century, sports events were held outdoors in fields and other public spaces. As the enclosure movement took place around the world, we see purpose-built facilities for sport being built. These facilities enclosed the playing area and ushered in the start of sport as a business through ticket prices and marketing and promotional efforts. Over the course of the twentieth century, stadia and other event facilities became more than functional sites to host events. They became destinations with their own parking, restaurants, and other entertainment amenities in addition to a place where games are played and events take place (Kidd 2013; Sage 1993). The style and architectural design can become artistic expressions of a local community such as in Seattle where the CenturyLink Field includes internal and external art from local area artists (Ansell 2013; CenturyLink Field 2013). They are also used as centerpieces of urban renewal projects, although the success of the renewal and economic impact on the local community can be difficult to quantify (Chapin 2004; Coates and Humphreys 2003; Jones 2002; Maennig and du Plessis 2009). Of course, such architectural and functional dynamism to account for environmental issues also comes with an environmental cost (Dolles and Söderman 2010).

What role, then, does sport play in the context of the natural environment? More specifically, how can sport personnel understand and take action over envi-ronmental issues? A strategic, integrated lens, following events in a moment and over time, allows this question to begin to be answered. However, many of the answers are answers with a question mark, as contextual variables shift and change. A starting point for this process is a dual-perspective track that looks at structural enablers and constraints to environmental causes and solutions. One perspec-tive is an outside-in one where the environment and related contextual elements (e.g., government laws and regulations) impact how an organization strategically plans and operates (Porter and Reinhardt 2007). A second perspective involves an inside-out view where sport organization personnel examine and understand how their efforts impact the environment (Porter and Reinhardt 2007). Most often, this takes place when environmental issues are first assessed within a sport organization and then again throughout the changed operation processes moving forward. The outside-in perspective is more difficult to address because it involves changes to environmental variables outside of the control of a sport organization. The flood of New Orleans and the surrounding communities impacted the professional sport teams and local intercollegiate programs in profound ways. However, the factors leading to the disaster, both man-made and occurring naturally, were out of the control of sport personnel. As a result, planning for the events that unfolded was nearly impossible or, at the very least, improbable.

The more common viewpoint with which to examine the impact sport has on the environment is to use the inside-out perspective (Porter and Reinhardt 2007). This view examines the substantial resources used to operate sport organizations and conduct sport events. For example, energy use, such as that to power lighting, communication equipment, and many other facets of a game experience, will continue to grow as stadia become more elaborate in their visual and entertainment content without concurrent investments in energy efficiency programs (Houghton 2007). Major League Baseball (MLB) led the major professional leagues in the United States by working to understand environmental issues related to its teams' games and stadia operations. In 2005, MLB personnel joined with counterparts at the NRDC to develop an environmental strategy. Other leagues soon followed. In the National Hockey League (NHL), the league and team personnel developed an overall environmental strategy and local (team-oriented) and national (league-oriented) initiatives. An example of a league-oriented initiative is a program called *Gallons for Goals* whereby, for each goal scored in the regular season, 1,000 gallons of water is restored to a dewatered river through a partnership with the Bonneville Environmental Foundation (National Hockey League 2014). In another example, the National Basketball Association (NBA) provides information and resources for classroom use during its annual *Green Week* (National Basketball Association 2014). Additionally, the NBA announced its Mosaic online tool to measure the environmental impact of team operations in conjunction with the NRDC and Renewable Choice Energy. "Mosaic will allow all NBA teams and venues to track, analyze and identify cost savings opportunities within their environmental footprint" (Environmental Leader 2013: 3).

The NRDC first developed metrics such as this with MLB and, later, the NHL in an effort to assist the league and team personnel with environmental assessment of their activities for improved strategic planning and information sharing among league teams (Hershkowitz 2010). In fact, the NHL developed a comprehensive strategy with the NRDC that incorporated the *Greening Advisor*, which "is a web-based resource customized for each team that offers environmental guidance and strategies to promote more sustainable practices for NHL team and arena operations" (Natural Resources Defense Council 2014a: 1). Over time, this evolved to include metrics for assessment of environmental efforts, a solar panel installation guide to all NHL teams, and a strategy to redistribute unused prepared food from league games (Natural Resources Defense Council 2014a).

Sport personnel, in conjunction with corporate partners who share similar environmental missions, conducted environmentally themed events. In the NBA, for example, the league conducted a contest with Sprint (a telecommunications company) where, during the 2013 Green Week, fans who pledged to recycle their old mobile devices were entered into a draw to win a trip for two to the 2013 Finals as the grand prize (Environmental Leader 2013). The partnership also produced a buyback program where fans recycling their telephones would receive credit towards Sprint services as well as other NBA-related prizes (Environmental Leader 2013). Sprint noted that this would save more than 20 million devices from entering landfills (Environmental Leader 2013). Other environmentally related events included team-level initiatives during games and in the community. This occurred among the NBA's properties: the NBA, the Women's National Basketball Association (WNBA), and the NBA Developmental League (D-League).

Beyond the United States, larger events have also undergone changes to integrate environmental issues into event activities. The Olympics, for example, has been integrating the natural environment into its strategies since 2000, providing guidance to environmental issues from bid to post-event. Data from the 2012 Summer Olympic Games in London, as just one example, showed that 10,500 athletes participated in the Games and approximately 500,000 people visited the United Kingdom to attend the Games in person and just to be a part of the Olympic experience (CNN 2012). Fédération Internationale de Football Association (FIFA) too has integrated environmental issues into its events. For example, estimates of energy consumption for each match of the 2006 World Cup noted that the matches used around 3 million kilowatt hours of energy and the fans at the games produced 5–10 tons of trash (FIFA 2013). That figure is important because it is a benchmark figure for FIFA, since that World Cup was the first one to use a pur-pose-developed environmental plan in the planning, building, and maintenance of the facilities for the tournament.

Intercollegiate athletics is also involved in these efforts (Casper et al. 2012; Jin et al. 2011). However, their involvement in environmental efforts began, as a whole, a bit later than the professional leagues. Since 2011, for example, the National Collegiate Athletic Association (NCAA) has worked with the NRDC to improve environmental issues associated with the Final Four. Activities at the Final Four related to fan experiences and event operations were developed. To reduce paper usage a mobile telephone application was created "to help fans locate events, find restaurants, make reservations etc. Printed fan guides were also elimi-nated" (Natural Resources Defense Council 2014b: 10). The NCAA, individual conferences, and individual athletics departments work together and individually to address environmental issues. The NCAA has also begun to partner with the NRDC in similar ways to the professional organizations and leagues.

If the conversation is moved from mega and large professional sporting events to smaller-scale events, then the continued impact of sport on the natural environ-ment can be seen. Despite larger, high-profile leagues, teams, and events getting more of the fan and media attention for environmental efforts, there are numerous sport events and related sport/recreational activities that contribute to environ-mental problems. Sport/recreational activities include golf, skiing, running, hiking, and similar activities and the sports played in and around them. Many of these types of organizations are also tourism oriented (e.g., ski resorts), meaning environmental impacts directly affect an organization's bottom line since poor infrastructure tends to dissuade people from visiting or re-visiting a venue (Burakowski and Magnusson 2012; Chalip and Costa 2005; Chalip et al. 2003; Flagestad and Hope 2001). Golf courses are an example of a sport facility set in nature that requires significant investments in land and development just to create the course. Golf is a fast-growing sport in many places around the world and new courses are being developed as rapid economic and social changes take place; but with this change comes a visible environmental impact (Tanner and Gange 2005; Terman 1997). As a result, many local communities, golf-course and property developers, and governing bodies such as the Professional Golfers' Association (PGA) in the United States are working independently and through coordinated efforts to improve the environmental performance of golf courses (Terman 1997). Once developed, the course must be maintained constantly to ensure a playing surface that satisfies the golfers. To achieve a satisfactory playing surface, course personnel must use pesticides to control insect populations, which then affect local plant and animal life. Further, there is a need to water the course, even with natural rainfall. It has even been put forth that golf courses, by their unique combination of nature and sport, can be developed in to wildlife habitats (Terman 1997). Ski resorts too are another example of the impact of sport on the environment. Ski-resort personnel must maintain a healthy amount of snow for skiers. When nature does not provide the necessary snow, then personnel have to generate it themselves (i.e., officials in Vancouver for the 2010 Winter Olympic Games). Manufactured snow becomes a hazard when wastewater is used to manufacture it (Schmidt 2006). Examples of this impact can go on and on, but the underlying factors remain.

Taking these two perspectives together helps sport-organization personnel understand, plan for, and take action to address environmental issues today, tomorrow, and in an uncertain future (Pfahl 2011). A strategic philosophy and approach to planning for environmental issues is necessary to move them from ad hoc activities and into a comprehensive organizational plan. In addition, the strategic elements extend into micro-level operational goals, objectives, and tactics.

Strategic action: the development of a collaborative sports world

The impact of sport and the environment becomes an important issue for sport personnel at every level to address. A community recreation coordinator in a small town has similar issues to that of personnel at the highest levels of professional or amateur sport (e.g., fields to maintain, water usage). However, the scale of environmental issues becomes an important issue when comparing environmental problems and solutions among sport organizations (e.g., Division I athletics department versus one at the Division III level or a MLB team compared to a Single A regional professional team). Scale involves the size of a sport organization's operations as well as the resources organization personnel have at their disposal to address the environmental issues at hand. Thus, environmental issues are inherently contextual, making a blanket analysis of them or among sport organizations a difficult task. Taking a strategic approach helps to move the discussion to a more common level: planning, goals, objectives, strategies, and tactics.

Often seen from environmental actions are cost savings from changing operations, community goodwill, and potential revenue generation opportunities. The cost savings can provide an operational benefit for a team in a community, but as the emphasis on environmental issues increases, there is more than just a financial stake in making sustainability a strategic component of sport operations. Friendliness emerges among team and league personnel in the sports world: a sense of cooperation formed around sport more than competition. While individual team and event examples will come later, it is useful to examine non-team or league-oriented actions taken by personnel in the sport industry. These examples are just that, examples. There are many other examples that can be given, and the ones offered here are not intended to be more than exemplars.

One recent step forward in the area of cooperation is in the form of the Green Sports Alliance (the Alliance). This organization "was formed in 2010 with a mission to help sports teams, venues, and leagues enhance their environmental performance" (Pfahl 2013: 8). "In February 2010, the concept of the Alliance began in a workshop where sport personnel, mainly from the Northwest United States, came together to discuss sustainability issues, share experiences, and to help each other address the environmental impacts of their teams and venues" (Pfahl 2013: 20). The founders of the Alliance include Jason Twill, the sustainability lead for Vulcan Inc., Dr Allen Hershkowitz, senior scientist and director of the Sports Project at the NRDC, and Paul Allen, co-founder of Microsoft and owner of the Seattle Seahawks and Portland Trailblazers and a part-owner of the Seattle Sounders. By working together, these people envisioned a coalition of organizations and personnel who could address environmental issues in their respective organizations. As the idea grew, additional partners were found in the form of personnel from the Seattle Mariners, Seattle Storm, Vancouver Canucks, Bonneville Environmental Foundation, Milepost Consulting, and the United States Environmental Protection Agency (Green Sports Alliance (GSA) 2013; Pfahl 2013). The GSA quickly expanded outside of the Pacific Northwest and now boasts over 170 teams and venues across the world as members (Green Sports Alliance 2013).

The Alliance is a coalition of willing partners in sport who wish to share best practices and information regarding environmental issues. Fostering cooperation and facilitating dialogue are central to the Alliance's mission and activities as they are not a governing or a certification body. From its earliest days, cooperation was a core value, and the Alliance has members from around the world (e.g., Australia, Shanghai, Sweden), although most are located in North America. The Alliance's work, while encompassing many professional venues and teams from around the world, is heavily focused on the major professional level of sport. This is a strategic decision made by Alliance personnel, although their work can find its way through the world of sport to other levels.

The NRDC, in addition to co-founding the Alliance and serving as its techni-cal environmental advisor, is also the principal environmental advisor to all major professional leagues, including MLB, the NBA, the NHL, Major League Soccer (MLS), the United States Tennis Association (USTA), the National Association for Stock Car Auto Racing (NASCAR), the National Football League (NFL), and the NCAA. Through its work in these areas (and beyond), the NRDC compiles data and case studies that provide guidance for sport personnel and oth-ers related to issue identification and other strategic elements in the form of the *Game Changer* report. The NRDC has also published a *Collegiate Game Changers* report specific to college athletics and recreation. Both of these reports are avail-able for download at the NRDC's website and contain an in-depth look at the issues facing sport personnel as well as success stories (Natural Resources Defense Council 2013).

While the Alliance and NRDC are working to coordinate efforts, individual venue and team personnel are pursuing environmental initiatives in their own way. Chelsea FC, a football team in the English Premier League, took steps to work with the local municipal government in London to improve its green efforts (Chelsea FC 2007). The Olympic Committee and FIFA have also developed plans for developing, implementing, and evaluating environmental impacts in the pro-cesses of hosting the Olympic Games and World Cup events respectively.

As another example of the different ways sport personnel are tackling envi-ronmental activities, Athletes for a Fit Planet (AFP) combines individual initiative and event planning to help road-racing events, among others, become more envi-ronmentally friendly. AFP "provides customized environmental consulting and on-the-ground support to organizers of events in North America and the UK. From road races and triathlons to golf and hockey tournaments we help you reduce your environmental footprint" (A Fit Planet 2013: 2). They help athletes, event planners, and companies improve their sustainability practices, but perhaps more importantly, they have members and partners pledge a commitment to sustainabil-ity for event planners to take and offer certification services for the environment friendliness of the event. In addition, they offer an events calendar to promote green events and organizations as well as to guide interested parties to events that share an environmental concern. In other words, they are facilitating community collaboration along the lines of the Alliance, but at a different, more micro-com-munity level. However, much work remains at various other levels and contexts (e.g., interscholastic sport, club sport, venues, stadia, events).

Conclusion

In conclusion, the issue of the environment is a human one transcending politics, economics, societies, cultures, and technologies. Yet, it impacts and is impacted by each of these areas. By examining the environmental impact of sport, we can also see the connections with economic growth and development, health and wellness, sustainable practices for resource usage, and many other related areas. Whether we are speaking about a community softball league or the Olympics, sustainability is becoming part of the strategic fabric of sport operations.

As sport personnel increase their awareness, knowledge, and understanding of environmental issues, they will see the strategic threads that are woven through the environmental issue at every level of their organizations. Working towards more environmentally preferable practices is an ongoing, constantly evolving process. However, with a strategic mindset, it will not be forgotten as new goals are set, new objectives formulated, and new tactics enacted across all fronts of sport operations.

In the end, the strategic inclusion of environmental issues into all aspects of organizational operations will eventually become routine and part of the fabric of sport business. Sport personnel have been a part of social change and awareness development for many social causes over the years, and the environment is the latest one. Sport personnel have the opportunity to serve as an unparalleled role model for society, the marketplace, and the world at large.

References

A Fit Planet. (2013) 'What we do'. Available online at www.afitplanet.com (accessed 23 July 2013).

Ansell, L. (2013) 'Artistic triumph'. *Stadia*, July: 50–3.

Burakowski, E. and Magnusson, M. (2012) *Climate impacts on the winter tourism economy in the United States*. New York: Natural Resources Defense Council.

Casper, J., Pfahl, M., and McSherry, M. (2012) 'Athletics department awareness and action regarding the environment: A study of NCAA athletics department sustainability practices'. *Journal of Sport Management*, 26: 11–29.

CenturyLink Field. (2013) 'Art at CenturyLink Field'. Available online at www. centurylinkfield.com/art-at-centurylinkfield (accessed 11 July 2013).

Chalip, L. and Costa, C. (2005) 'Sport event tourism and the destination brand: Towards a general theory'. *Sport in Society*, 8: 218–37.

Chalip, L., Green, B., and Hill, B. (2003) 'Effects of sport event media on destination image and intention to visit'. *Journal of Sport Management*, 17: 214–34.

Chapin, T. (2004) 'Sports facilities as urban redevelopment catalysts: Baltimore's Camden Yards and Cleveland's Gateway'. *Journal of the American Planning Association*, 70: 193–209.

Chelsea FC. (2007) 'Blues go green for London'. Available online at http://events.chelseafc. com/csr (accessed 23 July 2013).

CNN. (2012) 'London Olympics by the numbers'. Available online at www.cnn. com/2012/07/27/world/olympics-numbers (accessed 4 July 2013).

Coates, D. and Humphreys, B. (2003) 'Professional sports facilities, franchises and urban economic development'. *Public Finance and Management*, 3: 335–57.

Dolles, H. and Söderman, S. (2010) 'Addressing ecology and sustainability in mega-sporting events: The 2006 football World Cup in Germany'. *Journal of Management & Organization*, 16: 587–600.

Elliott, S. and Delpy Neirotti, L. (2008) 'Challenges of tourism in a dynamic island destination: The case of Cuba'. *Tourism Geographies*, 10: 375–402.

Environmental Leader. (2013) 'NBA to offset more than 10m pounds CO_2'. Available online at www.environmentalleader.com/2013/04/05/nba-to-offset-more-than-10m-pounds-co2 (accessed 10 April 2013).

Esty, D. and Winston, A. (2006) *Green to gold: How smart companies use environmental strategy to innovate, create value, and build competitive advantage*. New Haven, CT: Yale University Press.

FIFA. (2013) 'FIFA and the environment'. Available online at www.fifa.com/aboutfifa/socialresponsibility/environmental.html (accessed 13 March 2013).

Fineman, S. (1997) 'Fashioning the environment'. *Organization*, 8: 17–31.

Flagestad, A. and Hope, C. (2001) 'Strategic success in winter sports destinations: A sustainable value creation perspective'. *Tourism Management*, 22: 445–61.

Govindarajulu, N. and Daily, B. (2004) 'Motivating employees for environmental improvement'. *Industrial Management & Data Systems*, 104: 364–72.

Green Sports Alliance. (2013) 'About'. Available online at http://greensportsalliance.org/about (accessed 23 July 2013).

Harris, L. and Crane, A. (2002) 'The greening of organizational culture: Management views on the depth, degree and diffusion of change'. *Journal of Organizational Change Management*, 15: 214–34.

Hart, S. (1995) 'A natural-resource-based view of the firm'. *The Academy of Management Review*, 20: 986–1014.

Hart, S. and Milstein, M. (2003) 'Creating sustainable value'. *The Academy of Management Executive*, 17: 56–67.

Hershkowitz, A. (2010) 'Major League Baseball's important announcement'. Available online at http://switchboard.nrdc.org/blogs/ahershkowitz/major_league_baseballs_importa.html (accessed 4 April 2014).

Horne, J. (2006) *Sport in consumer culture*. New York: Palgrave.

Houghton, R. (2007) 'Balancing the global carbon budget'. *Annual Review of Earth and Planetary Sciences*, 35: 313–47.

Hums, M., Barr, C., and Gullion, L. (1999) 'The ethical issues confronting managers in the sport industry'. *Journal of Business Ethics*, 20: 51–66.

Inoue, Y. and Kent, A. (2012) 'Sport teams as promoters of pro-environmental behavior: An empirical study'. *Journal of Sport Management*, 26: 417–32.

Jin, L., Mao, L., Zhang, J., and Walker, M. (2011) 'Impact of green stadium initiatives on donor intentions toward an intercollegiate athletic programme'. *International Journal of Sport Management and Marketing*, 10: 121–41.

Jones, C. (2002) 'Public cost for private gain? Recent and proposed "national" stadium developments in the UK, and commonalities with North America'. *Area*, 34: 160–70.

Kidd, B. (2013) 'Toronto's SkyDome: The world's greatest entertainment centre'. *Sport in Society*, 16: 388–404.

Kitazawa, S. and Sarkis, J. (2000) 'The relationship between ISO 14001 and continuous source reduction programs'. *International Journal of Operations & Production Management*, 20: 225–48.

Lenskyj, H. (1998) 'Sport and corporate environmentalism: The case of the Sydney 2000 Olympics'. *International Review for the Sociology of Sport*, 33: 341–54.

Maennig, W. and du Plessis, S. (2009) 'Sport stadia, sporting events and urban development: International experience and the ambitions of Durban'. *Urban Forum*, 20: 61–76.

Mallen, C., Adams, L., Stevens, J., and Thompson, L. (2010) 'Environmental sustainability in sport facility management'. *European Sport Management Quarterly*, 10: 367–89.

Mallen, C. and Chard, C. (2011) 'A framework for debating the future of environmental sustainability in the sport academy'. *Sport Management Review*, 14: 424–33.

National Basketball Association. (2014) 'Reimagination!' Available online at www.bkfk. com/nba (accessed 4 April 2014).

National Hockey League. (2014) 'Gallons for goals'. Available online at www.nhl.com/ice/ eventhome.htm?location=/nhlgreen (accessed 4 April 2014).

Natural Resources Defense Council. (2013) 'Game changer: How the sports industry is saving the environment'. Available online at www.nrdc.org/greenbusiness/guides/ sports/game-changer.asp (accessed 23 July 2013).

Natural Resources Defense Council. (2014a) 'Smarter business: Greening the games'. Available online at www.nrdc.org/greenbusiness/guides/sports/nhl.asp (accessed 4 April 2014).

Natural Resources Defense Council. (2014b) 'National Collegiate Athletic Association'. Available online at www.nrdc.org/greenbusiness/guides/sports/ncaa.asp (accessed 4 April 2014).

Pfahl, M. (2010) 'Strategic issues associated with the development of internal sustainability teams in sport and recreation organizations: A framework for action and sustainable environmental performance'. *International Journal of Sport Management Recreation & Tourism*, 6: 37–61.

Pfahl, M. (2011) *Sport and the natural environment: A strategic guide*. Dubuque, IA: Kendall Hunt.

Pfahl, M. (2013) 'The environmental awakening in sport'. *Solutions*, 4: 67–76.

Porter, M. and Reinhardt, F. (2007) 'A strategic approach to climate change'. *Harvard Business Review*, 85: 22–6.

Sage, G. (1993) 'Stealing home: Political, economic, and media power and a publicly-funded baseball stadium in Denver'. *Journal of Sport & Social Issues*, 17: 110–24.

Schmidt, C. (2006) 'Putting the Earth in play: Environmental awareness and sports'. *Environmental Health Perspectives*, 114: A286–A295.

Sharma, S. (2000) 'Managerial interpretations and organizational context as predictors of corporate choice of environmental strategy'. *Academy of Management Journal*, 43: 681–97.

Sharma, S. and Vredenburg, H. (1998) 'Proactive corporate environmental strategy and the development of competitively valuable organizational capabilities'. *Strategic Management Journal*, 19: 729–53.

Shrivastava, P. (1995) 'Environmental technologies and competitive advantage'. *Strategic Management Journal*, 16: 183–200.

Tanner, R. and Gange, A. (2005) 'Effects of golf courses on local biodiversity'. *Landscape and Urban Planning*, 71: 137–46.

Terman, M. (1997) 'Natural links: Naturalistic golf courses as wildlife habitat'. *Landscape and Urban Planning*, 38: 183–97.

2

THEORETICAL FOUNDATIONS FOR UNDERSTANDING PRO-ENVIRONMENTAL BEHAVIOR IN SPORT

Yuhei Inoue

Overview

The purpose of this chapter is to provide theoretical foundations for understanding the pro-environmental behavior of individuals involved in sport, such as employees of sport organizations, athletes, and sport consumers. First, the chapter explains the definitions of pro-environmental behavior and classifies the behavior into specific types. Next, factors affecting one's decision to perform pro-environmental behavior as well as theoretical frameworks explaining the behavior are reviewed. This chapter concludes with suggestions on how both researchers and practitioners can use the reviewed information to further promote pro-environmental behavior in sport.

Introduction

The recent adoption of environmentally friendly practices in the sport industry is notable. For example, the majority of teams in the four major professional leagues in North America—Major League Baseball (MLB), the National Basketball Association (NBA), the National Football League, and the National Hockey League—have implemented energy efficiency programs (Natural Resources Defense Council, 2012). The Australian Football League invested AUD$13 million in the construction of an energy-efficient stadium, installing solar panels to cover 20 percent of its energy use (Singer, 2011), and Newcastle United of the English Premier League became the first carbon positive soccer team in the world by offsetting more carbon than the organization emits (*The Northern Echo*, 2012).

In all of the examples above, the sport organizations took a significant step toward sustainability because *individuals* within the organizations made a decision to engage in actions that would benefit the environment. In environmental psychology and other related academic fields, such actions are often referred to as *pro-environmental behavior*; understanding what this behavior entails as well as why people perform the behavior has been a focus of these fields (Steg and Vlek, 2009). The examination of pro-environmental behavior has been conducted among employees (e.g., Andersson et al., 2005; Brothers et al., 1994; Cordano et al., 2010) and consumers (e.g., Bagozzi and Dabholkar, 1994; Ölander and Thøgersen, 1995; Webb et al., 2008). Furthermore, a small but growing body of research has investigated pro-environmental behavior specific to the sport context (Babiak and Trendafilova, 2011; Casper and Pfahl, 2012; Casper et al., 2012; Inoue and Kent, 2012a, 2012b; Kellison and Kim, 2014; McCullough and Cunningham, 2011; Trendafilova and Babiak, 2013).

This chapter explains why and how individuals involved in sport, such as employees of sport organizations, athletes, and sport consumers, make a decision to engage in pro-environmental behavior. The next section defines pro-environmental behavior and classifies the behavior into specific types. This is followed by a review of factors that are found to influence pro-environmental behavior and theoretical frameworks useful to predict the behavior. This chapter concludes by explaining how the reviewed knowledge can be used to further promote pro-environmental behavior in sport.

Defining pro-environmental behavior

Pro-environmental behavior can be understood from two definitions (Stern, 2000): an impact-oriented definition and an intent-oriented definition. The impact-oriented definition focuses on the extent to which certain behavior has an actual impact on the environment, and thus "changes the availability of materials or energy from the environment or alters the structure and dynamics of ecosystems or the biosphere itself" (Stern, 2000: 408). On the other hand, the intent-oriented definition takes into account the possibility that some behavior could fail to produce the actual environmental impact, placing more emphasis on *intentions* to perform the behavior than the behavior itself (Stern, 2000).

These two definitions are important for different reasons (Stern, 2000). The impact-oriented definition is useful when identifying behavior that has significant environmental impact as a primary purpose. The intent-oriented definition, in contrast, should be used when a major aim is to understand and to influence given behavior by identifying one's motives or beliefs behind the behavior. Because the goal of this chapter is to understand how pro-environmental behavior can be promoted within a sport organizational context, the subsequent discussion examines pro-environmental behavior based on the intent-oriented definition.

According to the intent-oriented definition, pro-environmental behavior refers to actions that are undertaken with intent to benefit the environment and can be classified into three types (Dietz et al., 1998; Stern, 2000; Stern et al., 1999): environmental activism, non-activist behavior in the public sphere, and private-sphere environmentalism. First, *environmental activism* refers to active engagement in environmental movements, such as participation in environmental demonstrations and support for environmental protection organizations (Stern, 2000; Stern et al., 1999). For example, the participation of some top Kenyan long-distance runners in the United Nations Environment Programme (UNEP) Half Marathon, a running event that aimed to promote environmental conservation, illustrates this type of pro-environmental behavior (*Africa News*, 2013). Another example is the involvement of Billie Jean King, a former professional tennis star, in a public service announcement encouraging the use of public transportation as part of environmental efforts by the United States Tennis Association (Zeller, 2009).

Second, *non-activist behavior* encompasses environmental support in the public sphere that is less intense than environmental activism, but is still essential to the success of an environmental movement (Dietz et al., 1998; Stern, 2000; Stern et al., 1999). This type of behavior can be further split into environmental citizenship and policy support. *Environmental citizenship* incorporates environmental actions that involve low risk or are private, such as making financial contributions to environmental organizations, reading articles on environmental movements, and writing letters to government officials. This includes the efforts of Kelly Slater, an American professional surfer, to support the environment by making donations to environmentally conscious charities through his foundation (Kelly Slater Foundation, n.d.). On the other hand, *policy support* refers to the acceptance and support of environmental policies regardless of possible monetary (e.g., higher taxes) and material (e.g., regulations) sacrifices (Stern et al., 1999). Despite the costs associated with certification, for example, the Washington Nationals built Nationals Park in 2008 as the nation's first major professional sports stadium certified as Leadership in Energy and Environmental Design (LEED) Silver by the U.S. Green Building Council (Washington Nationals, n.d.). In addition, U.S. sport governing bodies, including MLB, the NBA, and the United States Tennis Association, have partnered with the Natural Resources Defense Council, a non-profit organization specializing in environmental advocacy, to implement league-wide environmental policies designed to integrate environmental management into their event operations (Natural Resources Defense Council, n.d.).

Finally, *private-sphere environmentalism* entails decisions on the use and disposal of products that have significant impact on the environment (Stern, 2000). This type of behavior can be further classified into three subtypes (Clayton and Myers, 2009): curtailment behavior, behavior choice, and technology choice. *Curtailment behavior* is concerned with individuals' effort to reduce their material and energy consumption, whereas *behavior choice* involves decisions to engage in behavior that has less environmental impact, such as recycling products and using public transportation. Furthermore, *technology choice* entails decisions on the purchase and use of technological innovations, such as renewable energy, hybrid cars, and energy-efficient appliances (Clayton and Myers, 2009). For example, efforts by the management of Newcastle United to save energy consumption to reduce the team's carbon emissions discussed earlier represents an example of curtailment behavior (*The Northern Echo*, 2012). As an example of behavior choice, both team staff and fans of the San

Francisco Giants have engaged in recycling and the use of sustainable materials at home games (Sygall, 2011). Moreover, organizers of the Formula One Singapore Grand Prix installed solar panels for track lighting, showing an example of technology choice (Chua, 2010). It is further noteworthy that the pro-environmental behaviors performed by consumers at sport events are primarily classified into private-sphere environmentalism. This highlights the role of sport organizations in serving as a platform to increase consumers' engagement in this type of pro-environmental behavior both at sport events and in daily lives (Inoue and Kent, 2012a, 2012b).

As shown in the examples provided in this section, the three behavioral types reviewed are useful to understand the pro-environmental behaviors of individuals involved in sport, regardless of whether they are employees of sport organizations, athletes, or sport consumers. One notable difference, however, may exist between the performance of pro-environmental behavior by individuals within organizations (primarily as employees) and by those outside organizations (primarily as athletes or consumers) with respect to the influence of external constraints (Stern, 2000). In organizational contexts, people may need to consider additional constraints, such as organizational commitment to sustainability (Andersson et al., 2005) and leaders' beliefs about environmental issues (Robertson and Barling, 2013), in deciding to perform pro-environmental behavior. This indicates the importance of understanding the determinants of pro-environmental behavior that are both internal and external to individuals. The next section thus reviews major internal and external factors that can affect one's engagement in pro-environmental behavior.

Factors affecting pro-environmental behavior

Several factors have been found to influence decisions to engage in pro-environmental behavior, which can be classified into two major categories (Clayton and Myers, 2009): (a) *internal factors*, which are related to personal characteristics; and (b) *external factors*, which are related to contextual characteristics. Using this classification, the present section summarizes empirical findings on how various factors affect pro-environmental behavior.

Internal factors

Internal factors encompass personal preferences or tendencies (Clayton and Myers, 2009). The first type of such factors is *attitudinal variables* including values, beliefs, and personal norms (Clayton and Myers, 2009; Stern, 2000). The importance of these variables is highlighted by the value–belief–norm (VBN) theory of environmentalism (Stern et al., 1999), a theoretical framework used to explain why people decide to perform pro-environmental behavior in various settings, including the context of sport management (Casper and Pfahl, 2012). According to this theory, personal norms to engage in certain pro-environmental behavior are the direct determinant of that behavior. These norms are, in turn, activated by both personal values and beliefs related to the environment (Stern et al., 1999). Therefore, a facility manager of a professional sport team would be more willing to adopt new energy-efficient technologies for team facilities if he or she has strong personal norms, values, and beliefs about environmental protection, although the actual adoption of such technologies would depend on various external factors, such as support from top management (see the discussion on external factors below).

The second type is *personal capabilities*, such as skills and knowledge necessary to perform certain pro-environmental behaviors, general personal capabilities (e.g., social status, money, literacy, power), and the availability of time (Stern, 2000). For example, the active participation of professional athletes in environmental programs, such as the UNEP's Sport and the Environment, may be influenced by the extent to which they are knowledgeable about environmental issues as well as establishing their status as successful athletes. Furthermore, the primary benefits of the partnerships between the Natural Resources Defense Council and U.S. sport governing bodies noted earlier can be explained by the potential of the partnerships to expand the knowledge and skills of sport personnel responsible for environmental management, allowing the governing bodies to successfully design and implement their environmental initiatives.

The third type is *emotions*, such as personal affinity for natural resources and both positive (e.g., happiness) and negative (e.g., fear) emotional states (Vining and Ebreo, 2002). For example, a spectator of a sport event may cooperate in a recycling program at the event because he or she has a high affinity for the natural environment, gains happiness from supporting the environment, and fears the negative consequences of environmental degradation. In relation to this factor, one important consideration is the ability of sport events to arouse spectators' emotion (Babiak and Wolfe, 2009). Given this ability, sport organizations may be able to increase spectators' participation in pro-environmental behavior by implementing activities designed to connect the emotion provoked at their events with support for environmental protection.

The final type of internal factors is *routines and habits*, which are especially important because persuading people to change behavior involves breaking old routines and habits (Stern, 2000). For example, even though a professional sport team encourages fans to use public transportation to attend its home games, those who are used to driving to games may have difficulty adopting the new practice; thus, the team would need to work with a local transit authority to promote the general use of public transportation in the community and make this mode of transportation more accessible to fans.

External factors

Pro-environmental behavior is further influenced by external factors, including: (a) *physical and social environmental constraints*, (b) *social norms*, (c) *incentives/punishment*, and (d) *information* (Clayton and Myers, 2009; Stern, 1999, 2000). First, some individuals may not have a choice to perform certain pro-environmental behavior because physical situations, such as lighting and thermostat settings, disallow them to do so. In addition, even though the choice is available, a lack of information regarding appropriate behavior may discourage people to adopt pro-environmental actions (Clayton and Myers, 2009). This applies to the case where an environmentally conscious person attends a sport event that does not set up any recycling bins; despite his or her environmental concern, the situation prevents that person from recycling materials at the event. It is further possible that the organizer's decision not to install recycling bins at this event has been affected by another environmental constraint, such as the lack of financial resources.

Second, evidence supports the effect of social norms on decisions to perform pro-environmental behavior (Cialdini et al., 1990; Clayton and Myers, 2009). Analysis of interviews with executives of North American professional sports organizations, for example, identified social expectations regarding corporate sustainability as a key driver for their organizations to adopt environmentally friendly practices (Babiak and Trendafilova, 2011; Trendafilova and Babiak, 2013). Given the impact of social norms, administrators of U.S. college athletic departments may likely incorporate environmental programs into event operations when their universities implement campus-wide green initiatives. The presence of such initiatives can establish norms to support the environment across campus, putting pressure on the athletic administrators to comply with the norms by adopting environmentally friendly practices.

Third, incentives and punishments are other important determinants of pro-environmental behavior (Clayton and Myers, 2009; Kazdin, 2009; McKenzie-Mohr and Smith, 1999; Stern, 1999). Incentives can take monetary and non-monetary forms (Stern, 1999). Monetary incentives are effective for influencing technology choice, such as the installation of solar panels in stadiums, because this subtype of behavior tends to require substantial financial sacrifices (Stern, 1999). Non-monetary incentives are often designed to influence individuals' behavior by providing them with convenience (Stern, 1999), such as picking up recyclable materials in seating areas to promote recycling among spectators during a game. On the other hand, punishment (e.g., fines) is effective for decreasing the tendency to perform certain behavior that can hurt the environment (Clayton and Myers, 2009). For example, city officials could require sport-event organizers to implement comprehensive recycling plans and thus reduce waste at their events by imposing fines on those failing to meet waste-reduction goals. Using punishment could, however, be problematic because it might encourage individuals to find a way to avoid detection or foster a sense of being controlled, resulting in resistance and hostility (Clayton and Myers, 2009).

Finally, information refers to an intervention designed to influence internal factors (Stern, 1999). Examples include prompts, feedback, and communication strategies (Clayton and Myers, 2009; McKenzie-Mohr and Smith, 1999; Stern, 1999). Prompts are messages that are used to remind people to engage in particular pro-environmental behavior; these reminders should ideally be located near places where the prompted behavior is performed (Clayton and Myers, 2009). For example, a message highlighting the importance of recycling can be placed next to recycle bins to promote recycling at stadiums. Feedback is another type of information that encourages individuals to perform pro-environmental behavior (Clayton and Myers, 2009; Kazdin, 2009). Existing studies indicated that the use of feedback can reduce about 5 to 17 percent of the energy consumption with enduring effects (Kazdin, 2009). Therefore, a facility operations director of a college athletic department could significantly decrease energy use by regularly providing employees responsible for individual facilities with feedback on whether they meet predetermined energy-reduction goals. Communication strategies, such as the use of credible message sources and the framing of messages, further affect pro-environmental decisions (Kazdin, 2009). Such strategies are especially useful when sport organizations attempt to promote participation in their environmental programs among such stakeholders as fans, corporate sponsors, and vendors.

Theoretical frameworks for pro-environmental behavior

This section discusses the main tenets and applications of three theoretical frameworks that are useful to explain the processes through which individuals make a decision to perform pro-environmental behavior: the theory of reasoned action (TRA) (Ajzen and Fishbein, 1980), the theory of planned behavior (TPB) (Ajzen, 1991), and the VBN theory (Stern et al., 1999). Of these theories, the TRA and the TPB are closely related with each other and thus discussed in the same subsection.

Theory of reasoned action/theory of planned behavior

The TRA views people as rational decision makers who consider the consequences of an action before they perform that action (Ajzen and Fishbein, 1980). From this view, the theory posits that one's decision to engage in a behavior is determined by one's intentions to engage in that behavior, suggesting the importance of identifying the determinants of such intentions. In particular, two factors are thought to have direct effects on behavioral intentions. The first factor is *attitude toward the behavior*, which refers to individuals' assessment of whether they are in favor of or against performing certain behavior. The second factor is *subjective norm*, or one's perception of how society expects one to engage in that behavior. In turn, attitude toward the behavior and subjective norms are influenced by two types of personal beliefs: *behavioral beliefs* and *normative beliefs*. Behavioral beliefs are the determinant of attitude toward the behavior, defined as personal beliefs about whether certain behavior can lead to positive or negative outcomes. In contrast, normative beliefs are the determinant of subjective norms, referring to one's beliefs about whether certain individuals or groups think that one should or should not engage in given behavior (Ajzen and Fishbein, 1980).

The TPB is an extension of the TRA and rests largely on the same theoretical propositions; the major difference from the TRA is the addition of a new psychological construct, *perceived behavioral control*, which refers to the perception of how easy or difficult performing certain behavior could be (Ajzen, 1991). Perceived behavioral control is determined by the extent of actual control (e.g., availability of resources and skills) over a behavior, influencing the behavior in two different ways. First, the construct directly influences the behavior by increasing one's effort to make a course of action successful. Second, it indirectly affects the behavior through behavioral intentions, together with attitudes toward the behavior and subjective norms.

In environmental psychology, both the TRA and the TPB have been used to predict various types of pro-environmental behavior (e.g., Bagozzi and Dabholkar, 1994; Kantola et al., 1983; Luzar and Diagne, 1999). For example, Bagozzi and Dabholkar (1994) attempted to predict consumer intentions to recycling based on the TRA; their findings were largely supportive of the theory because subjective norms and attitudes toward recycling explained about 30 percent of the variance in recycling intentions. In addition, Luzar and Diagne (1999) used this theory to investigate the determinants of wetland owners' decisions to participate in a voluntary environmental preservation program. Consistent with the theory, the study found a significant relationship between owners' attitude toward participating in the program and their actual participation (Luzar and Diagne, 1999).

A handful of environmental psychology studies have also used the TPB to explain pro-environmental behavior (e.g., Harland et al., 1999; Lam, 1999). In Lam (1999), the three determinants of behavioral intentions specified in the TPB—attitudes toward the behavior, subjective norms, and perceived behavioral control—collectively explained a substantial amount of the variance in pro-environmental behavior; they accounted for about 40 percent of the variance in intentions to reduce the use of water and about 25 percent of the variance in intentions to install water-saving appliances. The findings of Harland et al. (1999) also showed that each of the three constructs significantly explain intentions to perform various types of pro-environmental behavior, such as energy saving, the use of non-car vehicles, and environmentally friendly consumptions.

Furthermore, McCullough and Cunningham (2011) applied the TRA/TPB framework to the context of sport in their investigation of factors influencing the recycling intentions of spectators at a youth sport event. Their tested model included the three predictors of recycling intentions proposed by the two theories, including attitudes toward recycling, subjective norms, and perceived behavioral control. Results showed that the model accounted for 30 percent of the variance in spectators' intentions to recycle, providing support for the utility of the TRA/TPB in this context (McCullough and Cunningham, 2011). This finding indicates that in order for event organizers to promote recycling among spectators, it is essential to communicate the benefits of recycling (for attitude toward the behavior), social expectations about recycling (for subjective norm), and information on recyclable materials (for perceived behavioral control) through in-game announcements and other media (e.g., placing prompts on recycle bins).

Along with spectators, the three direct determinants of behavior—attitudes toward the behavior, subjective norm, and perceived behavioral control—are useful to describe the pro-environmental decisions of various people involved in sport. For example, consider a case of the construction of the Heavener Football Complex by the University of Florida Athletic Department in 2009 as the first athletic facility earning a LEED Platinum certification in the U.S. (Natural Resources Defense Council, 2013). Department staff's decision to support the construction of this facility can be explained by their attitudes, subjective norms, and perceived behavioral control with respect to the facility construction. First, it can be assumed that the staff developed positive attitudes toward the construction of the facility because of their behavioral beliefs that it would provide the department with positive outcomes, such as enhanced reputation and cost savings from improved efficiency in facility operations. Second, their subjective norms, or perceived social expectations, about the facility construction are attributable to the emphasis on campus sustainability by Bernard Machen, the university's president and "a founding signatory of the American College & University Presidents' Climate Commitment" (Natural Resources Defense Council, 2013: 39). Finally, the staff may have developed the perception of behavioral control about their involvement in sustainability by building the facility through their previous experience of implementing a successful game-day recycling program by working with the Office of Sustainability at the university (Natural Resources Defense Council, 2013). In turn, the development of attitudes, subjective norms, and perceived behavioral control collectively led the staff to formulate their intentions to support the building of the facility.

Despite their utility, several limitations of the TRA and the TPB have been identified (Boston University School of Public Health, 2013), with the following being the most relevant to the current discussion: both theories focus solely on the perception of social norms (i.e., subjective norms) and individualistic beliefs/ values (i.e., attitudes toward the behavior, perceived behavioral control) in predicting behavior, ignoring the effects of other internal factors (e.g., personal norms, non-individualistic values, emotion). This limitation has been explicitly addressed by the VBN theory (Stern, 1999, 2000; Stern et al., 1999). Specifically, while this theory also focuses on attitudinal variables, it recognizes that non-individualistic values and personal norms, which are neglected by the TRA and the TPB, can predict pro-environmental behavior (Stern, 1999). Detailed descriptions of the VBN theory are provided below.

Value–belief–norm theory

The VBN theory explains that pro-environmental behavior is a function of values, beliefs, and norms (Stern et al., 1999). *Pro-environmental personal norms*, or one's feelings of obligation to perform given pro-environmental behavior, are the direct predictor of the behavior. In turn, these norms are affected by three types of personal values relating to environmental concern (Stern, 2000): *biospheric values, altruistic values*, and *egoistic values*. Biospheric values refer to unselfish concern directed toward ecosystems or other species beyond the benefits to humans, and altruistic values refer to unselfish concern directed toward other humans (Dietz et al., 2005). In addition, egoistic values, or "the self-interest basis of environmental concern" (Dietz et al., 2005: 344), refer to individuals' concern about the environment because of its direct impact on their own lives and other important things.

Moreover, the relationships between the three values and pro-environmental personal norms are mediated by *new ecological paradigm* (NEP) and two personal beliefs—*awareness of consequences (AC) beliefs* and *ascription of responsibility (AR) beliefs* (Stern et al., 1999). NEP refers to "a view that human actions have substantial adverse effects on a fragile biosphere" (Stern et al., 1999: 85), and serves as the first mediator directly influenced by each of the three values. AC beliefs are personal beliefs that the biosphere and the non-human species are under threat, while AR beliefs are personal beliefs that one's own actions could increase or reduce the threat. AC beliefs are specified as the second mediator influenced by NEP, and AR beliefs are the subsequent third mediator that directly influences pro-environmental personal norms.

Studies by Stern and colleagues (e.g., Dietz et al., 1998; Stern et al., 1999) demonstrated a substantial explanatory power of the VBN theory. According to Stern et al. (1999), for example, this theory accounted for 19 to 35 percent of the variance in different types of pro-environmental behavior. Furthermore, Casper and Pfahl (2012) used the VBN theory to explain the pro-environmental behavior of U.S. undergraduate students in sport and recreation management by examining select constructs specified in the theory—biospheric values, NEP, and pro-environmental personal norms. Their analysis of survey data obtained from 341 students supported the application of the VBN theory to this particular population. Biospheric values positively influenced NEP, which in turn predicted pro-environmental personal norms. Furthermore, personal norms significantly explained students' engagement in curtailment and behavior choice as well as their opinions about the responsibility of businesses to incorporate environmental management into business operations (Casper and Pfahl, 2012).

To further understand the application of the VBN theory to sport settings, recall the case of the construction of the Heavener Football Complex by the University of Florida Athletic Department discussed earlier. The VBN theory suggests that athletic staff's decision to support the construction of the facility originally arose from their biospheric (concern about ecosystems), altruistic (concern about the welfare of the human society), and egoistic (concern about their self-interests) values. These values, in turn, activated their personal beliefs that (a) human actions can adversely influence a fragile biosphere (NEP), (b) the non-human species and ecosystems are under threat (AC beliefs), and (c) their own actions, such as the construction of an energy-efficient facility, can reduce the threat (AR beliefs). Finally, these beliefs led the staff to develop personal norms, or sense of obligation, to engage in pro-environmental action, influencing their support for the facility construction.

In summary, the strength of the VBN theory is to show that personal values, beliefs, and norms relating to pro-environmental action greatly influence the decision to engage in given pro-environmental behavior. This highlights the importance of fostering environmental consciousness among sport managers, athletes, and consumers to advance sustainability in the sport industry. On the other hand, the weakness of this theory is its inability to take into account the effects of personal capabilities, social norms, and attitudes, which are well explained by the TRA and the TPB. Given the strength and weakness of the VBN theory as well as those of the TRA and the TPB identified above, one suggestion is to integrate the three theories, as illustrated in Figure 2.1. The combined strengths of these theories based on this integration should help increase our ability to predict and explain individuals' pro-environmental behavior in sport settings.

Conclusions

This chapter aimed to provide theoretical foundations for understanding pro-environmental behavior pertaining to sport by reviewing existing research on this behavior in broad contexts and showing the application of the reviewed information to the sport context. To achieve this aim, the chapter first explained the definitions and classification of pro-environmental behavior. Based on the intent-oriented definition, pro-environmental behavior was defined as actions undertaken with intent to benefit the environment (Dietz et al., 1998; Stern, 2000; Stern et al., 1999). Moreover, the three types of this behavior were introduced, namely environmental activism, non-activist behavior in the public sphere, and private-sphere environmentalism. Next,

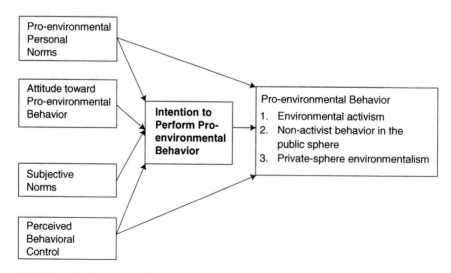

FIGURE 2.1 An integrative framework for understanding pro-environmental behavior

Note: this framework is developed by combining the theory of reasoned action (Ajzen and Fishbein, 1980), the theory of planned behavior (Ajzen, 1991), and the value-belief-norm theory (Stern et al., 1999).

the chapter identified various factors that have been found to affect one's decision to perform pro-environmental behavior based on the two major categories: internal factors and external factors. Internal factors entail personal preferences or tendencies, such as attitudinal variables, personal capabilities, emotions, and routines and habits, whereas external factors include contextual characteristics, such as constraints, social norms, incentives and punishment, and information. Finally, to demonstrate the interrelationships between these factors and further offer systematic views of how pro-environmental behavior can be explained, the three theoretical frameworks—the TRA (Ajzen and Fishbein, 1980), the TPB (Ajzen, 1991), and the VBN theory (Stern et al., 1999)—and their integration were discussed.

The information provided in this chapter offers a number of opportunities for researchers seeking to advance our understanding of pro-environmental behavior in sport as well as practitioners seeking to promote this behavior within their organizations and among athletes and consumers. Regarding research opportunities, the chapter shows that pro-environmental behavior is not unidimensional, but consists of different types of behavior. An analysis of the previous studies investigating pro-environmental behavior in sport (Casper and Pfahl, 2012; Inoue and Kent, 2012a, 2012b; McCullough and Cunningham, 2011), however, suggests that these studies focused on limited types of behavior, such as recycling. Therefore, future research should examine a wider range of pro-environmental behavior by asking such questions as: "Why do some professional athletes actively engage in environmental movements?"; "What factors affect a sport manager's decision to organize a charity event for an environmental organization?"; and "How can the use of public transportation be promoted among sport spectators?"

In addition, although the review of the environmental psychology literature reveals various internal and external factors that may influence pro-environmental behavior, sport management research has assessed the effects of only a few factors, such as attitudinal variables (Casper and Pfahl, 2012; Inoue and Kent, 2012b; McCullough and Cunningham, 2011) and communication strategies (Inoue and Kent, 2012a), suggesting the need for further investigation. For example, it has been argued that sport products are unique because of their ability to evoke emotions among consumers (Babiak and Wolfe, 2009). Given this, an important question is how emotions generated at a sport event would increase spectators' support for an environmental program implemented by event organizers. Also, investigations into the effects of both incentives and punishments on sport managers' decisions to adopt environmental programs and technologies would allow governments and government agencies (e.g., the United States Environmental Protection Agency) to further promote environmental management in the sport industry.

Furthermore, aside from some exceptions (Casper and Pfahl, 2012; McCullough and Cunningham, 2011), the application of the major theoretical frameworks for pro-environmental behavior (i.e., the TRA, the TPB, VBN theory) to the sport context is limited. Nevertheless, the utility of these theories is promising given that previous studies in sport (Babiak and Trendafilova, 2011; Kellison and Kim, 2014; Trendafilova and Babiak, 2013), though not directly referring to these frameworks, identified the determinants of pro-environmental behavior aligned with the frameworks, such as strategic motives (cf. egoistic values in the VBN theory) and the perception of social norms (cf. subjective norms in the TRA and the TPB). Consequently, further studies are encouraged to explicitly incorporate these theories into various types of pro-environmental behavior as well as different populations engaging in sport.

For sport practitioners, the current classification of pro-environmental behavior can be used to evaluate how their organizations progress toward achieving sustainability goals for specific behavioral types. For example, although a sport organization proactively addresses private-sphere environmentalism through its recycling activities and use of environmental technologies, its pro-environmental efforts could still be regarded as unsuccessful because of its failure to adopt practices related to environmental activism and non-activist behavior. Given complexities associated with sustainability (Kazdin, 2009), the assessment of organizations' environmental performance based on concrete behaviors is essential.

Using the information on the types of factors affecting pro-environmental behavior as well as the theoretical frameworks for explaining this behavior, sport practitioners can design and implement effective initiatives that increase engagement in pro-environmental behavior among their colleagues and customers. Specifically, the information on internal factors is useful to identify individuals who are more likely to support environmental programs by the organization. For example, surveys can be implemented to understand the personal characteristics of employees and customers (e.g., season-ticket holders) regarding environmental concern, such as their environmental values and knowledge and current practice of pro-environmental behavior. In addition, the information on external factors can be used to create an environment where both employees and customers are willing to engage in pro-environmental behavior promoted by the organization. Finally, the frameworks will allow sport practitioners to see the connections among different influencing factors and systematically evaluate the information related to pro-environmental behavior.

References

Africa News (2013) 'Environment; half-marathon to celebrate Nairobi as world's "environment capital"', February 1.

Ajzen, I. (1991) 'The theory of planned behavior', *Organizational Behavior and Human Decision Processes*, 50: 179–211.

Ajzen, I. and Fishbein, M. (eds) (1980) *Understanding attitudes and predicting social behaviour*, Englewood Cliffs, NJ: Prentice Hall.

Andersson, L., Shivarajan, S. and Blau, G. (2005) 'Enacting ecological sustainability in the MNC: A test of an adapted value–belief–norm framework', *Journal of Business Ethics*, 59: 295–305.

Babiak, K. and Trendafilova, S. (2011) 'CSR and environmental responsibility: Motives and pressures to adopt green management practices', *Corporate Social Responsibility and Environmental Management*, 18: 11–24.

Babiak, K. and Wolfe, R. (2009) 'Determinants of corporate social responsibility in professional sport: Internal and external factors', *Journal of Sport Management*, 23: 717–42.

Bagozzi, R. and Dabholkar, P. (1994) 'Consumer recycling goals and their effect on decisions to recycle: A means-end chain analysis', *Psychology and Marketing*, 11: 313–40.

Boston University School of Public Health (2013) *The theory of planned behavior*. Available online at: http://sphweb.bumc.bu.edu/otlt/MPH-Modules/SB/SB721-Models/SB721-Models3.html#limitationsofthetheoryofplannedbehavior (accessed April 7, 2014).

Brothers, K. J., Krantz, P. J. and McClannahan, L. E. (1994) 'Office paper recycling: A function of container proximity', *Journal of Applied Behavior Analysis*, 27: 153–60.

Casper, J. M. and Pfahl, M. E. (2012) 'Environmental behavior frameworks of sport and recreation undergraduate students', *Sport Management Education Journal*, 6: 8–20.

Casper, J. M., Pfahl, M. E. and McSherry, M. (2012) 'Athletics department awareness and action regarding the environment: A study of NCAA athletics department sustainability practices', *Journal of Sport Management*, 26: 11–29.

Chua, G. (2010) 'Greening the games: Sporting events around the world are getting more eco-conscious', *The Straits Times*, May 31.

Cialdini, R. B., Reno, R. R. and Kallgren, C. A. (1990) 'A focus theory of normative conduct: Recycling the concept of norms to reduce littering in public places', *Journal of Personality and Social Psychology*, 58: 1015–26.

Clayton, S. and Myers, S. (2009) *Conservation psychology: Understanding and promoting human care for nature*, Hoboken, NJ: Wiley-Blackwell.

Cordano, M., Marshall, R. S. and Silverman, M. (2010) 'How do small and medium enterprises go "green"? A study of environmental management programs in the U.S. wine industry', *Journal of Business Ethics*, 92: 463–78.

Dietz, T., Stern, P. C. and Guagnano, G. A. (1998) 'Social structural and social psychological bases of environmental concern', *Environment and Behavior*, 30: 450–71.

Dietz, T., Fitzgerald, A. and Shwom, R. (2005) 'Environmental values', *Annual Review of Environment and Resources*, 30: 335–72.

Harland, P., Staats, H. and Wilke, H. A. M. (1999) 'Explaining pro-environmental intention and behavior by personal norms and the theory of planned behavior', *Journal of Applied Psychology*, 12: 2505–28.

Inoue, Y. and Kent, A. (2012a) 'Investigating the role of corporate credibility in corporate social marketing: A case study of environmental initiatives by professional sport organizations', *Sport Management Review*, 15: 330–44.

Inoue, Y. and Kent, A. (2012b) 'Sport teams as promoters of pro-environmental behavior: An empirical study', *Journal of Sport Management*, 26: 417–32.

Kantola, S. J., Syme, G. J. and Nesdale, A. R. (1983) 'The effects of appraised severity and efficacy in promoting water conservation: An informational analysis', *Journal of Applied Social Psychology*, 13: 144–82.

Kazdin, A. E. (2009) 'Psychological science's contributions to a sustainable environment: Extending our reach to a grand challenge of society', *American Psychologist*, 64: 339–56.

Kellison, T. B. and Kim, Y. K. (2014) 'Marketing pro-environmental venues in professional sport: Planting seeds of change among existing and prospective consumers', *Journal of Sport Management*, 28: 34–48.

Kelly Slater Foundation (n.d.) *About us*. Available online at: www.kellyslaterfoundation.org/about-us.htm (accessed November 1, 2013).

Lam, S. (1999) 'Predicting intentions to conserve water from the theory of planned behavior, perceived moral obligation, and perceived water right', *Journal of Applied Social Psychology*, 29: 1058–71.

Luzar, E. J. and Diagne, E. (1999) 'Participation in the next generation of agriculture conservation programs: The role of environmental attitudes', *Journal of Socio-Economics*, 28: 335–49.

McCullough, B. P. and Cunningham, G. B. (2011) 'Recycling intentions among youth baseball spectators', *International Journal of Sport Management and Marketing*, 10: 104–20.

McKenzie-Mohr, D. and Smith, W. (1999) *Fostering sustainable behavior: An introduction to community-based social marketing*, Gabriola Island, BC: New Society Publishers.

Natural Resources Defense Council (2012) *Game changer: How the sports industry is saving the environment*. Available online at: www.nrdc.org/greenbusiness/guides/sports/files/Game-Changer-report.pdf (accessed November 1, 2013).

Natural Resources Defense Council (2013) *Collegiate game changers: How campus sport is going green*. Available online at: www.nrdc.org/greenbusiness/guides/sports/files/collegiate-game-changers-report.pdf (accessed April 10, 2014).

Natural Resources Defense Council (n.d.) *Smarter business: Greening the games*. Available online at: www.nrdc.org/greenbusiness/guides/sports (accessed April 6, 2014).

Ölander, F. and Thøgersen, J. (1995) 'Understanding of consumer behaviour as a prerequisite for environmental protection', *Journal of Consumer Policy*, 18: 345–85.

Robertson, J. L. and Barling, J. (2013) 'Greening organizations through leaders' influence on employees' pro-environmental behaviors', *Journal of Organizational Behavior*, 34: 176–94.

Singer, M. (2011) 'Arena gives teams, environment a sporting chance', *Australian Financial Review*, May 28: 20.

Steg, L. and Vlek, C. (2009) 'Encouraging pro-environmental behaviour: An integrative review and research agenda', *Journal of Environmental Psychology*, 29: 309–17.

Stern, P. C. (1999) 'Information, incentives, and pro-environmental consumer behavior', *Journal of Consumer Policy*, 22: 461–78.

Stern, P. C. (2000) 'Toward a coherent theory of environmentally significant behavior', *Journal of Social Issues*, 56: 407–24.

Stern, P. C., Dietz, T., Abel, T., Guagnano, G. A. and Kalof, L. (1999) 'A value–belief–norm theory of support for social movements: The case of environmental concern', *Human Ecology Review*, 6: 81–97.

Sygall, D. (2011) 'It ain't easy being green; the carbon debate', *The Sun Herald*, June 12: 66.

The Northern Echo (2012) 'Football club is "carbon positive"', December 6.

Trendafilova, S. and Babiak, K. (2013) 'Understanding strategic corporate environmental responsibility in professional sport', *International Journal of Sport Management and Marketing*, 13: 1–26.

Vining, J. and Ebreo, A. (2002) 'Emerging theoretical and methodological perspectives on conservation behavior'. In R. B. Bechtel and A. Churchman (eds) *Handbook of environmental psychology*, New York: Wiley, pp. 541–58.

Washington Nationals (n.d.) *Facts & figures*. Available online at: http://nationals.mlb.com/was/ballpark/information/index.jsp?content=facts_figures (accessed November 1, 2013).

Webb, D. J., Mohr, L. A. and Harris, K. E. (2008) 'A re-examination of socially responsible consumption and its measurement', *Journal of Business Research*, 61: 91–8.

Zeller, T., Jr. (2009) 'Sport events join efforts to go green; green inc', *The International Herald Tribune*, August 10: 18.

3

TEACHING SPORT MANAGEMENT AND THE NATURAL ENVIRONMENT

Michael E. Pfahl

This chapter examines the importance of the natural environment to sport education. The research conducted in this area is useful to existing sport managers, but without application into the curriculum, it becomes one of academic interest only. The tension between sport organization activities and the natural environment is a key part of the pre-hire socialization process that is higher education, especially for students interested in managing events and facilities. Thus, this chapter makes the case for including the sport–natural environment relationship into sport management curricula.

The beginning

With the inception of the American College and University Presidents' Climate Commitment (Climate Commitment) (American Colleges and University Presidents' Climate Commitment 2013; Emanuel and Adams 2011; Swearingen White 2009), American university and college personnel agreed to accept its guide to addressing on-campus sustainability issues. The work goes beyond only climate change and seeks to develop change mechanisms throughout campus units to reconfigure the entire natural footprint of a campus. While this will not occur overnight, the agreement does provide a starting point for university and college personnel (i.e., sustainability coordinators) to begin to interact with campus unit management personnel and develop strategic plans to change campus operations. As of 2014, over 600 colleges and university presidents signed the Climate Commitment (American College and University Presidents' Climate Commitment 2013). Institutional personnel across all university units are beginning to take stock of their environmental footprint (e.g., developing strategic plans) to achieve general benefits (e.g., corporate or community partnerships), operational benefits (e.g., revenue generation, cost savings), and other future benefits (e.g., goodwill) (Osmond et al. 2012; Pfahl 2011a; Swearingen White 2009; Vaughter et al. 2013).

With numerous on-campus efforts (e.g., recycling programs) and increasing attention given to the issue at campus recreation and athletics department sporting events (Casper et al. 2014), students at universities and colleges across America are ensconced in environmental activities, making an increased pedagogical presence of the natural environment in sport an important undertaking (Casper and Pfahl 2012). One key area in this process is the athletics department. Athletics department personnel at all levels of intercollegiate athletics are being asked to examine their role in greening the campus (Casper et al. 2012; Inoue and Kent 2012; Jin et al. 2011).

Awareness and action in context

The issue of sport's impact on the environment is one that works between awareness and action (Johnson and Mappin 2005). To a certain extent, students will have been made aware of various environmental issues as they matriculated through school and just simply growing up, although awareness of issues and depth of understanding will vary. Awareness of environmental issues means a person is both aware of the issues in the first place and has a level of understanding as to how these issues work in a particular context, both of which are individually and socially understood (Bamburg and Möser 2007; Spaargaren 2003; Szagun and Pavlov 1995). Consequences of environmental actions are also understood to various extents by students drawing upon broader and deeper moral and normative behaviors (Dunlap et al. 2000; Hansla et al. 2008; Stern 2000).

The environmental actions of students on campus are often individual oriented although with group actions commonly found in food waste reduction or recycling programs (Lounsbury 2001). The diversity of university and college campuses makes generalizing among student behaviors difficult and measuring environmentalist behaviors challenging. However, in the field of sport management, environmental issues are important and salient, making them ideal for inclusion in the curriculum.

A sport management curriculum is a pre-hire anticipatory socialization stage where students are preparing themselves for personal and career challenges within the sports industry (Casper and Pfahl 2012). The sport management major plays a significant role in shaping an individual's perceptions of a career track even if many of the forces at work in determining that track are not planned by the individual (e.g., chance meeting at a conference). The traditional description of organizational socialization processes has been a stage model (Feldman 1976; Jablin 1985, 1987), with individuals progressing through the choice of career paths (vocational organizational socialization, VOCS), moving into pre-entry, then entry/hire, encounter, metamorphosis (adopting/adapting), and finally exit stages (Jablin 1987). However, the stage model has been called into question because of the underlying presumption of linearity inherent in it (Hess 1993; Kramer and Noland 1999). Hess (1993) argued that a socialization process is likened more to overlapping clusters of events than it is to step-by-step stages. In his view, there is less discrete separation between sub-processes within the overall socialization process.

Early research showed the values, beliefs, and norms framework of under-standing environmental actions can work within the sport management education context, but showed specifically that personal values are important to environ-mental perspective development and issue understanding (Casper and Pfahl 2012). Additionally, personal norms were significant in terms of shaping perceptions and taking action (Casper and Pfahl 2012). One point of emphasis that illustrates the potential for overlapping processes is that of information-seeking. Information-seeking is especially important in the early aspects of a career decision-making process as the style and substance of the information and its source will influence the career perspective of the information seeker (e.g., perceptions of barriers and supports, self-efficacy). As *pre-managers*, the academic work done has the potential to shape future actions in the sport industry.

Engaging with the natural environment

The applied and experiential nature of sport management education often meant faculty members would use course-based (and beyond) learning opportunities to provide opportunities for students to learn and to apply skills and ideas in a sport context (e.g., event, internship) (Pauline and Pauline 2008; Southall et al. 2003). With roots going back to the writings of Dewey (1997) and James (2000), experiential learning (Kolb 1984; Kolb et al. 2001) is a combination of processes and outcomes resulting in an individual becoming an active part of the learn-ing process, both in the activity and through sense-making reflections about the experience (Dewey 1997; Light and Dixon 2007). In other words, "Knowledge is continuously derived from and tested out in the experiences of the learner" (Kolb 1984: 27). These experiential learning opportunities are being enhanced by emerging computer-mediated communication (CMC) elements bringing separate and connected online and offline opportunities to bear (Boyer 1990; Kolb 1984; Palmer 1998). Light and Dixon (2007) encouraged a shift from in-class lectures to engaging experience because they believed traditional content is not as strong without application and understanding of how to analyze situations in a critical manner and build in flexible thinking that adapts strategy and tactics to changing contextual conditions. Faculty members who work to balance what students need to know with co-construction and self-discovered experiences find themselves at an important intersection of theory and practice (Chalip 2006; Frisby 2005; Pastore 2003).

Experiential learning is not about mindless conduct of an activity, but is designed to weave theoretical and applied materials with an individual's reflexive thought processes in order to co-construct/co-produce learning and knowledge. Experiential learning can take place at the individual or group level, through indi-vidual and group interpretation of experiences. The result is that students can develop skills, engage in industry work experiences, and develop a better under-standing of the complex issues facing sport managers on a daily basis (Irwin et al. 2007; Parkhouse 1996; Pauline and Pauline 2008).

The natural environment provides opportunities for such experiential learning, as the environment touches all aspects of organizational operations in both conceptual and tangible ways. Conceptually, natural environment issues are a part of meta-level strategic decision making. Concepts such as the *triple bottom line* allow students and sport professionals alike to see how environmental issues are important to all organizational activities. For example, if a marketing manager is planning an activation event or community outreach program (e.g., 3–on-3 tournament in a park), it would be environmentally irresponsible to bring substantial amounts of paper and non-recyclable materials if the sport organization is supposed to be committed to environmental ideals. In a tactical sense, students in sport management can immediately apply environmental ideas and theories within their classroom work or related support activities. In keeping with a 3-on-3 basketball tournament, should a student organization organize one to raise money for a trip, they would be able to plan for environmental issues and utilize classroom knowledge about sustainable event practices as they prepare their event.

Internship and practicum experiences can also enhance the role of the environment in a sports management program. Sport organizations of all types understand the value of environmental responsibility, but they can also be encouraged to provide experiential opportunities for students (Pfahl 2011b). An internship or practicum can be had with facilities on campus or can be arranged with a sport organization. Ideally, sport organization personnel would develop an internship track that allows for two interns (or more) to manage internal and external engagement opportunities related to the environment (Pfahl 2011b). As sustainability in sport takes hold, such a situation should come to fruition. Additionally, university and college campus sustainability departments can be places where volunteer opportunities are developed. As athletics department and sustainability department personnel grow closer in their operations, opportunities on campus to work in this space will grow (Casper et al. 2012; Pfahl et al. in press; Trendafilova et al. 2013).

Thus, the natural environment provides a valuable strategic aspect to studies of sport management. Further, as there is no finish line for environmental activities (e.g., temporal nature of a marketing activity at an event), there is no shortage of possible engagement points with this issue. It never goes away and it must always remain at the top of the mind in strategic planning. Students, therefore, can utilize principles learned over time within and across courses within and outside of a sport management curriculum. Additionally, other university units can provide support for these efforts in many ways, including guest speakers, certificate program options, and case materials. The inclusion of the natural environment within various components of a sport management curriculum ultimately develops a student's theoretical and applied understanding of what managing a sport organization involves.

Changing curricula

When describing curricular change possibilities, it is important to discuss the issue of advocacy versus the examination of strategic issues. The issue of the natural environment is one that breeds divisiveness and debate. While not unhealthy in an academic setting, it is important to remember that the sport industry is already undertaking environmental initiatives as part of community outreach and a social contract that encourages sport personnel to *give back* to the local community (and beyond) (Carroll and Shabana 2010; Mohr et al. 2001; Smith and Alcorn 1991). Too often the environmental issue is politicized or only emphasizes one aspect (e.g., climate change). A holistic approach and balanced understanding of issues within the context will help students see why actions are needed (e.g., energy usage and cost savings) to improve sport organization performance and fan engagement and experiences, and to fulfill social contracts.

To accomplish this, a broad and holistic perspective is needed to examine environmental issues in the sport context. The Commission on Sport Management Accreditation outlines core Common Professional Component areas that guide their accreditation process: social, psychological, and international foundations of sport management (sport management principles, sport leadership, sport operations management/event and venue management, and sport governance); ethics in sport management, sport marketing and communication, and finance/accounting/economics (principles of sport finance, accounting, economics of sport, and legal aspects of sport); and integrative experience (strategic management/policy, internship, and capstone experience) (COSMA 2010). Through this lens, it is possible to see how natural environment issues can be integrated into sport management curricula. Further, it is important to recall that theoretical discussions can be supported with applied learning opportunities as facilities, sport and otherwise, are available for project-oriented work as well as field trips and site visits. Sport management faculty members can, and must, integrate the following principles into any curriculum:

- sensible application: meet students where they are at and teach where you are at (i.e., provide resources and open discussions);
- integrated and strategic progression: environmental literacy, environmental responsibility, and environmental advocacy;
- engagement oriented: include opportunities for students to give their perspective, but not always publicly (e.g., reflection papers, case studies, readings and reactions in class);
- broad focus: cases are everywhere (pedagogical familiarity), but more than what you would do? Include contextual analysis to understand the whys and hows of problem development prior to implementation.

A first key area is one that is possibly the most intangible and challenging. The natural environment, and the enactment of sport within it, makes for important and useful discussions in governance and ethics (Giacalone and Thompson 2006; Kashyap et al. 2006; Moberg 2006). Case studies (e.g., Major League Baseball green initiatives, Japanese Nippon Professional Baseball, NCAA and the Natural Resources Defense Council partnership) can be undertaken to outline the scope and substance of natural environmental issues and ideologies within sport (Natural

Resources Defense Council 2012, 2013). Case studies and video content are available about environmental change efforts in sport, and these can be used to understand the oversight and ethical nature of environmental efforts in sport.

Second, marketing coursework can be enhanced through the need to understand fan engagement with environmental issues (e.g., messaging, activation efforts, community outreach). Teams such as the Philadelphia Eagles and the Seattle Mariners spent a great deal of time and effort creating fun activities and learning opportunities for fans to undertake in and around games. Further, sponsorship studies in this area will elicit opportunities to understand how corporations and non-profit organizations utilize sport as a platform for engagement with fans about sustainability and environmental efforts while offering team personnel new revenue-generating opportunities.

Third, facility and event management contexts can be studied for a variety of reasons. The most obvious one is that facilities and events have an environmental impact. Examinations into the ways the impacts occur and are managed (e.g., planning and construction) offer a deep dive into environmental issues. Further, there are policy and process lessons that can be taught as students investigate ways to not only understand environmental issues associated with facility and event management, but also managing them into the future. The environmental issue is one that has no end point, so there is a need to discuss and to study how management, maintenance, and destruction of facilities take place.

Finally, capstone experiences, as well as others throughout a curriculum, can be enhanced with activities to understand the strategic planning processes associated with environmental issues in sport. All aspects of an organization's operations are touched by environmental issues (e.g., human resources and hiring, financing and budgeting, law and regulation compliance), making the issue one that can run through both entire curricula and individual classes. Without a final end point, the environment offers another route to understanding and engaging in strategic and tactical work, a stalwart of sport management education.

A conclusion, but not an end

Sport and the natural environment play an important role in shaping the elements of the communities in which sport organization personnel operate. Sport management students, as pre-managers (Casper and Pfahl 2012), require the most comprehensive and immersive experiences possible to prepare them for a career in the sport industry. With the multiplicity of linkages between sport organization and event operations and the environment, it is imperative that sport management curricula integrate the natural environment into its course and extracurricular work. Developing an understanding, a focus on, and even a passion for sustainability in sport requires a holistic approach to teaching (i.e., inside and outside of the classroom) that interconnects intellect, application, philosophy, and emotions into an immersive set of applied experiences that result in a transformative learning experience (Shrivastava 2010).

References

American Colleges and University Presidents' Climate Commitment. (2013) *Signatories list.* Available online at www.presidentsclimatecommitment.org/signatories/list (accessed 1 April 2013).

Bamburg, S. and Möser, G. (2007) 'Twenty years after Hines, Hungerford, and Tomera: A new meta-analysis of psycho-social determinants of pro-environmental behavior'. *Journal of Environmental Psychology*, 27: 14–25.

Boyer, E. (1990) *Scholarship reconsidered: Priorities of the professorate.* Princeton, NJ: The Carnegie Foundation for the Advancement of Teaching.

Carroll, A. B. and Shabana, K. M. (2010) 'The business case for corporate social responsibility: A review of concepts, research and practice'. *International Journal of Management Reviews*, 12: 85–105.

Casper, J. M. and Pfahl, M. E. (2012) 'Environmental behavior frameworks of sport and recreation undergraduate students'. *Sport Management Education Journal*, 6: 8–20.

Casper, J. M., Pfahl, M. E., and McSherry, M. (2012) 'Athletics department awareness and action regarding the environment: A study of NCAA athletics department sustainability practices'. *Journal of Sport Management*, 26: 11–29.

Casper, J. M., Pfahl, M. E., and McCullough, B. (2014) 'Intercollegiate sport and the environment: Examining fan engagement based on athletics department sustainability efforts'. *Journal of Issues in Intercollegiate Athletics*, 7: 65–91.

Chalip, L. (2006) 'Toward a distinctive sport management discipline'. *Journal of Sport Management*, 20: 1–21.

COSMA. (2010) *COSMA accreditation manual.* Available online at www.cosmaweb.org/accreditation-manuals.html (accessed 18 September 2014).

Dewey, J. (1997) *Democracy in education.* New York: Free Press.

Dunlap, R., Van Liere, K., Mertig, A., and Emmet Jones, R. (2000) 'Measuring endorsement of the New Ecological Paradigm: A revised NEP scale'. *Journal of Social Issues*, 56: 425–42.

Emanuel, R. and Adams, J. N. (2011) 'College students' perceptions of campus sustainability'. *International Journal of Sustainability in Higher Education*, 12: 79–92.

Feldman, D. C. (1976) 'A contingency theory of socialization'. *Administrative Science Quarterly*, 21: 433–52.

Frisby, W. (2005) 'The good, the bad, and the ugly: Critical sport management research'. *Journal of Sport Management*, 19: 1–13.

Giacalone, R. and Thompson, K. (2006) 'Business ethics and social responsibility education: Shifting the worldview'. *Academy of Management Learning & Education*, 5: 266–77.

Hansla, A., Gamble, A., Juliusson, A., and Gärling, T. (2008) 'The relationships between awareness of consequences, environmental concern, and value orientations'. *Journal of Environmental Psychology*, 28: 1–9.

Hess, J. A. (1993) 'Assimilating newcomers into an organization: A cultural perspective'. *Journal of Applied Communication Research*, 21: 189–210.

Inoue, Y. and Kent, A. (2012) 'Sport teams as promoters of pro-environmental behavior: An empirical study'. *Journal of Sport Management*, 26: 417–32.

Irwin, R. L., Southall, R. M., and Sutton, W. A. (2007) 'Pentagon of sport sales training: A 21st century sport sales training model'. *Sport Management Education Journal*, 1: 18–39.

Jablin, F. M. (1985) 'An exploratory study of vocational organizational communication socialization'. *Southern Journal of Communication*, 50: 261–82.

Jablin, F. M. (1987) 'Organizational entry, assimilation, and exit'. In F. M. Jablin, L. L. Putnam, K. H. Roberts, and L. W. Porter (eds), *Handbook of organizational communication* (pp. 679–740). Newbury Park, CA: SAGE.

James, W. (2000) *Pragmatism and other writings*. New York: Penguin Books.

Jin, L., Mao, L., Zhang, J., and Walker, M. (2011) 'Impact of green stadium initiatives on donor intentions toward an intercollegiate athletic programme'. *International Journal of Sport Management and Marketing*, 10: 121–41.

Johnson, E. and Mappin, M. (2005) *Environmental education and advocacy: Changing perspectives of ecology and education.* Cambridge: Cambridge University Press.

Kashyap, R., Mir, R., and Iyer, E. (2006) 'Toward a responsive pedagogy: Linking social responsibility to firm performance issues in the classroom'. *Academy of Management Learning & Education*, 5: 366–76.

Kolb, D. A. (1984) *Experiential learning: Experience as the source of learning and development.* Englewood Cliffs, NJ: Prentice-Hall.

Kolb, D. A., Boyatzis, R. E., and Mainemelis, C. (2001) 'Experiential learning theory: Previous research and new directions'. In R. Sternberg and L. Zhang (eds), *Perspectives on Thinking, Learning, and Cognitive Styles* (pp. 227–47). New York: Routledge.

Kramer, M. and Noland, T. (1999) 'Communication during job promotions: A case of ongoing assimilation'. *Journal of Applied Communication Research*, 27: 335–55.

Light, R. and Dixon, M. A. (2007) 'Contemporary developments in sport pedagogy and their implications for sport management education'. *Sport Management Review*, 10: 159–75.

Lounsbury, M. (2001) 'Institutional sources of practice variation: Staffing college and university recycling programs'. *Administrative Science Quarterly*, 46: 29–56.

Moberg, D. (2006) 'Best intentions, worst results: Grounding ethics students in the realities of organizational context'. *Academy of Management Learning & Education*, 5: 307–16.

Mohr, L. A., Webb, D. J., and Harris, K. E. (2001) 'Do consumers expect companies to be socially responsible? The impact of corporate social responsibility on buying behavior'. *Journal of Consumer Affairs*, 35: 45–72.

Natural Resources Defense Council. (2012, September) *Game changer: How the sports industry is saving the environment.* Available online at www.nrdc.org/greenbusiness/guides/sports/files/Game-Changer-report.pdf (accessed 20 March 2013).

Natural Resources Defense Council. (2013) *Collegiate game changers: How campus sport is going green.* Available online at www.nrdc.org/greenbusiness/guides/sports/files/collegiate-game-changers-report.pdf (accessed 7 November 2013).

Osmond, P., Dave, M., and Prasad, D. (2012) *Transforming universities into green and sustainable campuses: A toolkit for implementers.* Nairobi, Kenya: United Nations Environment Programme.

Palmer, P. (1998) *Courage to teach: Exploring the inner landscape of a teacher's life.* San Francisco, CA: Jossey-Bass Inc.

Parkhouse, B. (1996) *The management of sports: Its foundation and application.* St. Louis, MO: Mosby-Year Book.

Pastore, D. (2003) 'A different lens to view mentoring in sport management'. *Journal of Sport Management*, 17: 1–12.

Pauline, G. and Pauline, J. S. (2008) 'Teaching sport sponsorship activation through a client-based experiential learning project'. *Sport Management Education Journal*, 2: 19–37.

Pfahl, M. (2011a) 'Strategic issues associated with the development of internal sustainability teams in sport and recreation organizations: A framework for action and sustainable environmental performance'. *International Journal of Sport Management, Recreation & Tourism*, 6: 37–61.

Pfahl, M. (2011b) *Sport and the natural environment: A strategic guide.* Dubuque, IA: Kendall Hunt.

Pfahl, M., Casper, J., Trendafilova, S., McCullough, B. P., and Nguyen, S. N. (in press) 'Crossing boundaries: An examination of sustainability department and athletics department collaboration regarding environmental issues'. *Communication & Sport.*

Shrivastava, P. (2010) 'Pedagogy of passion for sustainability'. *Academy of Management Learning & Education,* 9: 443–55.

Smith, S. M. and Alcorn, D. S. (1991) 'Cause marketing: A new direction in the marketing of corporate responsibility'. *Journal of Services Marketing,* 5: 21–37.

Southall, R. M., Nagel, M. S., LeGrande, D., and Han, P. (2003) 'Sport management practica: A metadiscrete experiential learning model'. *Sport Marketing Quarterly,* 12: 27–36.

Spaargaren, G. (2003) 'Sustainable consumption: A theoretical and environmental policy perspective'. *Society & Natural Resources,* 16: 687–701.

Stern, P. (2000) 'Toward a coherent theory of environmentally significant behavior'. *Journal of Social Issues,* 56: 407–24.

Swearingen White, S. (2009) 'Early participation in the American College and University Presidents' Climate Commitment'. *International Journal of Sustainability in Higher Education,* 10: 215–27.

Szagun, G. and Pavlov, V. (1995) 'Environmental awareness: A comparative study of German and Russian adolescents'. *Youth & Society,* 27: 93–112.

Trendafilova, S., Pfahl, M. E., and Casper, J. (2013) 'The case of NCAA athletic departments'. In J. L. Paramio-Salcines, K. Babiak, and G. Walters (eds), *Routledge handbook of sport and corporate social responsibility* (pp. 105–18). New York: Routledge.

Vaughter, P., Wright, T., McKenzie, M., and Lidstone, L. (2013) 'Greening the ivory tower: A review of educational research on sustainability in post-secondary education'. *Sustainability,* 5: 2252–71.

SECTION II
Strategic approach

4

STRATEGIC MANAGEMENT

Jonathan M. Casper

The purpose of this chapter is to explore how managers make decisions when it comes to environmental actions. Three broad management implications will be covered: awareness, knowledge, and action. The environmental strategic planning process based on the managerial decision-making model for initiating environmental actions is then described.

Importance of strategic management and environmental sustainability

The rationale for sport organization personnel to account for the natural environment is sound. Based on statistics presented in Chapter 1, the environmental footprint of sport is large and significant. At the most basic level, many of the sports that are played today are outdoors. As we need clean air to breathe, clean water to drink, and a healthy climate in which to live, we need to account for resources related to sport consumption as they are linked to all other aspects of life; in fact nature is the ultimate resource of all economic value ([Natural Resources Defense Council] NRDC, 2012).

Sport managers must recognize this and have the *ability and willingness* to take action. Decision-makers must devote the same level of effort to keeping natural capital intact as they do to more traditional capital (NRDC, 2012). The growing environmental movement and increased resources available to address environmental issues (e.g., Green Sports Alliance) for sport originations has helped with driving the integration of environmental sustainability within sport organization operations (Thibault, 2009; Trendafilova et al., 2013). These statements gain further credibility as every commissioner of a professional sport league in the United States has made a commitment to environmental stewardship and are actively encouraging teams in their leagues to incorporate sustainable measures into their operations (NRDC, 2012). While this demonstrates progress, the adoption of sustainability initiatives does not ensure success. This is particularly true for organizations that view sustainability only in terms of its public-relations value. It has been shown that such narrowly focused or shallow sustainability programs do not last (Blackburn, 2007). Environmental sustainability within sport operations needs to have the support of managers and be strategically planned out.

Fundamental to all management decisions is a thorough justification of why chosen operational actions will work (e.g., management strategy) and how such actions link to operational goals and objectives (e.g., revenue generation, cost reduction). The decisions made by sport managers are based not only on prior organizational knowledge and research, but on personal values and beliefs (Stern, 2000). The emerging role of the natural environment in sport challenges sport managers to understand their own views on the environment (e.g., it is not an issue; he or she is a passionate advocate) and on the enabling and constraining elements within their operational context (e.g., university guidelines or mandates; governmental regulations) (Hums et al., 1999).

Like their counterparts in the traditional corporate world, sport managers are in a liminal position in which they must balance their presence as change agents with their responsibilities to fulfill organizational missions, whether voluntary or directed (Bohdanowicz, 2006; Rivera and De Leon, 2005; Spaargaren, 2003). Similarly, sport managers, especially those with direct authority over areas with significant environmental elements (e.g., a facility manager), are now held accountable and measured by different standards (Hums et al., 1999; Mascarenhas, 2009). The current environmental movement is driving a need to know more about the environmental impact of a sport organization, but most have other priorities to balance against any environmental strategic planning or action (Casper et al., 2012). In sport, this becomes even more complicated. For example, a U.S. collegiate athletic director must balance goals related to monitoring teams and players, scheduling games and events, fundraising and budgeting, and hiring and supervising personnel. For many sport organization personnel, the ultimate objective is having a winning program/team, and if operational activities do not relate or seem extraneous to that goal they may be marginalized. As environmental issues are integrated into strategic planning processes in sport organizations, sport managers must become more aware and knowledgeable about environmental issues in order to balance (and satisfy) competing stakeholder requirements through the actions they take.

Awareness, knowledge, and action

One of the fundamental issues of environmental action in sport operations is to understand the processes that preceded how a successful greening program was implemented. While resources to accomplish green programs are now available, individual-level changes may first need to happen for a manager to seek resources. A manager whose values and beliefs about environmental sustainability are negative will probably not even seek out resources and information. So the main issue is change needs to happen at an individual level. Additionally, for many, seeing is believing. Elements of social proof (informal social influence) from seeing actions and results inside and outside the sport organization may influence values and beliefs. By identifying specific information about an individual's environmental values, beliefs, awareness, and knowledge, which precede actions, sport managers will begin to better understand how to incorporate environmental issues into long-term planning and daily operations for a more sustainable approach to sustainability and the environment.

The literature reveals connections between awareness and action, which makes understanding environmentally related core values, beliefs, and awareness of sport managers an important part of the overall evaluation as to whether environmental actions will be taken. Individual perspectives about environmental issues are as varied as the people who hold them (Starkey and Crane, 2003). Educational, contextual, and personal interest levels of environmental issues vary within a person (e.g., awareness of recycling, but minimal knowledge of air pollution issues). These perspectives are developed (and change) over time and are used when sport and managers begin making strategic decisions in line with changing competitive environment contexts (Hums et al., 1999). Such variation means there can never be a single approach to environmental activities because of the variation in awareness and knowledge of the individual(s) involved in them. This is further complicated by the continual change that takes place within a given context (i.e., sport team). Simply looking at environmental outcomes as a measure of success is incomplete unless there is a commensurate examination of the context in question and the awareness, knowledge, and actions of the individual(s) involved.

Greater understanding of an individual's awareness and knowledge of environmental issues helps to evaluate decision-making processes about environmental issues as well as the success of environmental actions taken (Nicolaides, 2006). Further, it helps to create a holistic framework for analyzing the environmental actions from an organizational perspective (Figure 4.1).

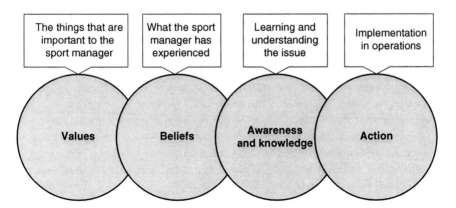

FIGURE 4.1 Holistic understanding of environmental issues

Source: created by author.

Values and beliefs

Examination into linkages between environmental values, beliefs, awareness, knowledge, and action is an important part of literature related to the environment (Schmidt, 2006; Stern, 2000). From a strategic managerial perspective, values and beliefs help to contextualize decision-making processes. Improved contextualization helps to address why choices were made.

Values are principles, standards, or qualities that an individual or group of people hold in high regard (i.e., they are things that are important to you). These values guide the way we live our lives and the decisions we make. At its core, a value is commonly formed by a particular belief that is related to the worth of an idea or type of behavior. Some people may see great value in saving the world's rainforests; however, a person who relies on the logging of a forest for their job may not place the same value on the forest as a person who wants to save it (e.g., not caring for sustainability of the forest or differing in the perspective of what constitutes sustainable logging) (State of New South Wales, 2009). Past research has suggested that it is important that we do not influence manager decisions based on *our* values. We should always work from the basis of supporting the manager's values (State of New South Wales, 2009). For pro-environmental behavior, values placed on different targets (e.g., self, people in general, or the biosphere) direct attention toward value-congruent information, which affects the willingness to support environmental protections (Steg et al., 2005). For example, if a manager recognizes or is shown that fans expect pro-environmental actions, they may be willing to direct resources, time, and efforts even if their values are not similar (e.g., example of social proof).

Beliefs come from real experiences (i.e., they are what you believe to be true from what you have experienced). Our values and beliefs affect the quality of our work and all our relationships because what you believe is what you experience (State of New South Wales, 2009). It is assumed that environmental behavior results from the beliefs individuals have about the relationship between humans and the environment (Steg et al., 2005). When it comes to strategic sustainable actions, due to it being relatively new, a sport manager may not have real experiences, so may rely on their values more than beliefs in future actions.

Values and beliefs can be symbiotic, but also in conflict with each other. Experiences that we have that match our values will reinforce each other and appear to be *correct*. Experiences that contradict our values raise questions of the experience and of our values. The tension between the two helps to foster our awareness of issues around us and the constant interplay of our experiences and values. An outcome of this tension is our attitude toward something. However, the intricacy of our attitude is related to our ability to be aware of the complexities of a given context or situation (i.e., awareness levels).

Awareness

As we delve further in management decision-making, awareness of the environmental issues and ways to confront the issues becomes important. Awareness, formed from our values and beliefs, refers to an individual's understanding of the *basic elements* within an issue, not simply being aware an issue exists (Morrone et al., 2001; Pfahl, 2011). For example, a manager is aware of pollution created by sport-event tailgating and understands the causes. Awareness of environmental issues comprises sensitivity to the existence of the issues and an appreciation of how these issues are enacted in a particular context. A manager must have situational awareness to understand the impact of environmental action and who is impacted. Within a sport context this can comprise a variety of elements (e.g., budgets, group interactions). Each of these elements influences strategic and operational awareness, decisions, and, ultimately, action(s) taken (Spaargaren, 2003). A highly aware perspective is needed to seek out information about an environmental issue and to take environmental action(s) (Bamburg and Möser, 2007; Harland et al., 1999; Manstead, 2000; Schwartz, 1977). In our case, we seek to inform managers about environmental awareness, understanding the fragility of our environment and the importance of its protection.

Knowledge

Knowledge refers to an individual's depth of understanding about the environmental issues he or she must deal with at any given moment. Whether examined from a strategic or operational perspective, environmental issues are present in sport or recreation contexts. How aware he or she is to the importance of an issue and the level of knowledge he or she has about it determines the action(s) taken (Spaargaren, 2003). This means awareness of an issue does not directly mean knowledge of an issue. One can be aware a problem exists (e.g., pollution) and care about prevention/reduction, but unless there is an integrated, systemic perspective employed by an individual sport manager (e.g., understanding how pollution is generated), true knowledge of the issue is not developed (Bamburg and Möser, 2007; Harland et al., 1999; Manstead, 2000; Schwartz, 1977). The move from awareness to knowledge is driven by an individual's ability to observe and to understand the complexities of a given context at a given moment while also taking into account historical aspects (e.g., past decisions) and future implications (e.g., impact on organizational operations) associated with it (Horne, 2006; Johnson, 2001). In other words, a breadth and depth of understanding (i.e., knowledge).

However, managerial awareness, knowledge, and action is enabled and constrained by contextual factors no matter the level of knowledge obtained (Deetz, 1992; Foucault, 2001). As noted earlier, these contextual factors produce a tension between values and understanding experiences as well as between an individual's personal value(s) and the organizational needs for which he or she is responsible. Within this changing context, decisions must be made leading to environmental action(s) (Hansla et al., 2008; Stern, 2000).

Action

Environmental actions can take many different forms. For many sport managers, actions will take place in the context of daily activities such as office operations, facility and event management, and personal practices (e.g., reduced printing). In the corporate world, environmental reporting and environmental audits and reports are issued to explain actions taken to interested stakeholders (Jose and Lee, 2007; Wilmshurst and Frost, 2000). However, this practice is less common in the sport world. What exactly sport managers do and know is critical towards developing an understanding of the effectiveness of current practices, be they game-day recycling efforts or large-scale university/organizational initiatives, and the ability to report and to communicate them effectively (Nicolaides, 2006; Pfahl, 2011).

Strategic planning activities and operational actions related to environmental issues focus on internal and external aspects of organizational operations (Etzion, 2007; Vastag et al., 1996). Having a clearer understanding of awareness and knowledge by individual sport and recreation managers will assist in determining the appropriateness and usefulness of actions taken (e.g., recycling efforts, purchasing choices) (Nicolaides, 2006).

Developing a strategic sustainability plan

To help with changing values and beliefs and create awareness and knowledge of why accounting for environmental sustainability is important in sport organization operations, a strategic plan should be developed. What most sport managers will want to know is *what* it is they are being asked to do and *why* it is important for the organization to achieve it (Blackburn, 2007). A strategic framework encourages dialogue, explains change, and can be an effective way of planning for sustainability within complex sport organizations (Hart, 1995; Pfahl, 2011). A strategic plan provides awareness and knowledge, allowing emphasis to go into creating the action. The steps to creating a plan outlined in this chapter are a model for environmental planning and decision-making (Table 4.1). The steps for developing a strategic plan are summarized from the Planning for Sustainability Guide (2009) by Natural Step, an international non-profit sustainability consulting firm. We have also incorporated recommendations from the NRDC Game Changer Reports (2012, 2013) into the structure and substance of the plan. Readers who would like to get more information on the specifics of this process are encouraged to view the free reports.

The Natural Step Sustainability Starter Guide:
www.naturalstep.ca/planning-for-sustainability-a-starter-guide

NRDC Report: Game Changer:
www.nrdc.org/greenbusiness/guides/sports/files/Game-Changer-report.pdf

TABLE 4.1 Strategic planning process

Section	Description	Suggested tasks
Getting ready	Assess how prepared your organization is to engage in a sustainability-driven change initiative.	1. Form a team. 2. Assess governance and decision-making practices.
Step A—Awareness	Establish a shared understanding among a core team of people of global sustainability challenges and how they are relevant to your organization's success.	3. Evaluate and build awareness of the relevance of sustainability to your organization. 4. Develop a common language and understanding around sustainability.
Step B—Baseline analysis	Analyze at high level the social and environmental impacts of your organization.	5. Create an inventory of assets that you can build from in your sustainability initiative. 6. Conduct a sustainability impacts analysis for your organization. 7. Evaluate stakeholder relationships with respect to how they can help and hinder your organization's sustainability initiative.
Step C—Compelling vision	Create a compelling vision and long-term strategic goals to guide your organization towards sustainability.	8. Synthesize your learning from Step B into "strategic goals."
Step D—Down to action	Brainstorm potential solutions to bring you closer to your vision; prioritize first steps and quick wins; and develop the first draft of a strategic plan to capture short-, medium-, and long-term measures toward success.	9. Set performance indicators and targets. 10. Brainstorm opportunities for action. 11. Screen and prioritize the potential actions. 12. Create an action implementation table.
Step E—Continuing the journey	Embed strategic planning into ongoing processes that support your organization's movement toward sustainability.	13. Periodically review the plan. 14. Report to stakeholders and celebrate success. 15. Ensure ongoing integration of sustainability concepts.

Source: Recreated with permission from Natural Step (2009).

Establishing a team

While often the initial greening movement within sport organizations begins with an individual or *champion*, the ones that are most successful incorporate the culture of the organization, and this requires a team (NRDC, 2012; Pfahl, 2010, 2011). Successful environmental initiatives take the coordination of many stakeholders and, while it may take an individual to have the onus to get something started, it takes a team to have a successful green program. The stakeholders involved in sport organizations can be complex, so it is important to identify major decision-makers at the table.

A strong core team will have:

- a cross-section of people from different departments or programs who perform diverse tasks within the organization;
- a diverse skill-set, including communications, networking, reporting, marketing, business development, etc., and the participation of influencers (people who influence decision-makers);
- time mapped out in each individual's work plan to participate in this project.

Step A: awareness—establishing a shared understanding

The major parts of awareness in the strategic process are evaluating and building awareness of the relevance of sustainability within the sport organization and developing a common language and understanding around sustainability. Building awareness often starts with a dialogue of what some of the challenges the organization is facing are and how sustainability can help address the challenges. This leads to identification of where sustainability applies to the organization, and should go beyond the business (or cost savings) case and look at internal operation and human resources to the perceptions of the sport organization brand. Next, the desired common language around sustainability is to move from old behaviors, norms, values, and beliefs to a new way of thinking. This means making sure the team has a firm understanding of sustainability and how to strategically move forward.

Step B: baseline analysis—overall impacts of organization

Within the baseline analysis, the sustainability team should create sustainability initiative inventory. This includes identification of current initiatives (e.g., green games), programs (e.g., stadium recycling program), relationships, policies, or other actions already being undertaken. Within this process the team can look for particular assets that can be built upon or leveraged. After the inventory there is identification of the current environmental impacts of the organization. Simplified, these may include impacts to degradation of land, water, and air. After a thorough analysis, the team may prioritize impacts that are more significant than others and identify those that they have control over. Lastly, the team should look at key stakeholders that can affect and influence the organization sustainability initiatives.

This includes brainstorming on what stakeholders stand to lose or gain from sustainability initiatives and what stakeholder actions could affect their success (e.g., BASF sponsorship of Sustainable Saturdays at Seattle Mariners games).

Step C: compelling vision—vision and long-term goals for guidance

As with any strategic plan, the research conducted in the prior steps guides the rationale of strategic goals. As the sustainability team looks at the past steps, there may be some very clear goals that will lead to success in environmental sustainability. This may be based on connection and relationships with stakeholders to give direction, or they may be based on agreement from the team on a certain direction to go. In any case, strategic goals need to address sustainable outcomes.

Step D: down to action—make a plan with emphasis on first steps

Once the goals and objectives have been clearly identified, it is time for action. This is often done by identifying performance indicators (or metrics) that will be quantifiable if the sustainability plan is successful. It is also important to note that any indicator development should be done prior to beginning an action and should be done in conjunction with any stakeholders (e.g., utility company) to ensure what is measured is what is sought. With any indicator, realistic targets should be identified. For example, by tracking environmental data such as energy and water use, you can assess performance and identify opportunities for improvement. Additionally, by quantifying successes and documenting progress, you will inspire further investment by staff, partners, fans, and sponsors.

The team can then brainstorm for specific opportunities for action to meet a performance indicator. The first step is to create strategies (i.e., what you want to do) and tactics (i.e., how you are going to do it) that are measurable. For many sport organizations just starting out, the NRDC recommends starting with efforts that have the fastest return on investment and meet goals that the team have established. These "low hanging fruits" may show more immediate success and attract interest in other greening opportunities.

Step E: continuing the journey—a sustainable sustainability plan

With any environmental action, evaluation and continuation is important. You want to be able to understand if what you did actually worked, especially when time and resources are invested. In many cases this can be done in the prior steps. When an environmental action is planned, there needs to be someone responsible for the action, the tasks are laid out, a budget is agreed upon, and there are markers made for progress and completion.

For many actions this can be measurable (e.g., achieving a 98 percent landfill diversion rate), but for others, evaluation may be more difficult (e.g., fan education). In any case, actions need to have periodic reviews, there needs to be continued meetings of the green team, and you must ensure stakeholder involvement.

Another important continuing metric is to report successes. This needs to be done both internally and externally. To do so, you can prepare a sustainability report that communicates progress to achieve sustainability goals, also making sure to provide opportunities for staff and stakeholders to remain involved, and especially in sport this means communicating success to fans. Greening initiatives provide opportunities for fans to interact with the team and the community. Publicizing actions and success can yield great fan response and may lead to additional opportunities through further efforts such as sponsorship initiatives.

Conclusions

The first step toward green sport programs is strategic management. Sport managers must go through a decision-making process whereby they understand the environmental footprint that their organization has, are willing to take steps to minimize where possible, and then create a strategic plan that includes major stakeholders in the origination to implement actions. To get to this stage we must understand the manager's values and beliefs. Understanding that managers may not have pro-environmental values and beliefs and may even view barriers such as cost and time prohibitive to creating a greening program, it is important to help with the generation of awareness and knowledge of what the organization can do. This may be done by communicating the values of key stakeholders that are part of the organization (e.g., fans or employees) or education on what other sport organizations are doing to increase knowledge.

References

Bamburg, S., and Möser, G. (2007) 'Twenty years after Hines, Hungerford, and Tomera: A new meta-analysis of psycho-social determinants of pro-environmental behavior', *Journal of Environmental Psychology*, 27: 14–25.

Blackburn, W. R. (2007) *The sustainability handbook*. Washington D.C.: Earthscan.

Bohdanowicz, P. (2006) 'Environmental awareness and initiatives in the Swedish and Polish hotel industries—survey results', *Hospitality Management*, 25: 662–82.

Casper, J., Pfahl, M., and McSherry, M. (2012) 'Athletic department awareness and action regarding the environment: A study of NCAA athletic department sustainability practices', *Journal of Sport Management*, 26: 11–29.

Deetz, S. (1992) *Democracy in an age of corporate colonization: Developments in communication and everyday life*. Albany, NY: State University of New York Press.

Etzion, D. (2007) 'Research on organizations and the natural environment, 1992–present: A review', *Journal of Management*, 33: 637–64.

Foucault, M. (2001) *Fearless speech* (ed. by J. Pearson). Los Angeles, CA: Semiotext(e).

Hansla, A., Gamble, A., Juliusson, A., and Gärling, T. (2008) 'The relationships between awareness of consequences, environmental concern, and value orientations', *Journal of Environmental Psychology*, 28: 1–9.

Harland, P., Staats, H., and Wilke, H. (1999) 'Explaining proenvironmental intention and behaviour by personal norms and the theory of planned behaviour', *Journal of Applied Social Psychology*, 29: 2505–28.

Hart, S. (1995) 'A natural-resource-based view of the firm', *The Academy of Management Review*, 20: 986–1014.

Horne, J. (2006) *Sport in consumer culture*. New York: Palgrave Macmillan.

Hums, M., Barr, C., and Guillon, L. (1999) 'The ethical issues confronting managers in the sport industry', *Journal of Business Ethics*, 20: 51–66.

Johnson, S. (2001) *Emergence: The connected lives of ants, brains, cities, and software*. New York: Scribner.

Jose, A., and Lee, S-M. (2007) 'Environmental reporting of global corporations: A content analysis based on website disclosures', *Journal of Business Ethics*, 72: 307–21.

Manstead, A. (2000) 'The role of moral norm in the attitude–behaviour relation'. In D. Terry and M. Hogg (eds), *Attitude, behaviour, and social context: The role of norms and group membership* (pp. 11–30). Mahwah, NJ: Lawrence Erlbaum.

Mascarenhas, B. (2009) 'The emerging CEO agenda', *Journal of International Management*, 15: 245–50.

Morrone, M., Mancl, K., and Carr, K. (2001) 'Development of a metric to test group differences in ecological knowledge as one component of environmental literacy', *The Journal of Environmental Education*, 32: 33–42.

Natural Resources Defense Council (NRDC). (2012) *Game changer: How the sports industry is saving the environment*. Available online at www.nrdc.org/greenbusiness/guides/sports/files/Game-Changer-report.pdf (accessed 16 April 2014).

Natural Resources Defense Council (NRDC). (2013) *Collegiate game changers: How campus sport is going green*. Available online at www.nrdc.org/greenbusiness/guides/sports/files/collegiate-game-changers-report.pdf (accessed 16 April 2014).

Natural Step. (2009) *Planning for sustainability: A starter guide*. Available online at www.naturalstep.ca/planning-for-sustainability-a-starter-guide (accessed 16 April 2014).

Nicolaides, A. (2006) 'The implementation of environmental management towards sustainable universities and education for sustainable development as an ethical imperative', *International Journal of Sustainability in Higher Education*, 7: 414–24.

Pfahl, M. (2010) 'Strategic issues associated with the development of internal sustainability teams in sport organizations: A framework for action and sustainable environmental performance', *International Journal of Sport Management, Recreation, and Tourism*, 6(C): 37–61.

Pfahl, M. (2011) *Sport and the natural environment: A strategic guide*. Dubuque, IA: Kendall Hunt.

Rivera, J., and De Leon, P. (2005) 'Chief executive officers and voluntary environmental performance: Costa Rica's certification for sustainable tourism', *Policy Sciences*, 38: 107–27.

Schmidt, C. (2006) 'Putting the Earth in play: Environmental awareness and sports', *Environmental Health Perspectives*, 114: A286–A295.

Schwartz, S. (1977) 'Normative influence on altruism'. In L. Berkowitz (ed.), *Advances in experimental social psychology*, 10 (pp. 221–79). New York: Academic Press.

Spaargaren, G. (2003) 'Sustainable consumption: A theoretical and environmental policy perspective', *Society & Natural Resources*, 16: 687–701.

Starkey, K., and Crane, A. (2003) 'Toward a green narrative: Management and the evolutionary epic', *Academy of Management Review*, 28: 220–37.

State of New South Wales. (2009) *Personal values, belief, and attitudes.* Available online at http://sielearning.tafensw.edu.au/MCS/CHCAOD402A/chcaod402a_csw/knowledge/values/values.htm (accessed 16 April 2014).

Steg, L., Dreijerink, L., and Abrahamse, W. (2005) 'Factors influencing the acceptability of energy policies: A test of VBN theory', *Journal of Environmental Psychology*, 25: 415–25.

Stern, P. (2000) 'New environmental paradigm: Toward a coherent theory of environmentally significant behavior', *Journal of Social Issues*, 56: 407–24.

Thibault, L. (2009) 'Globalization of sport: An inconvenient truth', *Journal of Sport Management*, 23: 1–20.

Trendafilova, S., Pfahl, M., and Casper, J. (2013) 'CSR and environmental responsibility: The case of NCAA athletic departments'. In K. Babiak, J. Paramino-Salcines, and G. Walters (eds), *The Routledge handbook of sport and corporate social responsibility* (pp. 105–18). London: Routledge.

Vastag, G., Kerekes, S., and Rondinelli, D. (1996) 'Evaluation of corporate environmental management approaches: A framework and application', *International Journal of Production Economics*, 43: 193–211.

Wilmshurst, T., and Frost, G. (2000) 'Corporate environmental reporting: A test of legitimacy theory', *Accounting, Auditing and Accountability Journal*, 13: 10–26.

5

MANAGEMENT AND LEADERSHIP RELATED TO SPORT AND THE ENVIRONMENT

Lisa Delpy Neirotti

The purpose of this chapter is to provide a foundation on the origins of sport environmental initiatives and the leaders that follow. Furthermore, it provides an understanding of what were and still are the motivating factors for sport organizations, venues, and events to work toward minimizing their environmental footprints as well as some of the resources available to assist in these efforts. Finally, this chapter discusses the importance for sport employees at all levels to recognize and act on ways to reduce environmental impacts.

Early connections between sport and the environment

The need to consider the environmental footprint among sport venues, events, and organizations began with the United Nations Environment Programme (UNEP) in 1994. After the Barcelona Olympics proved that organized planning of the Games could further social and economic causes, the UNEP began working with the Olympic Movement to inspire similar progress for environmental causes. The Olympic Movement went as far as to include the environment in its charter, alongside sports and culture (UNEP 2014).

The UNEP divides sports' impact on the environmental movement into two broad categories: integrating environmental considerations into sports management and practices, and using the social capital of sports' global popularity to promote awareness and positive practices (UNEP 2014). The UNEP liaises with Olympic hosts to ensure sound environmental planning is utilized in all aspects of event organization. Agenda 21 was established to endorse sustainable practices among players and audiences alike through major sports figures.

Shortly after the UNEP movement, the United States Golf Association (USGA) began considering the environmental impacts of courses. In 1996, the USGA published a series of voluntary principles to produce "environmental excellence in golf course planning and siting, design, construction, maintenance and facility opera-tions" (USGA 2014: 1). The principles were created in conjunction with a variety of nonprofit organizations and organizations representing various environmental or golf interests including the American Farmland Trust, Audubon International, SENES Oak Ridge, Inc., Center for Risk Analysis, the EPA, and the American Society of Golf Course Architects (USGA 2014). The flexibility of the guidelines allowed for the specifics of each unique physical, economic, and social environ-ment (USGA 2014).

Taking action: integrating sustainability into sport operations

Since 2004, the Natural Resources Defense Council (NRDC) has worked closely with sport personnel in the sports greening movement. The NRDC collaborates with professional and collegiate sports leagues, teams, venues, sponsors, own-ers, and organizations to promote sustainable practices in all aspects of the sports industry. The NRDC supplies free technical resources and outreach programs to bring awareness and methods to teams, athletes, and sports fans nationwide. They provide technical and market guidance "focused on energy efficiency, renewable energy, water conservation, waste reduction and recycling, healthy food, safer chemicals and the procurement of environmentally preferable paper products, as well as other products and services" and an online *Greening Advisor* to teams and managers (NRDC 2014).

The owners of the Philadelphia Eagles were the first movers among team leader-ship to promote large-scale sustainability changes in the running of their franchise. Christina Lurie, the wife of team owner Jeffrey Lurie, began the Eagle's Go Green energy conservation program in 2003. Team personnel determined they could save resources and money for an upfront investment in time and dedication. The Eagles and their owners designed their own institutional practices with the NRDC to promote environmental stewardship, from the types of resources they procure and the energy they save, to deliberate infrastructure design, to the sustainable businesses they support, and additional impact-offset and awareness programs they sponsor. What began as a simple recycling program has grown to an organization-wide initiative with minimal additional costs (Eagles 2010; NRDC 2014).

Environmental leadership and management action in sport

Leaders need to be aware of the growing resources available to assist in their efforts to make change. As Christina Lurie pointed out, we "are not environmen-tal experts by trade, however we have learned from the best in the business and our experiences along the way have grown each of us into authorities on green-ing a business, a building and a fan-base" (US Green Building Council 2013: 4). New resources—institutional and structural—are popping up for this movement as initial advocates gain experience, cultivate their practices, and share them with the like-minded. As more industry leaders realize this, more advancement can be made across the sports industry as a whole. Organization personnel will be able to utilize more trained incoming hires (e.g., educated in sport facility management and green practices) as well as tap into internal and external sources of expertise. The point about education is important as more sport management programs develop green elements within a given curriculum and diverse hires are made from a variety of backgrounds (e.g., environmental science). A key issue is identifying the organization's needs in a strategic manner to determine short-, medium-, and long-term needs and action areas. Then, the human resource element and external skill assistance can be determined clearly. In other words, they need to know what they do not know to address the situation.

The first professional league-wide partnership with the NRDC came from Major League Baseball in 2005 with the implementation of greening policies (NRDC 2014). To jumpstart the initiative, the NRDC posted its Greening Advisor online guide, beginning with baseball and expanding to meet the particular characteristics each of basketball, football, hockey, soccer, lacrosse, and tennis as more sports expressed interest. MLB remains the most organized among the leagues, providing members with the Team Greening Program, a league-wide environmental protection strategy, and a NRDC Team Greening Advisor that will work with each individual club. To further individual efforts, other non-profit organizations and universities provide tools to assist these initiatives. Some of these include the Green Sports Alliance, the George Washington University Green Sports Score Card, Sport England, and sport-based fundraisers for various environmental causes. These third-party consultants help organizations recognize and implement environmental improvements. Such inter-organizational cooperation aids in skill development and information transfer and dissemination. Leaders in a sport organization's green effort must understand how to find and to leverage such relationships in order to more effectively lead individual change processes, both from an internal organization perspective down to managing and leading individuals in the change efforts. The relationship is symbiotic and incorporates leadership and followership moments for each organization's personnel.

The Green Sports Alliance was co-founded in 2010 by Vulcan Inc. and the Natural Resources Defense Council. It began its work with several Pacific Northwest teams, facilitating communication between the teams' venue operators and executives and environmental scientists to "exchange information about better practices and develop solutions to their environmental challenges that are cost-competitive and innovative" (Green Sports Alliance 2014: 1). They host a yearly summit to share movement leaders' progress and innovation with industry participants. Over 600 industry stakeholders will attend to discuss and learn ways to advance the green sports movement.

After the initial GSA Summit in 2010, other organizations started hosting similar conferences. The Leadership in Greening the Sports Industry Conference was hosted by the Wharton Initiative for Global Environmental Leadership (Wharton

IGEL), the NRDC, and the Wharton Sports Business Initiative (WSBI). The conference explored "the best business practices for sports organizations to improve environmental performance and become leaders in sustainable development" (The Wharton School 2014: 1).

In addition to the growth of nonprofits and national conferences, universities and other organizations are educating and initiating greening advancements in sports industries. The George Washington University provides a Green Sports Score Card, a voluntary assessment tool to "help sport entities … determine their respective environmental profiles, how they compare with similar entities, and how they can improve their environmental practices over time" (GW University 2014: 1). The Green Sports Score Card helps identify a range of essential practices in sports events and pinpoint particular practices for their environmental improvement. The Card supplies support, direction, and expertise for sports entities committed to reducing their environmental impact.

Similarly, Sport England was founded to improve social health through sports and work to create healthy habits through sport (Sport England 2014). This provides online planning tools and guidance notes across a variety of sustainable practices: a Sports Facility Calculator, a series of Active Design notes, and a Planning Contributions Kitbag. Its Facilities Improvement Service includes a web-based planning guidance toolkit for local authorities to develop needs assessment tools and skills to plan and implement sport activities (Sport England 2014).

The Vancouver Organizing Committee for the 2010 Olympic Winter Games (VANOC) and the International Academy of Sports Science and Technology (AISTS) co-developed a Sustainable Sports and Events Toolkit (SSET) online. The creators collaborate with upcoming event planners to design the events in accordance with sustainable practices and analyze recent and current events as active case studies. SSET aims to "give sport organizations the tools required to incorporate sustainability organizationally and to plan and execute sustainable sport events" (VANOC, AISTS 2010: 1). The kit covers eight objectives in eight chapters: 1) Create a Sustainable Commitment and Strategy, 2) Management, 3) Site Selection and Construction, 4) Site, Venue, and Office Management, 5) Community and Supply Chain, 6) Transportation and Accommodation, 7) Catering, Food, and Beverage, and 8) Marketing and Communication (VANOC, AISTS 2010). Each chapter is supplemented by objectives, action items, and performance indicators that structure the process of greening large-scale sporting events. This approach is an important one given the short-term nature of the Olympic Games and the multiple levels of administration between organizing committees and front-line personnel. Such a plan translates into management actions, leadership opportunities, and knowledge transfer, which, in turn, provide leadership and management opportunities throughout an organization, especially for organizational personnel close to the ground and managing daily sustainability activities.

The Environmental Protection Agency (EPA) has numerous resources and guidelines for reducing the environmental impact of sports functions and collects data to provide goals and comparisons. The World Wildlife Fund's Panda Nation is partially funded by sports-based fundraisers, inspiring athletes and sports fans to preserve endangered species and their natural habitats.

The Council for Responsible Sports, founded in 2007, provides objective third-party verification of "the socially and environmentally responsible work event organizers are doing, and actively supports event organizers who strive to make a difference in their communities" by "supporting," "certifying," and "celebrating" events and sporting bodies that minimally or positively impact local environments and communities (CRS 2014: 1).

A growing number of teams are also aiming for third-party certification of their stadiums through the U.S. Green Building Council's LEED (Leadership in Energy and Environmental Design) program. Penn State constructed the first LEED certified stadium in 2006 (Cooper 2009). Nationals Park, the first certified professional stadium, followed in 2008. The building won a Silver Rating for its mixture of active and passive resource conservation design (Cooper 2009). The stadium tackles both environmental and conservation concerns and urban revitalization through unique and methodical design. The stadium was a brownfield redevelopment project that borders the Anacostia River—victim of urban and agricultural pollution—and is accessible to a variety of local public transportation routes (Washington Nationals 2014). The designers and inhabitants of the stadium also chose to utilize a minimum of 10 percent recycled building materials, regionally produced supplies, habitat-appropriate landscaping plant material, and water and energy conserving fixtures (Washington Nationals 2014). The ballpark additionally includes a ground and storm water filtration system that ensures both sources of water are thoroughly treated for chemical and organic debris before being released into the local watershed (Washington Nationals 2014).

While the green sports advancement has grown among national sports leagues and teams, the international greening initiative has continued to grow as well. Green initiatives have been an important part of the Olympics since 1994. The Fédération Internationale de Football Association, FIFA, has as well implemented greening initiatives since 2006. Beginning with the 2006 World Cup in Germany, FIFA began to incorporate measurable environmental initiatives into its planning. In 2006, the goal was to "reduce the negative environmental impacts of the tournament" (Carbon Footprint). FIFA established Green Goal, an environmental program tasked with addressing the issues within environmental protection in order to oversee the operations of the 2006 World Cup. Green Goal was created to pursue "the reduction in the consumption of potable water, the avoidance and/or reduction of waste, the creation of a more efficient energy system and an increase in the use of public transport to FIFA events" (Football Stadiums). It was the first time in the history of the tournament that mitigating environmental issues was incorporated into the tournament strategy as an official task. Following 2006, FIFA maintained its commitment to the environment, and Green Goal was incorporated into both the 2010 World Cup and the 2011 Women's World Cup. Each time they built upon everything they had learned from the previous tournament. To further cement its stance on environmental protection, FIFA has now mandated that environmental matters be included in the World Cup bidding process, starting with the 2018 and 2022 bids (Al-Madhoun et al. 2014).

As a part of FIFA's comprehensive sustainability strategy, it has continued its pursuit of the use of green stadiums through the Green Goal program. The initiative for green stadiums is a continuation of the program established for the 2006 World Cup and was considered very successful. One objective for the 2014 World Cup was for all the stadiums to be LEED certified. LEED certification can be obtained by an independent study that rates a facility's environmental performance. As of August 2014, seven out of twelve 2014 World Cup stadiums had achieved LEED Certification, with Belo Horizonte achieving the highest standard of LEED Platinum and the National Stadium in Brasilia also seeking this level (Foster 2014).

For the 2014 World Cup, FIFA passed along everything it has learned in the past and built upon it. Its goal was to have more than just energy-efficient stadiums. In order to be truly sustainable there must also be a sound management team involved, and FIFA invested its resources to ensure that the stadiums would be run with sound managerial practices for many years to come. Beginning in August 2013, FIFA held workshops for stadium owners and managers to educate them on green practices like storing rainwater, installing efficient appliances, distributing package-free foods and merchandise, the re-use of beverage containers, and the utilization of renewable energy (Al-Madhoun et al. 2014).

As exemplified by FIFA, a positive strategy for sport organizations yet to consider the environment is to begin small and build on successes. If an environmental champion is not apparent among the executive team, demonstrate through the collaboration of outside resources the financial upside as well as the positive public relations benefits an environmental plan could offer. Develop a strong case based on comparisons of like organizations, with financials and a turn-key strategy. Success is often found in educating leaders and capturing their interest.

Conclusion

With sustainability and environmental operations not having a final destination or a final finish line, executive actions and strategic planning will ebb and flow with changing leadership, current and long-term issues, and needs within a sport organization. Although vision and support from top executives is helpful, sport managers and other personnel must be aware of the overall environmental impact of their organization's activities and begin to see micro- and macro-level strategic and tactical areas for change. Everyone, no matter their organizational role, can play a part in the environmental activities of an organization. While not every role is equal or as consistent (e.g., sustainability director), leadership opportunities will continue to present themselves. Historical information showed how sport organization personnel have grown the need to incorporate environmental issues into sport organization life. In order for them to take actions appropriate for a current situation, and to plan for longer-term ones, it is important that proper leadership and management mechanisms are in place so that individual initiative and leadership can be demonstrated.

References

Al-Madhoun, R., Baisch, J., Cooper, C., Granucci, D., Kachikwu, B., Leyton, D., Martin, C., and Parrish, A. (2014). 'Impacts of the 2014 FIFA World Cup'. Term paper, George Washington University, Washington, DC.

Cooper, C. (2009). *Green (LEED) Stadiums*. Available online at http://bleacherreport.com/articles/275434-green-leed-stadiums

CRS. (2014). *About CRS*. Available online at www.councilforresponsiblesport.org/about-crs-2

Eagles. (2010). *Gogreen Playbook*. Available online at http://prod.static.eagles.clubs.nfl.com/assets/docs/2010_Playbook_Gogreen.pdf

Foster, R. (2014). *The New Cathedrals of Football*. Available online at http://cities-today.com/2014/08/new-cathedrals-football

Green Sports Alliance. (2014). *Green Sports Alliance*. Available online at http://greensportsalliance.org

GW University. (2014). *GW Green Sports Scorecard, Version 2.0 Information Page*. Available online at https://www.surveymonkey.com/s/greenscorecard2

NRDC. (2014). *Natural Resource Defense Council*. Available online at www.nrdc.org

Sport England. (2014). *About Us*. Available online at www.sportengland.org

The Wharton School. (2014). *Leadership in Greening the Sports Industry Conference*. Available online at http://igel.wharton.upenn.edu/research/leadership-in-greening-the-sports-industry-conference

UNEP. (2014). *About UNEP, Sport and the Environment*. Available online at www.unep.org/sport_env/about.aspx

USGA. (2014). *Environmental Principles for Golf Courses in the United States*. Available online at www.usga.org/course_care/articles/environment/general/environmental-principles-for-golf-courses-in-the-united-states

US Green Building Council. (2013). 'Session spotlight: The Philadelphia Eagles go green'.

VANOC, AISTS. (2010). Sustainable Sport and Event Toolkit (SSET).

Washington Nationals. (2014). *Green Ballpark*. MLB Advanced Media, LP. Available online at http://washington.nationals.mlb.com/was/ballpark/information/index.jsp?content=green_ballpark

6

HOW DO ENVIRONMENTAL POLICIES FIT WITHIN LARGER STRATEGIC PLANNING PROCESSES?

Lynn Crowe

Overview

This chapter explores how environmental policies fit within larger strategic processes relevant to sport management and development. It identifies key policy areas such as environmental impact assessment, sustainable land use planning, environmental protection and visitor impact management. Good practice and guidelines which will enable sport managers to integrate their work with these environmental policies are explored. Detailed guidance on design and longer-term management and maintenance to enhance and protect the natural environment are provided.

Introduction

Sustainable development, at its most simplistic, seeks to balance economic development with social equity and environmental protection. There are many complex academic debates surrounding the definition of the term sustainable development, but a particularly relevant and useful approach for the sport and recreation manager is summarised by Wheeler: 'sustainable development is development that improves the long-term health of human and ecological systems' (Wheeler 2013: 30).

One of the most influential reports on the problems of unrestrained economic growth was the 1987 report of the World Commission on Environment and Development, chaired by the Norwegian Prime Minister, Gro Harlem Brundtland. Following the release of the Brundtland Commission report *Our Common Future* in 1987 and the United Nations Rio de Janeiro Earth Summit conference in 1991, calls for sustainable development entered the official mainstream internationally.

The Rio summit also marked the first international attempt to draw up action plans and strategies for moving towards a more sustainable pattern of development. One of the main products of the Rio summit was Agenda 21 – a non-binding, voluntarily implemented action plan for the UN, other multilateral organisations and individual governments around the world that could be executed at local, national and global levels (Elliot 2012). Following the Rio Earth Summit, national programmes, such as the *Sustainable America* report of the President's Council on Sustainable Development in 1991, attempted to establish sustainable development directions for particular countries (cited in Wheeler 2013).

As national and local governments implemented their own Agenda 21 programmes to demonstrate their commitment to sustainable development, sports institutions, teams and sponsoring organisations have had to recognise the need to better understand the environmental impacts of the activities they sponsor, host and regulate. This has been considered alongside debates that have encompassed the social impacts of major sporting events and of associated facilities; for example, the imposition of environmental costs (noise, congestion, pollution, etc.) on existing populations and businesses (see, for example, Collins *et al.* 2009).

For example, the UK government launched a new strategy for sustainable development, *Securing the Future*, in March 2005. All UK government departments now share responsibility for making environmentally sustainable development a reality. In turn, Sport England (2013a) (the UK government's main agency promoting sport in England) prepared a Sustainable Development Strategy which reviews the contribution of Sport England in meeting the government's national sustainable development goals. The Strategy commits Sport England to actively promote environmental objectives and strengthen environmental advice in its published design guidance.

In addition to international and national policies advocating sustainable development, there is now the specific urgency around our response to climate change. The UK government has produced guidance to other agencies, businesses and developers to encourage them to plan and adapt to potential changes. Extreme events, such as the flooding which occurred throughout the UK in late 2012 or the drought of early 2012, are likely to become more frequent and more severe in the coming decades, bringing potential disruption to the economy (UK CCRA 2012). However, future climate and economic circumstances are uncertain, and with uncertainty comes risk that needs to be accounted for. In response to this uncertainty, the UK government has published its National Adaptation Programme (HM Government 2013), which encourages all organisations to consider the impacts of climate change when planning, designing and implementing new initiatives. Thus, sporting bodies at all levels and in all nations are recognising the need to integrate their plans and policies with the increasing focus on sustainability and environmental management. What might this mean in practice?

Sustainability planning for sport and recreation

Wheeler (2013) advocates a major shift in the planning and managing of different activities and resources, which historically have often been undertaken in very narrowly focused sectors by compartmentalised professions, and he refers to this approach as sustainability planning. Sustainability planning is a holistic outlook that emphasises the relationships between the different elements of human and natural systems, works across disciplinary boundaries, and operates across different scales of planning.

Sport and recreation managers are part of this process. They also need to look beyond the confines of their own discipline and explore the importance of planning new projects and initiatives strategically, integrating the development and management of sports facilities with associated environmental objectives and land management strategies.

There are a number of principles that can be followed to ensure that new projects enhance and protect the natural environment are far as possible. These principles have been recently articulated in guidance from the UK government to its own sports agencies (Sport England 2013c), but would apply to similar agencies in any country.

The importance of strategic planning

If sports and recreation managers are to integrate their proposals into a wider sustainable context, then they need to reflect on the local, regional and national planning policy frameworks in their own constituencies. Wheeler (2013) provides an excellent overview of sustainability planning in practice. He explains how environmental review legislation, such as the National Environmental Policy Act in the United States and subsequent state environmental policy acts, have required since the 1970s a relatively contextual evaluation of proposed projects. These frameworks require public agencies, and occasionally private developers, to consider a wide range of environmental impacts, traffic and historical records, housing, recreation and cultural resources. Agencies compile and analyse this information within environmental impact statements and assessments according to the legal requirements of their area.

In the UK, a similar approach is advocated through the National Planning Policy Framework, the UK government policy which requires local planning authorities to contribute to and enhance the natural and local environment, and ensure that development is sustainable (Department of Communities and Local Government 2012).

In many jurisdictions, an Environmental Impact Assessment (EIA) might be needed if proposed developments are either significant in scale or have an impact on protected landscapes or habitats. The International Association of Impact Assessment (IAIA) defines EIA as the process of identifying, predicting, evaluating and mitigating the biophysical, social and other relevant effects of development proposals prior to major decisions being taken and commitments made (International Association of Impact Assessment n.d.: n.p.). Strategic environmental assessment (SEA) is a systematic decision process, aiming to ensure that environmental issues are considered effectively in policy, plan and programme making (Fischer 2007). It should be a structured, rigorous, participative and open process, often prepared by public planning authorities and at times private bodies. The European SEA

Directive 2001/42/EC requires that all member states of the European Union should have ratified the Directive into their own country's law by 21 July 2004 (Strategic Environmental Assessment Information Service 2013).

At a strategic level, many local planning authorities will be required by their own statutory legislation to provide development plans which set out a clear vision of the development potential of their area. This will generally include consideration of residential and economic development needs, transport and waste management, environmental designations and protected areas, alongside recreation and leisure policies. Many such policies advocate a strategic approach to the provision of green space to provide a range of public benefits – often a network of natural areas, green corridors and other land which can contribute to what has become known as 'green infrastructure' (see, for example, Natural England 2009).

Green infrastructure – although far from a new concept – was first identified in the 1990s in the United States as a strategic, multi-scale approach to land conservation and land use planning, with particular emphasis on the life-support functions of natural processes or ecosystems (Natural England 2009). Defined in the UK's National Planning Policy Framework as 'a network of multi-functional green space, urban and rural, which is capable of delivering a wide range of environmental and quality of life benefits for local communities' (Department of Communities and Local Government 2012: n.p.), green infrastructure can provide a range of informal and formal recreation opportunities, as well as a much broader range of so-called ecosystem services such as climate change and flood regulation, biodiversity enhancement, and water catchment management.

Strategic needs assessment and visitor impact management

In terms of conflicts between environmental protection and sport and recreation provision, many people working in this area remain focused on the potential impacts of participants on the resource itself and regard recreation as a major problem to be managed. This perception is contrary to much of the available evidence (see for example House of Commons 1995). It appears that concern about direct damage to the natural environment from recreational use is often more of a philosophical standpoint, rather than a conclusion based on any hard data. Other pressures – agricultural intensification, urban development, extensive pollution – can be far more significant in terms of impacts on our environment (English Nature 2003).

Many researchers now believe that the focus on achieving a balance between sport and recreation and environmental protection is no longer as relevant to current leisure and sport management practices as had previously been thought. Indeed, in most cases, it is possible to meet the demand for leisure and to promote further opportunities through sensitive planning and management based on a series of principles contained within established frameworks. Rather than discussing a balance or compromise between these two objectives, it is far better to aim to achieve the best of both worlds.

Elson *et al.* (1995) conclude that six major factors are pivotal in good management practice:

- understanding the state of the environment – establishing baseline environmental conditions on site, and an agreed view of the nature of any impacts;
- clarity of purpose – setting unequivocal objectives forming a realistic framework for future action;
- participatory management – regarding management as a process, guided by regular engagement with and negotiations between relevant interests;
- importance of voluntary agreements – the operation of restraint and self-policing by clubs and governing bodies;
- local involvement – regular liaison and negotiation with local populations and sports organisations;
- monitoring and review – a conscious, systematic process which informs future management decisions, and any changes in direction to site management.

Outdoor recreation managers are generally faced with an environmental resource used by a multitude of individuals and organisations, with many different interests and concerns. An early approach to the issue of potential conflict was the concept of carrying capacities – 'the level of recreation use an area can sustain without an unacceptable degree of deterioration of the character and quality of the resource or the recreation experience' (Countryside Commission 1970, cited in Hall and Page 2002: 135). However, the chief problem in utilising this concept lies in what different individuals and groups construe as unacceptable recreational use. Not only is this an issue when related to social and perceptual factors, but it is also true of ecological change. Indeed, it has been notoriously difficult to provide any empirical evidence which can confidently demonstrate causal links between numbers of participants and environmental change.

Despite carrying capacity being highly elusive to implement successfully due to these difficulties, many practitioners continue to refer to it as a useful concept. However, there are other techniques which may be more useful in the field – a range of Visitor Planning Frameworks that seek to achieve the best of all worlds (Crowe 2005). One of these alternatives is a framework known as Limits of Acceptable Change (LAC). Instead of asking *How much is too much?*, the LAC approach rephrases the question by asking *How much change is acceptable?* (Newsome *et al.* 2002). The concept was first developed by Stankey and McCool (1984) in response to perceived difficulties in establishing a numerical recreational carrying capacity for wilderness and white water rivers in protected landscapes in the US. In the UK, Sidaway (1991) has simplified the LAC process into four steps:

- detailed objectives to be agreed for each site by interested agencies and individuals;
- thresholds for deterioration (i.e. the limits of acceptable change) to be agreed in advance;

- regular, systematic measurements to be taken so that management can monitor change;
- management responses triggered when these values are exceeded, also agreed in advance.

The emphasis is very different from the carrying capacity concept, and particularly highlights the need for robust and up-to-date user and visitor needs assessments, as well as effective monitoring of environmental change.

The LAC approach has been used extensively in North America, Australia and New Zealand (see Case Study 6.1).

CASE STUDY 6.1: THE BOB MARSHALL WILDERNESS COMPLEX, MONTANA, USA – VISITOR MANAGEMENT PLANNING

An excellent case study is found at the Bob Marshall Wilderness Complex, Montana, USA (United States Forest Service 2013).

The Bob Marshall Wilderness Complex, in north central Montana, is managed by the US Forest Service (USFS). It comprises 600,000 hectares of temperate forest and attracts 25,000 visitors a year, primarily from June to November. June to September is dominated by backpacking and horse-supported backcountry trips. In the autumn, most use is for big game hunting.

In 1982, the USFS embarked on a planning effort based on the Limits of Acceptable Change process, largely because of the perceived need to involve the public more closely in the management process. It involved continuous public participation through a taskforce consisting of a range of stakeholders: the public, scientists and managers. The process took five years. The LAC framework focused effort on addressing how much change in wilderness, biophysical and social conditions was acceptable. By designing a public participation process that incorporated the full range of values involved in the Wilderness area, participants developed a set of management actions that were effective in reducing and controlling human-induced impacts, and achieved the social and political acceptability necessary for implementation.

The plan has three broad characteristics:

1 It establishes four zones designed to protect the pristine character of the wilderness, yet realistically permits some trade-offs between recreation use and human-induced impacts.
2 It identifies indicator variables – things to monitor to ensure conditions remain acceptable and things to use to establish the effectiveness of actions implemented to control or mitigate impacts. For each indicator, quantifiable standards exist, indicating what limit of change from the natural baseline is acceptable in each zone.

3 It indicates for each zone the management actions in order of their social acceptability. This gives the manager a choice of tools and determines what management action will be most acceptable in controlling impacts. This procedure encourages the least intrusive management action first.

Some of the management actions implemented have been successful at reducing impacts on the ground, while other actions have caused unexpected results that have actually led to the degradation of the overall resource condition in some locations. Lessons learnt include the following:

Education/enforcement – direct visitor contacts by experienced wilderness rangers are important to educate the public about the value of wilderness.

Prepare for potential shifts in visitor use – e.g. due to fire activity – managers need to prepare for increased pressure from the public in popular locations not impacted by fire.

Encourage the proper 'Leave-No-Trace' principles for camping – encouraging future users to camp at already popular sites, because research shows that approximately 90 per cent of the resource impact to a previously unused location is caused in the first four nights of use.

Closing campsites can lead to a net increase in resource impact – temporary closure of campsites for 'rehabilitation' has not led to an improvement in their condition. Campsite rehabilitation needs to minimise the future expansion of a site.

Coordination among commercial services – active work with guides to minimise overlap of itineraries reduces the likelihood of organised groups being at the same place at the same time.

Stock holding facilities – temporary hitch rails or high-lines encourages stock holding in more durable areas and reduces the spread of resource damage.

Overall, the implementation of the LAC process at the Bob Marshall Wilderness Complex has been regarded as a success, and the planning and management activities continue today, as does the involvement of the task force.

One of the most critical aspects of developing a LAC approach has been establishing stakeholder endorsement and support. Stakeholders from the local tourism sector and communities can provide valuable input to determining desired outcomes, and are usually essential in providing the economic and political support necessary to ensure programmes can be effectively delivered and monitored.

Site management strategies and techniques

Visitor management frameworks also require the implementation of effective site management actions to implement policies aimed at reducing the impact of users on the environment. Sidaway (1991) has suggested that the following techniques are generally worth considering:

- zoning;
- regulating access;
- self-regulation, voluntary codes and voluntary agreements;
- information and interpretation;
- monitoring and review.

One of the key strategies for managing the environment is through zoning. This involves recognising smaller zones or units within areas, each with prescribed levels of environmental protection and certain levels and types of use. Most planning frameworks include identifying and managing zones over large areas. But this process can also work effectively at a detailed, site level.

Zoning helps to provide choice for visitors, as well as clarifying future intentions. Zoning can be used to separate incompatible uses in space and time (spatial and temporal zoning). Spatial zoning might segregate different recreational uses, such as motorised and non-motorised users on water or land, or horse riders and cyclists on multi-user routes. An example of temporal zoning might include limiting access to particular areas of a site, such as a nature reserve during bird-nesting seasons.

The provision, location, style and quality of site infrastructure are key components of the management of visitors and of regulating access. Infrastructure provides an indication of the quality of management and can be an interface between organisations and visitors. But the first question must be – do we need any infrastructure at all? Particularly in more natural areas, there may be special qualities such as a sense of wilderness, which should not be sacrificed. Often, people services – such as a ranger service or educational service – can be more effective in resolving management issues than new infrastructure.

However, infrastructure may be needed. The general issues that relate to the use of such tools include (adapted from Keirle 2002):

- the design of the item – as reflected in its function and anticipated users;
- the nature of the site, and location of the item;
- creation of local distinctiveness – through selection of appropriate materials, scale and design;
- costs – both of the initial installation and long-term maintenance requirements;
- robustness (for example, against vandalism);
- needs of participants with disabilities;
- health and safety issues.

The acceptance of responsibility for protecting the environment by participants themselves is one of the most effective measures. Self-regulation is most successful when there is an affinity of interests between the participants. This is usually more easily achieved when most participants belong to the same organisation or club, which can then negotiate use with a landowner or public body. It can, however, lead to difficulties of exclusive agreements between a limited group of stakeholders. For example, attempts to resolve conflicts surrounding access to water by both anglers and canoeists have been made through the development of access arrangements between either or both of these groups and the waterway owners. However, even where voluntary agreements between these groups can be negotiated, often the needs of the informal participant, with no access to special arrangements or information, can remain unclear and ambiguous.

High-quality information, both on and off site, is needed to enable participants and spectators to make informed decisions; whereas interpretation might be needed to help visitors to understand and enjoy a site. Keirle (2002) outlines a range of information that can be provided at recreation sites and the variety of methods for providing that information. He also suggests how information provision can be used to influence users:

- where people go – by providing information we can influence the sites that people go to, or the locations within sites that people go to;
- when people go – by letting people know about opening times, or the timing of events;
- how people get to a site – provision of clear information on how to get to a site by car, public transport or bike;
- what they do when they get to the site – what are the attractions of the site and how do they get to them?;
- who goes to a site – information can be targeted at particular market segments.

Interpretation goes beyond just information provision. An early definition of interpretation states that it is 'An educational activity which aims to reveal meanings and relationships through the use of original objects, by first-hand experience, and by illustrative media, rather than simply communicate factual information' (Tilden 1957: 8). Good interpretation enhances enjoyment and understanding as well as adding to the visitors' experience; interpretation can also develop visitors' understanding and support for the managers' role, and their objectives and policies.

Monitoring and review is now an accepted stage in any programme or project management cycle, although all too often it is still under-resourced and ineffectively used. Managers need to accurately evaluate the performance of their decisions in terms of implementing policies, and reflect on the results of such monitoring to then increase the effectiveness of their work. As part of this process, managers should ask themselves *what will success look like?*, and consider how their objectives are to be measured. At a local level, managers need to collect input, output and outcome data – each of these will assist in evaluating the success of any project.

Often by demonstrating a contribution to wider public benefits, the sport and recreation manager can also enhance the justification of their work. This may be particularly important in the public sector, where competing priorities for scarce resources increases the pressure on leisure budgets. So monitoring the wider public benefits which participation provides becomes an important tool for the sport and recreation manager.

Good facility design and management

Environmental policies are meaningless without detailed action plans and proposals for implementation which successfully put into practice their defined strategic targets. In the sport and recreation sector, these can often be achieved through the good design of new facilities and better long-term management. Sport England (2007) has produced a detailed guide to provide practical information to assist the design and management of sports, recreation and leisure facilities to promote the UK's commitments to delivering environmentally sustainable development.

The aim of the guide is to encourage clients, designers, contractors and facilities managers to embrace the environmental sustainability policies developed by government, and to treat sustainability as an integral concern from the inception of any project. This Sport England guide (2013b) covers every phase of a project from the development of a vision for sustainability shared between client and design team, through to good practice in the day-to-day operation of the completed facility.

While some principles, like energy conservation, are fundamental, there are many emerging technologies that are undergoing rapid development. Many of the issues are posed in the form of questions, challenging the delivery team to assess feasibility in the context of a specific project. The following areas provide a useful checklist (adapted from Sport England 2007):

- client and design team vision;
- transport arrangements;
- site appraisal and renewable energy;
- protecting and enhancing biodiversity;
- building design;
- construction elements;
- low environmental impact materials and components;
- lighting, heating and ventilation systems;
- water conservation measures;
- commission and hand-over arrangements;
- longer-term management practices.

There are many examples of sporting organisations developing their own good practice in terms of sustainable design. The Olympics movement has recently led the way (IOC n.d.).

The Vancouver Organizing Committee (VANOC) for the Winter Olympics in 2010 was the first Organising Committee to create a Sustainability Department. For VANOC, sustainability meant managing the social, economic and environmental impacts and opportunities of the Vancouver Olympic Games to create lasting benefits both locally and globally. To achieve this, VANOC established a set of six corporate-wide sustainability performance objectives, including accountability; environmental stewardship and impact reduction; social inclusion and responsibility; aboriginal participation and collaboration; economic benefits; and sport for sustainable living.

The London 2012 Organising Committee (LOCOG) produced the London 2012 Sustainability Plan (London 2012 Olympic Delivery Authority n.d.). The Plan was a framework for how LOCOG and its partners would address sustainability, and reflected the Organising Committee's ambition to deliver a truly sustainable Olympic Games. The Plan was structured according to five priority themes:

- climate change;
- waste;
- biodiversity;
- inclusion;
- healthy living.

A report compiled for the Economic and Social Research Council (ESRC 2010) suggests that it is still too early to fully assess the sustainability of the London 2012 Games. However, the London 2012 Olympic Delivery Authority (n.d.) published its own achievements, which include:

- reusing or recycling 98 per cent of demolished materials, and transporting 63 per cent (by weight) of construction materials to the site by rail or water;
- establishing a new energy infrastructure to reduce carbon emissions;
- optimising the opportunities for efficient water use and creating more than 100 hectares of open space, designed to reduce the risk of flooding in the river valley and enrich the biodiversity of the area;
- relocating species, including birds, bats and lizards, and cleaning over a million cubic metres of soil;
- setting itself, and its contractors working on the Olympic Park, a comprehensive range of targets that were embedded in systems, processes, tools and the culture of the project.

Ensuring stakeholder involvement and community participation

Sustainable development depends on economic and social sustainability, as well as environmental. The involvement of local people and, indeed, all relevant stakeholders, in the design and management of projects and facilities, can help to ensure that environmental objectives are met.

An effective sport or leisure manager will base their decision-making on sound evidence about their customers' needs and demands, and on the special characteristics of their resource. In order to develop clear objectives, owned and shared by all stakeholders, it is essential that information and data is gathered from all those with an interest in a site. The different aspects of a site to be monitored must be agreed and performance measures decided in advance. All of these issues require resources in terms of staff time and finance. Both internal and external stakeholders should be involved in all stages of the process. External facilitators might be required to ensure the process is a full and open engagement with all stakeholders (see Case Study 6.2).

CASE STUDY 6.2: THE STANAGE FORUM, PEAK DISTRICT NATIONAL PARK, UK – STAKEHOLDER INVOLVEMENT

An excellent example of this approach is provided by the Stanage Forum located in the Peak District National Park in the UK (Peak District National Park Authority n.d.).

The Stanage/North Lees Estate is owned and managed by the Peak District National Park Authority (NPA). Its landscape value is exceptional, with internationally rare heather moorland and blanket bog, and its recreational value is equally outstanding. The Estate receives over half a million visitors per year, with a wide range of activities including walking, cycling, hang-gliding and paragliding, and bird watching. Stanage Edge is perhaps best known as an internationally important gritstone climbing edge, arguably one of the birth-places of the sport.

In 2000, the NPA wished to review the Management Plan for the Estate. It was perceived that there were real conflicts between the various activities on the Estate, and its management for conservation and farming interests. Rather than embark on a traditional process involving the production of a draft plan followed by various consultation exercises, the NPA began with a blank sheet of paper and commissioned an independent facilitator to guide the subse-quent process.

A website was established with an on-line discussion board to enable as wide a debate as possible. An open public meeting was held, attended by over 70 people, in August 2000. This wider Forum agreed a set of consensus-building principles in order to develop a shared vision for the Plan and a steering group was created. The Steering Group framed a number of specific problems, which were then discussed in smaller technical groups. The emphasis was on consen-sus building and improving understanding in order to reach agreed solutions.

Over the next two years, large amounts of time were voluntarily given by individuals and groups contributing to the shared development of the Stanage/North Lees Estate Management Plan. A total of 285 people received the Forum newsletter, and in total 135 different people attended public events. From the first Forum event in August 2000 up to the production of the draft plan at the end of June 2002, there were 21,300 hits on the Forum website. The final ten-year Management Plan was agreed in October 2002.

Since then there have been notable successes. The rare *mountain black-bird*, the Ring Ouzel, is now successfully breeding on the Edge following close co-operation with local climbers to avoid their nesting sites. Difficult negotia-tions between different groups over the legal use of a byway by motorised vehicles has led to the agreement of voluntary codes of conduct by the motor-ing groups, including speed limits and other restrictions (although this issue remains particularly contentious). An annual public forum reviews progress and continues to seek to encourage anyone with an interest in the area to become involved in its future management.

Due to the nature of land ownership and land use, the range of stakeholders with an interest in any sport or recreation development is likely to be large. Equally, resources are often limited, and this can lead to managers focusing on those stakeholders with the *loudest voice*, or where traditional relationships are already well established (such as with significant non-governmental organisations, national sports bodies and known user groups). Particular difficulties are faced in trying to work with *hard to reach* groups, such as the elderly or young people, spatially or socially isolated groups, and other minorities who may not be formally represented or organised.

Considerable support may be needed to enable some participants to engage meaningfully. Managers need to be creative and imaginative in reaching a wider audience and enabling them to engage as fully as possible. This could mean developing partnerships with groups not normally associated specifically with sports activities such as community groups or youth services. Wider social benefits can also be achieved by promoting community use of existing sports facilities, particularly on school sites and other educational establishments.

Conclusions

The natural environment is a hugely important sport and leisure resource, in all its many and varied forms. There is increasing recognition that the use of the natural environment for leisure can bring a range of important public benefits, not just to individuals but also to society more generally. Increasingly, these public benefits are included within a wider range of public benefits, defined as *ecosystem services* by the United Nations (United Nations Millennium Ecosystem Assessment 2005). The wider benefits to society of a healthy and well-managed environment underline the importance of maintaining and enhancing that environment. Thus, sport development must also be achieved through sustainable planning and sustainable management in order to achieve the long-term health of both humans and ecosystems.

References

Collins, A., Jones, C., and Munday, M. (2009) 'Assessing the environmental impacts of mega sporting events: Two options?', *Tourism Management*, 30: 828–37.

Crowe, L. (2005) 'Promoting outdoor recreation in the English National Parks: Guide to good practice', *Countryside Agency CA214*.

Department of Communities and Local Government (2012) 'National Planning Policy Framework'. Available online at https://www.gov.uk/government/publications/national-planning-policy-framework--2 (accessed 20 November 2013).

Economic and Social Research Council (ESRC) (2010) *Olympic Games Impact Study – London 2012 Pre-Games Report*. Available online at www.uel.ac.uk/geo-information/documents/UEL_TGIfS_PreGames_OGI_Release.pdf (accessed 20 November 2013).

Elliott, J.A. (2012) *An introduction to sustainable development*, Abingdon: Routledge.

Elson, M., Heaney, D., and Reynolds, G. (1995) *Good practice in the planning and management of sport and active recreation in the countryside*, England: Sports Council and Countryside Agency.

English Nature (2003) 'Publications and products'. Available online at http://publications.naturalengland.org.uk/publication/81071?category=20003 (accessed 12 March 2013)

Fischer, T. B. (2007) *Theory and practice of strategic environmental assessment*, London: Earthscan.

Hall, C. M. and Page, S. J. (2002) *The geography of tourism and recreation: Environment, place and space*, London: Routledge.

HM Government (2013) 'National adaptation programme – Making the country resilient to a changing climate'. Available online at https://www.gov.uk/government/uploads/system/uploads/attachment_data/file/209866/pb13942-nap-20130701.pdf (accessed 8 August 2013).

House of Commons (1995) *Environment committee report on the environmental impact of leisure activities*, London: HMSO.

International Association of Impact Assessment (n.d.) Available online at www.iaia.org (accessed 20 November 2013).

International Olympics Committee (IOC) (n.d.) 'Sport and Environment Commission'. Available online at www.olympic.org/sport-environment-commission?tab=games (accessed 27 August 2013).

Keirle, I. (2002) *Countryside recreation site management: A marketing approach*, London: Routledge.

London 2012 Olympic Delivery Authority (n.d.) 'Sustainability'. Available online at http://learninglegacy.independent.gov.uk/themes/sustainability/index.php (accessed 20 November 2013).

Natural England (2009) *Green infrastructure guide*, Natural England, NE176. Available online at www.naturalengland.org.uk (accessed 7 May 2014).

Newsome, D., Moore, S. A., and Dowling, R. K. (2002) *Natural area tourism: Ecology, impacts and management*, Clevedon: Channel View Publications.

Peak District National Park Authority (n.d.) 'Stanage forum'. Available online at www.peakdistrict.org/index/looking-after/stanage.htm (accessed 20 November 2013).

Sidaway, R. (1991) *Good conservation practice for sport and recreation*, 37, England: Sports Council and Countryside Commission.

Sport England (2007) *Environmental sustainability: Promoting sustainable design for sport*, England: Sport England. Available online at www.sportengland.org/media/32366/Environmental-sustainability.pdf (accessed 8 August 2013).

Sport England (2013a) 'Planning for sport'. Available online at www.sportengland.org/facilities-planning/planning-for-sport (accessed 6 August 2013).

Sport England (2013b) 'Planning for sport development management'. Available online at www.sportengland.org/media/166625/planning-for-sport_development-management-june-2013.pdf (accessed 6 August 2013).

Sport England (2013c) 'Planning tools and guidance'. Available online at www.sportengland.org/facilities-planning/planning-for-sport/planning-tools-and-guidance (accessed 20 November 2013).

Stankey, G. H. and McCool, S. F. (1984) 'Carrying capacity in recreation settings: Evaluation, appraisal and applications', *Leisure Science*, 6: 453–73.

Strategic Environmental Assessment Information Service (2013) 'About SEA'. Available online at www.sea-info.net (accessed 8 August 2013).

Tilden, F. (1957) *Interpreting our heritage* (3rd edition), Chapel Hill, NC: The University of North Carolina Press.

UK Climate Change Risk Assessment (UK CCRA) (2012) 'Government report'. Available online at https://www.gov.uk/government/publications/uk-climate-change-risk-assessment-government-report (accessed 20 November 2013).

United Nations Millennium Ecosystem Assessment (2005) 'Guide to the millennium assessment reports'. Available online at www.unep.org/maweb (accessed 20 November 2013).

United States Forest Service (2013) 'Home page'. Available online at www.fs.fed.us/r1/flathead/wilderness/bmwcomplex.shtml (accessed 20 November 2013).

Wheeler, S. M. (2013) *Planning for sustainability: Creating liveable, equitable and ecological communities*, Abingdon: Routledge.

7

CORPORATE SOCIAL RESPONSIBILITY AND THE ENVIRONMENT IN THE SPORT INDUSTRY

Sylvia Trendafilova and Sheila Nguyen

Overview

This chapter covers the concept of Corporate Social Responsibility (CSR) and how it is perceived in the realm of sport. More specifically, the reader will learn about the three components of CSR, emphasizing the environmental component as it is an area that has recently received growing attention in the sport industry. Further, the chapter presents some examples of environmental programs in various sport settings around the world. Additionally, the strategic decisions behind the adoption of environmental initiatives are discussed as well as some of the regulating bodies involved in these decisions. The chapter concludes with a summary of the current state of CSR in sport and suggestions of what the future might look like.

Introduction

Corporate Social Responsibility is defined as the "economic, legal, ethical, and discretionary expectations that society has of organizations at a given point in time" (Carroll and Buchholtz, 2003: 36). In other words, organizations have moral, ethical, and philanthropic responsibilities in addition to their responsibilities to earn a fair return for investors and comply with the law. Being socially responsible means that a corporation identifies with its stakeholder groups and incorporates their needs within the day-to-day decision-making process. CSR-related actions are usually not required by law and the overarching goal is to contribute to some social good that benefits society (Carroll, 2000; McWilliams and Siegel, 2000).

The origin of Corporate Social Responsibility dates back to the 1930s, but its nature and scope has changed over time. The academic foundation of this concept is based on the book *Social responsibilities of the businessman* by Bowen (1953), in which it is assumed that businesses are moral agents and should operate within guidelines set by society. Throughout the twentieth century, the study of CSR continued with the work of Davis (1960), Preston and Post (1975), and Jones (1980), suggesting that CSR should be viewed as a process and not a static concept. This new view not only expanded the knowledge of CSR, but also led to the development of Carroll's (1991) hierarchical model, categorizing CSR along four layers of responsibilities, economic, legal, ethical, and discretionary, and suggesting that these components of the model are not mutually exclusive. Although Carroll's model provided a comprehensive description of CSR, more recently Niskala and Tarna (2003) developed a model that offers a multidimensional view of CSR by incorporating three broad areas: economic, environmental, and social. Their model emphasizes the importance of conducting business in a balanced way by addressing relevant issues in all three areas.

The importance of social responsibility in business settings is illustrated by world-wide efforts to develop and implement CSR programs and initiatives. For example, the European Commission is one of the major leaders in CSR efforts in Europe, initiating new strategies and organizing a forum to discuss the progress of these efforts (European Commission, 2009). Efforts to incorporate CSR initiatives into daily business practices have reached Australia as well. In fact, despite internal resistance to CSR, Australian companies have not cut CSR budgets and continue to expand those activities (Welford, 2009). Research has examined the corporate social and environmental responsibility of businesses in Europe, North America, Australia, New Zealand, Africa, Asia, and the Middle East and has concluded that political, social, and economic factors influence those activities (Baughn et al., 2007). For example, French and Dutch businesses are highly committed to environmental management, while firms in the United States are focusing more on philanthropic programs and volunteerism. In addition, mandatory regulations in Europe require businesses to annually report their environmental performance and to disclose the implementation of their environmental policies. A similar regulatory system exists in Australia where companies are required to report corporate governance practices.

Corporate Social Responsibility: sport and strategy

Since CSR activities are usually not required by law, for the most part they are philanthropic in nature. However, in recent years CSR has been viewed not only as a philanthropic engagement, but as a strategic approach as well, where business decisions are made to achieve social and strategic distinction (Porter and Kramer, 2006). Moreover, a strategic approach has the potential for a business to gain stability when changes are anticipated and to avoid financial and reputation risks (Bonini et al., 2006). Pohle and Hittner (2008) studied business leaders around the world and discovered that CSR practices are utilized as a strategic platform for growth and differentiation. While traditional business corporations have been placing an emphasis on CSR activities and, further, environmental accountability, sport has emerged as a unique platform for CSR (Coady et al., 2007).

The natural environment has become an important CSR consideration and, as evidenced in CSR research, environmental sustainability in both management and marketing literature is converging because of shared environmental, economic, and social concerns among managers and experts in marketing (Montiel, 2008). Recent research supports this and indicates a growing number of programs being adopted in major league professional sports in the United States (Babiak, 2010; Robinson, 2005; Sheth and Babiak, 2010). Consider the recent partnerships formed by the Natural Resources Defense Council (NRDC) with North American professional and collegiate sports, and similarly those relationships like the one developed between the United Nations Environmental Programme (UNEP) and the Indian Premier League (IPL) in 2010 (UNEP and IPL, 2010). The Environmental Protection Agency (EPA) has also played an active role in the growth of adopted programs, particularly in advising the sport industry on issues related to resource use (e.g., water and energy) and on more sustainable field and turf management (EPA, 2013). The NRDC professional and collegiate sport partnerships are well documented through highlighted cases via the respective systems (NRDC, 2012, 2013). For example, the key achievements documented by the NRDC among professional sports include such outcomes as having all league commissioners publicly committing to environmental stewardship, all major concessionaires developing environmentally preferable menus, and all leagues actively involved in educating their fans. Similarly, with the influence of the NRDC, the top three adopted sustainability considerations include 119 collegiate recreation departments and 97 collegiate athletics departments who have recycling bins in public spaces; there are 99 and 78 collegiate recreation and athletic departments, respectively, who boast office recycling programs, and 94 and 69 collegiate recreation and athletic departments who have bike racks and other infrastructure to promote bicycle commuting (see NRDC, 2013 for a full report on outcomes).

Sport entities are incorporating strategic corporate partnerships into their CSR programs, hoping to generate favorable brand imaging, fan loyalty, ticket sales, and sport development (Sports Philanthropy Project, 2007), with these efforts becoming increasingly institutionalized and formalized (Babiak and Trendafilova, 2011; Babiak and Wolfe, 2009). Sports organization personnel are making efforts to integrate CSR practices into their daily operations (Babiak and Wolfe, 2006; Brietbarth and Harris, 2008; Walters and Chadwick, 2009). CSR strategic programs usually achieve two objectives: 1) create a positive social impact, and 2) enhance the organization's brand, reputation, and in some cases its bottom line. In addition, a good CSR strategy helps employee engagement, innovation, and stakeholders' collaboration. Therefore, sport organizations have begun to view CSR efforts as the better option than traditional marketing relations as a means to increase consumer patronage and develop a positive brand image (Walker et al., 2011).

The natural environment: a CSR concern within the sport industry

Specific to the environment, professional sport teams and leagues are trying to understand the negative impact they have on the natural environment and are developing strategies to address relevant issues in order to mitigate this impact (Babiak and Wolfe, 2006). This new CSR environmental focus in sport is driven by changing societal values and increased engagement with and expectations by a variety of stakeholders (Babiak and Trendafilova, 2011; Horne, 2006). For example, Babiak and Trendafilova (2011) interviewed senior sport executives and discovered that seeking legitimacy by conforming to institutional pressures and expectations was one of the main motives that affected the decision to adopt environmental initiatives. Furthermore, these types of CSR practices could have economic and legitimacy benefits for a sport organization (Babiak and Trendafilova, 2011; Pfahl, 2010).

Trendafilova and Babiak (2013) specifically studied environmentally related CSR practices among professional sport teams in North America, and found that teams and leagues recognized their environmental initiatives as being central to strategic planning and related to their other CSR programs, resulting in internal benefits to the organization (e.g., employee engagement, image enhancement) as well as external benefits (e.g., new sponsors, customers, the environment). Environmentally focused CSR programs could benefit both the sport organization and society as a whole. Sport organizations often operate teams, venues, and events that are resource intensive (Babiak and Trendafilova, 2011). Thus, strategies to reduce the social, environmental, and financial costs glean a number of attractive outcomes for the sport organization and simultaneously their communities and stakeholders. These benefits could be successfully achieved by leveraging key stakeholders such as the media, to communicate a focus on the environment and educate fans.

The rise of environmental CSR in the sport industry is evident not only in the United States, but around the world as well. For example, FIFA has established a Green Goal Program, with the aim of organizing a climate-neutral World Cup (FIFA, 2009). Further, the International Olympic Committee (IOC) made the decision to incorporate the environment as the third *pillar* of Olympism alongside sport and culture (Cantelon and Letters, 2000). In collaboration with the IOC, the United Nations is actively involved in promoting sustainable sport, by organizing global forums on sport and the environment, focusing in particular on corporate environmental responsibility (UNEP, 2008).

While professional sports have been the main high-profile drivers behind the inclusion of environmental sustainability on the CSR agenda, National Collegiate Athletic Association (NCAA) schools' athletic departments are also integrating the environment into their planning process in order to most efficiently utilize scarce resources and to address the negative impact sport events and facilities have on the environment (Pfahl, 2010, 2011). With strategic emphasis on environmental actions, athletic departments can generate additional revenue and connect more closely with the local community. This close relationship could lead to the development of strategic partnerships and to attracting new and unconventional sponsors (e.g., supply chain, packaging, etc.). The key outcomes for most of these examples demonstrate that CSR is viewed as a strategic investment, and the scope of activities associated with CSR should continue expanding by including the protection of the natural environment. This strategic approach to managing the natural environment has the potential to bring both short-term and long-term benefits to the sport organization.

Table 7.1 provides examples of those who have integrated their efforts at a strategic level. This is not the case for many other examples where environmental sustainability efforts are in their infancy or are still managed ad hoc. As clearly articulated by Porter and Kramer (2006), "if, instead, corporations were to analyze their prospects for social responsibility using the same frameworks that guide their core business choices, they would discover that CSR can be much more than a cost, a constraint, or a charitable deed – it can be a source of opportunity, innovation, and competitive advantage" (p. 2).

Environmental CSR in various sport settings

The daily operations of sport entities and the conduct of the athletics contests require the consumption of energy and water consumption and production of a variety of wastes, often in significant amounts. To address these issues and to minimize the adverse effect their operations have on the natural environment, sport professionals at all levels turned their attention to environmental CSR initiatives (Babiak and Trendafilova, 2011; Babiak and Wolfe, 2006, 2009; Brietbarth and Harris, 2008; Sheth and Babiak, 2010; Smith and Westerbeek, 2007).

For example, the major professional leagues in North America have each initiated environmental programs and some have partnered with the NRDC. Programs such as the Greening Advisors program are used to implement systems, structures, and processes by which to engage in greening activities. A team at the leading edge of these efforts is the Philadelphia Eagles of the National Football League (NFL), with their owner being at the forefront of the adoption and implementation of environmental programs. Their stadium is the first in the United States capable of generating 100 percent of its energy from renewable sources: solar panels, biodiesel/natural gas generator, and 14 wind turbines (NRDC, 2012). In addition, the team has a comprehensive recycling program and recycles plastic, aluminum, and paper products. Interestingly, the Eagles have even adopted a forest in Pennsylvania.

Following the example of the Philadelphia Eagles, other teams and leagues have adopted green initiatives. San Antonio Spurs of the National Basketball Association (NBA) incorporated environmental programs as their main CSR platform and purchased wind energy to power stadium and practice facilities. Every year around the Super Bowl, the NFL organizes tree planting in the local community hosting the event. In Major League Baseball (MLB), the Houston Astros are making efforts to compost their food waste and to recycle plastic and cardboard at their stadium.

TABLE 7.1 Examples of key actions and outcomes of environmental efforts

Organization/ venue	Driving force	Key action(s)	Outcomes
Los Angeles Staples Center	"When you realize that this is truly a priority to our organization, you have to look for ways to do that. Beginning with the planning and design of STAPLES Center in 1998, this has always been our way of life," says Bill Pottorff, Vice President of Engineering for STAPLES Center and Nokia Theatre L.A. Live.	Adoption of innovative clean technology ISO 14001 certification process Strategic partnerships with high-profile tenants	Save an average of $55,000 a year in energy costs Reduce direct water costs by $28,200 a year 90% of cleaning products have green certifications
The Philadelphia Eagles (NFL)	"This commitment makes good business sense, but more importantly, it helps our Eagles organization to fulfill our role as a community champion by inspiring others to take a step forward and 'Go Green!' to help save our wonderful planet," say Jeffrey and Christina Lurie, owners of the Philadelphia Eagles.	Construction design considerations Environmentally minded procurement policies Organization-wide commitment to their environmental sustainability journey	Reduced electricity consumption by more than 33% Cut water waste by 21% All requests for proposals (RFPs) mandate that vendors propose green-certified materials as standard
University of Colorado Boulder	"Key to our sports greening collaboration is the clear desire of students to move in this direction," says Dave Newport, director of CU-Boulder's Environmental Center.	Employment of recycling and composting efforts Design focus on energy efficiency, green building design, and turf management Net-zero energy and zero-waste strategies	Innovation: first of its kind tea-compost irrigation system 78.5% waste diversion rate Implementation of a successful Green Stampede tailgating materials recovery program

Source: National Resources Defense Council Report (2012).

Other examples of environmental practices by sport teams include water-conserving fixtures, bicycle parking, convenient access for public transit users and pedestrians, and recycled building materials (Green Sports Alliance, 2012). Due to the essence of the game and the requirements for their facilities, the National Hockey League (NHL) focuses specifically on reducing water consumption. The NHL developed and implemented an online measurement tool, complete with specific metrics, for all NHL venue personnel to track and to analyze data related to waste, energy usage, and water consumption. This initiative has encouraged sport venues across North America to decrease the environmental impact and to bring awareness of the resources used and the financial costs incurred (NHL Green, 2012).

In addition to professional sports, intercollegiate athletics personnel in the United States have also started paying attention to the environment, and athletics departments among the NCAA schools are strategically planning green initiatives. Athletics department personnel are beginning to understand and to examine their role in campus environmental activities, the illustration of which is the American College and University Presidents' Climate Commitment (ACUPCC) (Swearingen White, 2009). This area of sport combines internal initiatives within athletics departments with the need to work with broader university requirements such as those of the ACUPCC.

For example, many NCAA schools are following in the footsteps of the University of Colorado, the first Football Bowl Subdivision (FBS) school to launch a zero-waste program for waste reduction at football games. The program also addresses the energy used in powering the stadium, team travel, and other football-related activities. Similarly, the University of Tennessee has established the recycling program Good Sports Always Recycle in an effort to promote recycling at all sporting events. The program operates with the assistance of corporate sponsors Eastman Kodak, Coca-Cola, Waste Connections, and Food City. North Carolina State University formed the Sustainability in Athletics Committee, which includes key university and athletics department personnel, campus sustainability office personnel, and faculty members. The committee incorporated environmental sustainability as part of the university-wide strategic plan. Florida State University and Penn State have also implemented a recycling program at their football games, targeting the concourses inside the stadium, along with the tailgate areas and parking lots. Through the efforts of this program, Florida State University collected over 32 tons of recyclable material during the 2010 football season alone (Florida State University, 2011).

Outside of the United States, there are a number of initiatives being led by the sport industry. With the IOC officially committing efforts to address the natural environment as a social responsibility, the 2010 Winter Olympics Vancouver Organizing Committee and the 2012 London Olympic Games Organising Committee adopted holistic approaches (social, economic, and environmental) in managing the Games. Both organizing committees developed a sustainability policy, which included a reporting system in Vancouver (Coady et al., 2007) and a sustainability legacy in London (London 2012's sustainability legacy lives on, 2012). The IPL partnered with the UNEP in 2010 to send a "clear and powerful signal to millions upon millions of spectators and fans: namely that if we all bat together, we can score fours and sixes for a more sustainable future," Achim Steiner, Executive Director, UNEP (UNEP and the IPL, 2010).

In Australia, the natural environment conditions (e.g., drought, floods, etc.) have impacted the sport industry and have forced the industry to respond. Their efforts have been motivated by environmental necessity, government mandate, and more recently as a recognized social responsibility. For example, Simonds Stadium, a multi-purpose sporting venue and home to teams and leagues such as the Geelong Football Club (Australian Football League), A-League, Super Rugby, Rugby League, Super-X, Domestic First Class Cricket, and Nitro Circus, has been an active participant in considering opportunities for environmentally responsible built environment developments. It was originally built in 1941 on Crown-owned land, and since 2005 has been managed by the City of Greater Geelong. Recent developments saw venue personnel introduce a number of physical changes to the facility in order to minimize its environmental footprint. Two key areas of interest during the changes were water and energy savings. To accomplish these goals, systems were introduced to harvest storm water, to implement a drought-tolerant turf playing surface, and to install dual flush cisterns and flow-restricted showerheads. For lighting, LED lighting in netball courts, sensor lighting within the stadium, and CBUS lighting control systems have been implemented. In implementing these changes, Simonds has been able to save at least 20 megaliters of water per year and plan to increase the stadium's capacity by installing more LED lighting and managing the lighting towers and overall energy consumption. Through these efforts, the City of Greater Geelong hopes to review their waste management practices along with improving their community awareness and education efforts to position themselves as leaders in this space. As Natalie Valentine, the manager of Simonds Stadium and coordinator of Sport Venues (City of Greater Geelong, Victoria, Australia), sums it up:

> Simonds Stadium Management and the City of Greater Geelong are committed to ongoing developments and improvements, assisting in identifying the Stadium as environmentally friendly, sustainable and a leader in the industry. With a captive audience of over 34,000 at any given event, we are aware that the changes and improvements we make within our stadium and the education we provide our clients and spectators results in a direct benefit to the wider community.
>
> (Personal interview, November 11, 2013)

Examples such as these from around the world demonstrate the tactical implementation of CSR initiatives related to the environment. However, strategic management leadership of the efforts remains critical for the long-term sustainability of these efforts.

Protecting the environment: regulation and leadership

The sport industry has experienced a diffusion of environmental initiatives over the past ten years, and the motives behind the strategic decisions to include the environment as a core component of the overall CSR efforts are multifaceted. Growing social expectations, increasing affluence, and globalization play a role in determining the future of CSR. The current trend is for organization personnel to increasingly implement more and expand current environmental initiatives into their CSR efforts as a strategic necessity to preserve organizational legitimacy in the face of changing social values (Vidaver-Cohen and Simcic Brønn, 2008). This focus on the environment and greening programs will continue to be on the agenda of many sport organizations not only because of the ongoing shift in social values related to environmental issues, but also because of new expectations (e.g., financial performance, adherence to governmental regulations) from a variety of stakeholders.

Interest groups, government agencies, and corporate partners are developing their own CSR agendas and, in their partnerships, sport organizations are responding to maintain mutually beneficial relationships (Nguyen et al., 2014). Improving the financial performance of an organization, for instance, is determined to a large degree by the satisfaction of the stakeholders' interests. Therefore, addressing these new expectations is critical to an organization's planning processes over time. The adoption of environmental CSR activities is often associated with some initial cost (rather large in some instances, such as solar panels), which could affect management decisions about which specific programs to adopt first and how to strategically distribute limited resources.

Although most environmental CSR activities in the sport industry are voluntarily driven, recent government regulations require that new facilities meet specific environmental standards, thus forcing sport organizations to carefully plan and comply. In some markets, the Leadership in Energy and Environmental Design (LEED) certification, established by the United States Green Building Council (USGBC), is understood as the standard of design and development. Several professional teams have obtained LEED certification for the facilities in which they play. For example, the Orlando Magic (NBA) was the first new arena in the NBA to be LEED certified. Similarly, the Washington Nationals (MLB) play in a new green stadium (LEED Silver certified). LEED, while a USGBC certification, is not only limited to North American facilities, but has made its way to other parts of the world, as evidenced at Melbourne and Olympic Parks, more well known as the home of the Tennis Grand Slam Circuit's Australian Open. In its AUS$700 million major 15-year redevelopment project, the Eastern Plaza Project (where the National Tennis Centre is located) has recently achieved LEED Gold Certification; the new Margaret Court Arena will also be pursuing LEED certification in this development plan (Melbourne and Olympic Parks, 2014).

Other regulating bodies that have supported built environmental sustainability decisions include the Global Reporting Initiative (GRI), which creates and shares sustainability reporting guidelines for voluntary use in reporting their environmental impact (www.globalreporting.org), and also the International Organization for Standardization (ISO), which houses the ISO 14000 family that "addresses various aspects of environmental management...[and] provides practical tools for companies and organizations looking to identify…and improve their environmental performance" (iso.org, 2009). Further, there are several industry partners that assist the sport industry in making better environmental decisions across their business in areas such as procurement and waste management (e.g., Forestry Stewardship Council, Natural Resources Defense Council, Environmental Protection Agency, etc.).

Along with the growing opportunities for certification and regulation, the sport industry has positioned itself as a leader in the movement and has made it their responsibility to address environmental sustainability. Environmentally focused CSR programs appear to be perceived not only as strategic but as a value driver as well, with many benefits that are not reflected in traditional financial terms (Babiak and Trendafilova, 2011). Considering the shifting social consciousness around environmental issues and the social bonds or contracts sport organizations have with local communities, sport organizations have positioned themselves to strategically take advantage of these opportunities in taking the lead in making environmental sustainability a CSR priority.

References

Babiak, K. (2010) 'The role and relevance of corporate social responsibility in sport: A view from the top', *Journal of Management and Organization*, Vol.16, No.4, pp.528–49.

Babiak, K. and Trendafilova, S. (2011) 'CSR and environmental responsibility: Motives and pressures to adopt sustainable management practices', *Corporate Social Responsibility and Environmental Management*, Vol.18, No.1, pp.11–24.

Babiak, K. and Wolfe, R. (2006) 'More than just a game? Corporate social responsibility and Super Bowl XL', *Sport Marketing Quarterly*, Vol.15, pp.214–22.

Babiak, K. and Wolfe, R. (2009) 'Determinants of corporate social responsibility in professional sport: Internal and external factors', *Journal of Sport Management*, Vol.23, No.6, pp.717–42.

Baughn, C. C., Bodie, N. L. and McIntosh, J. C. (2007) 'Corporate social and environmental responsibility in Asian countries and other geographical regions', *Corporate Social Responsibility and Environmental Management*, Vol.14, No.4, pp.189–205.

Bonini, S., Mendoca, L. and Oppenheim, J. (2006) 'When social issues become strategic', *McKensey Quarterly*, Vol.2, pp.20–32.

Bowen, H. R. (1953) *Social responsibilities of the businessman*, New York: H&R.

Brietbarth, T. and Harris, P. (2008) 'The role of corporate social responsibility in the football business: Towards the development of a conceptual model', *European Sport Management Quarterly*, Vol.8, No.2, pp.179–206.

Cantelon, H. and Letters, M. (2000) 'The making of the IOC environmental policy as the third dimension of the Olympic movement', *International Review for the Sociology of Sport*, Vol.35, pp.294–308.

Carroll, A. B. (1991) 'The pyramid of corporate social responsibility: Toward the moral management of organizational stakeholders', *Business Horizon*, July–August, pp.39–48.

Carroll, A. B. (2000) 'Ethical challenges for business in the new millennium: Corporate social responsibility and models of management morality', *Business Ethics Quarterly*, Vol.10, No.1, pp.33–42.

Carroll, A. B. and Buchholtz, A. K. (2003) *Business and society: Ethics and stakeholder management* (5th ed.), Australia: Thomson South-Western.

Coady, L., Snider, S., Duffy, A. and Legg, R. (2007) 'Corporate social responsibility for the Vancouver 2010 Olympic and Paralympic winter games: Adopting and adapting best practices', *Corporate Social Responsibility Review*, Autumn, pp.11–15.

Davis, K. (1960) 'Can business afford to ignore social responsibilities?', *California Management Review*, Vol.2, No.3, pp.70–6.

EPA (2013) 'Green sports news and events'. Available online at http://www2.epa.gov/green-sports/green-sports-news-and-events (accessed 22 March 2014).

European Commission (2009, 10 April) 'Community social responsibility forum'. Available online at http://ec.europa.eu/enterprise/policies/sustainable-business/corporate-social-responsibility/index_en.htm (accessed 30 April 2009).

FIFA (2009) Available online at www.fifa.com (accessed 24 May 2009).

Florida State University (2011) 'Garnet and gold goes green'. Available online at www.sustainablecampus.fsu.edu/Our-Programs/Garnet-Gold-Goes-Green (accessed 29 October 2011).

Green Sports Alliance (2012) Available online at http://greensportsalliance.org (accessed 17 January 2013).

Horne, J. (2006) *Sport in consumer culture*, New York: Palgrave Macmillan.

ISO.org (2009) 'International organization for standardization 26000'. Available online at http://isotc.iso.org/livelink/livelink/fetch/2000/2122/830949/3934883/3935096/07_gen_info/faq.html (accessed 29 December 2009).

Jones, T. (1980) 'Corporate social responsibility revisited, redefined', *California Management Review*, Vol.22, No.3, pp.59–67.

London 2012's sustainability legacy lives on (2012) Available online at www.olympic.org/news/london-2012-s-sustainability-legacy-lives-on/205777 (accessed 8 October 2013).

McWilliams, A. and Siegel, D. (2000) 'Corporate social responsibility and financial performance: Correlation or misspecification?', *Strategic Management Journal*, Vol.21, No.5, pp.603–9.

Melbourne and Olympic Parks (2014) 'Melbourne Park masterplan'. Available online at www.mopt.com.au/about/melbourne-park-masterplan (accessed 26 March 2014).

Montiel, I. (2008) 'Corporate social responsibility and corporate sustainability: Separate pasts, common futures', *Organization and Environment*, Vol.21, No.3, pp.245–69.

Nguyen, S., Trendafilova, S. and Pfahl, M. (2014) 'The Natural-Resource-Based View of the firm (NRBV): Constraints and opportunities for a Green Team in professional sport', *International Journal of Sport Management*, Vol.15, No.4, pp.485–517.

NHL Green (2012) 'NHL Green, NHL Foundation launch "Gallons for Goals" to restore water to freshwater streams'. Available online at www.nhl.com/ice/news.htm?id=612208&navid=DLjNHLjMicrosite-NHLGreen (accessed 19 August 2013).

Niskala, M. and Tarna, K. (2003) *Yhteiskuntavastuuraporttointi (Social responsibility reporting)*. Gummerus Oy, Helsinki, Finland: KHT Media.

NRDC (2012) 'NRDC report, game changer: How the sports industry is saving the environment'. Available online at www.nrdc.org/greenbusiness/guides/sports/files/Game-Changer-report.pdf (accessed 23 February 2013).

NRDC (2013) 'NRDC report, collegiate game changers: How campuses are going green'. Available online at www.nrdc.org/greenbusiness/guides/sports/files/collegiate-game-changers-report.pdf (accessed 25 March 2014).

Pfahl, M. E. (2010) 'Strategic issues associated with the development of internal sustainability teams in sport and recreation organizations: A framework for action and sustainable environmental performance', *International Journal of Sport Management Recreation and Tourism*, Vol.6, pp.37–61.

Pfahl, M. E. (2011) *Sport and the natural environment: A strategic guide*, Dubuque, IA: Kendall Hunt.

Pohle, G. and Hittner, J. (2008) 'Attaining sustainable growth through corporate social responsibility'. Available online at http://blog.gcase.org/2008/11/20/attaining-sustainable-growth-through-corporate-social-responsibility (accessed 2 June 2009).

Porter, M. E. and Kramer, M. R. (2006) 'Strategy and society: The link between competitive advantage and corporate social responsibility', *Harvard Business Review*, Vol.84, No.12, pp.78–92.

Preston, L. E. and Post, J. E. (1975) *Private management and public policy*, Englewood Cliffs, NJ: Prentice-Hall.

Robinson, R. (2005) 'Sports philanthropy: An analysis of the charitable foundations of major league teams', Unpublished master's thesis. California: University of San Francisco.

Sheth, H. and Babiak, K. (2010) 'Beyond the game: Perceptions and priorities in corporate social responsibility in the sport industry', *Journal of Business Ethics*, Vol.91, No.3, pp.433–50.

Smith, A. C. T. and Westerbeek, H. M. (2007) 'Sport as a vehicle for deploying corporate social responsibility', *The Journal of Corporate Citizenship*, Vol.25, pp.43–54.

Sports Philanthropy Project (2007) 'Sports Philanthropy Project helps teams and athletes partner with community groups to promote health and well-being', Report to Robert Wood Johnson Foundation.

Swearingen White, S. (2009) 'Early participation in the American College and University Presidents' Climate Commitment', *International Journal of Sustainability in Higher Education*, Vol.10, No.3, pp.215–27.

Trendafilova, S. and Babiak, K. (2013) 'Understanding strategic corporate environmental responsibility in professional sport', *International Journal of Sport Management and Marketing*, Vol.13, No.1–2, pp.1–26.

UNEP (2008) Available online at www.unep.org/sport_env (accessed 9 April 2009).

UNEP and IPL (2010) 'Batting for the environment'. Available online at www.unep.org/sport_env/IPL.aspx (accessed 8 October 2013).

Vidaver-Cohen, D. and Simcic Brønn, P. (2008) 'Corporate citizenship and managerial motivation: Implications for business legitimacy', *Business and Society Review*, Vol.113, No.4, pp.441–75.

Walker, M., Kent, A. and Jordan, J. S. (2011) 'An inter-sport comparison of fan reactions to CSR initiatives', *Journal of Contemporary Athletics*, Vol.5, No.1, pp.1–19.

Walters, G. and Chadwick, S. (2009) 'Corporate citizenship in football: Delivering strategic benefits through stakeholder engagement', *Management Decision*, Vol.47, No.1, pp.51–66.

Welford, R. (2009) 'The state of CSR in Australia', *CSR Asia Weekly*, Vol.5, pp.4–5.

8

PRESSURES FROM STAKEHOLDERS TO IMPLEMENT ENVIRONMENTAL SUSTAINABILITY EFFORTS

An overview

Brian P. McCullough

Introduction

Stakeholders within the sport industry have a certain degree of influence on organizations. By way of applying various forms of pressure on the organization, legitimate stakeholders can influence a wide array of organizational aspects including attracting a quality work force (Greening and Turban 2000), managerial decision making (Frooman 1999), and various initiatives that become integrated into the organizational identity (Scott and Lane 2000). Imperative initiatives that have been forwarded by stakeholders consist of diversity issues (Smith et al. 2001), work–family life balance (Guest 2002), and environmental sustainability (Reed 2008).

Environmental sustainability has emerged as a growing emphasis of organizations across various industries and, as the focus of this chapter, within the sport industry. While environmental sustainability might be viewed as a social issue movement (Orlitzky et al. 2011), in previous chapters the case has been made for the environmental impact across the sport industry and, specifically, among individual sport organizations. Academic research followed suit among sport management scholars in response to this integration of environmental management and the sport industry (for a review see Mallen and Chard 2011).

Previous research conceptualized the pressures for sport organizations to implement environmentally sustainable business practices (Babiak and Trendafilova 2011; McCullough and Cunningham 2010). These pressures can influence organization personnel to change their operations to include environmental sustainability efforts into their daily and game day operations. However, to maintain organizational legitimacy, the sport entity should work to appease the demands of the stakeholders (Scott and Lane 2000). For example, as more individuals live in more environmentally sustainable ways, they would expect that their daily activities and actions would follow suit. With that being said, these individuals can apply pressure on the organizations that they interact with (e.g., sporting events and venues) to implement environmental sustainability efforts (e.g., recycling, composting, carpooling/ride share, energy efficiency, renewable energy resources). For instance, in Colorado, Citizens for Colorado's Future applied pressure on the city of Denver after it was awarded an Olympic bid to host the 1976 Winter Games. This group was concerned about the development surrounding the Olympic Games and the subsequent environmental impact. Voters in the state overwhelmingly decided to decline the Olympic bid by a two to three margin (Chappelet 2008). As a result of these potential pressures, sport organizations need to be aware of various stakeholder groups and cognizant of their demands while determining ways to respond to those specific pressures.

To this end, this chapter will address the role of stakeholders in the environmental sustainability efforts of sport organizations. In the following section, stakeholders will be defined to provide a framework to understand these groups and individuals. Then, a theoretical foundation will be used to define the pressures stakeholders can place on sport organizations to implement environmental sustainability into the organization. Lastly, specific examples will be provided to demonstrate the role of stakeholders as sport organizations implement environmental sustainability efforts.

Stakeholders

In order to address the concerns or pressures of stakeholders, the concept of a legitimate organizational stakeholder must be framed. The definitions for what constitutes an organizational stakeholder have varied across the literature. Donaldson and Preston (1995) describe a stakeholder as an individual or group that has a legitimate connection to a specific organization. Furthering the concept, Freeman defines a stakeholder as "any group or individual who can affect or is affecting the achievement of the firm's objectives" (Freeman 2010: 25). From these conceptualizations and definitions, we can take away that stakeholder groups have an interest in aspects of the organization in one form or another. Freeman (2010) identifies traditional and non-traditional stakeholder groups, both of which need to be considered given the ever-changing business environment concerning social responsibility or lack thereof of organizations (e.g., environmental sustainability).

Needless to say, traditional stakeholders have received the majority of the attention within the literature when exploring the genre of literature surrounding stakeholders. These stakeholder groups include: suppliers, owners, shareholders, customers, and employees. These specific groups have been identified through traditional views of production models. There are inputs (suppliers), a process that is influenced by shareholders/owners and employees, and ultimately the recipient of the organization's output—customers. Given the evolving nature of business today in and out of the sport industry, other stakeholder groups have been included as legitimate stakeholder groups.

Freeman (2010) also argued that organization personnel who might not be involved in the decision-making process might be indirectly affected by decisions concerning environmental sustainability or the lack thereof. This expanded view of stakeholder groups includes the addition of governments, political groups, communities, and trade associations. Although this is not an exhaustive list, this list will serve as a basis for understanding the influence of stakeholders on sport organizations in environmental sustainability efforts. To this point, when considering the environmental impact of an organization, the environment has been argued to be a legitimate stakeholder.

For example, when examining the role of stakeholders in the Sydney Olympics, dubbed the Green Games, Kearins and Pavlovich (2002) identified stakeholders as those with an interest in incorporating environmental sustainability into the 2000 Summer Olympiad. The Green Games were influenced by several stakeholder groups such as the Royal Australian Institute of Architects, the Royal Australian Planning Institute, the Housing Industry Association and Auburn Municipal Council, Greenpeace Australia, sponsors of the Olympic Games, academics, and other environmental groups. These stakeholder groups all had their own perspective, or agenda, to promote and create an environmentally sustainable mega event. However, the concept of what makes up a sustainable mega event had not been done before.

As a result, and due to the pressure and influence of these groups, the overall concept of the Olympiad's attempt to incorporate environmental sustainability came to fruition. These national and international groups formed an Environmental Committee where their viewpoints could be shared and form the foundation for a sustainable Olympic bid. Based on each individual group's priorities (e.g., waste management, carbon emissions, sustainable construction), "the committee ... developed comprehensive environmental guidelines which were circulated in draft form and finally published in September 1993 (Sydney Olympics 2000 Bid Ltd., 1993)" (Kearins and Pavlovich 2002: 158).

The environment as a legitimate stakeholder

A major conflict arises among the various views of stakeholder theory and its application to various groups that may claim to be legitimate stakeholders. While these theories address certain aspects of the groups or individuals that have a legitimate claim on an organization, these varying perspectives ultimately conflict with one another. As noted by Orts and Studler, "the broader one conceives stakeholder theory to extend, the deeper the conflicts among stakeholder interests will become; the greater number of different stakeholders one recognizes, the more divergent and irreconcilable their interests" (Orts and Studler 2002: 219). One specific area where these conflicts arise is whether or not the natural environment has a legitimate claim for being a stakeholder. While traditional stakeholders take the form of individuals and groups, non-traditional stakeholders, within the context of this chapter, take the form of the natural environment itself.

Phillips and Reichart (2000) argued that despite the dependent nature of the organization and the natural environment, the natural environment does not have a claim for being a legitimate traditional stakeholder, while others have argued that traditional stakeholder groups (e.g., Greenpeace; Natural Resources Defense Council or NRDC) voice the concerns related to the environmental impact of organizations. The natural environment should receive ample consideration as being affected by organizations as these organizations achieve their business objectives (Jacobs 1997; Starik 1995). Regardless of whether the environment by itself is a traditional stakeholder or not, managers have an ethical obligation to occupy a natural environment and use natural resources responsibly. Under this pretense, the natural environment will not be treated as a traditional stakeholder by itself but rather as a factor that is represented by groups or individuals as a non-traditional stakeholder, thus adhering to Freeman's (2010) conceptualization of stakeholders as those who affect or can affect the organization from achieving its objectives.

Theoretical conceptualization of stakeholder influence

Within the sport management literature, there are two theoretical perspectives that demonstrate the influence that stakeholder groups or individuals have on sport organizations and sustainability efforts. McCullough and Cunningham (2010) use deinstitutionalization theory (Oliver 1992) to conceptualize the pressures that might prompt sport organization personnel to move away from business practices that might not consider or account for environmental impacts. This conceptual framework can be used to gauge the three categories of pressure (i.e., political, functional, social) that can be applied to influence sport organizations to move away from environmentally damaging practices to implement environmental sustainability efforts. Additionally, Babiak and Trendafilova (2011) examined the pressures and motivations for sport organizations to implement environmental sustainability initiatives using a corporate social responsibility (CSR) lens. These two perspectives are discussed below, specifically in terms of the role of stakeholder pressures to implement environmental sustainability efforts among sport organizations.

McCullough and Cunningham (2010)

Deinstitutionalization theory (Oliver 1992) explains how previously institutionalized behaviors erode and give way under political, functional, and social pressures to new business practices. McCullough and Cunningham (2010) apply this theoretical framework to explain the erosion of behaviors that, whether implicit or explicitly, ignore the environmental impact of sport organizations. The conceptual framework explains that political, functional, and social pressures will lead to the implementation of green initiatives or environmental sustainability efforts. Under McCullough and Cunningham's framework, the influence of pressures is moderated by upper management consistent with upper echelon theory (Hambrick and Mason 1984), which states that the organization processes and behaviors are slowed or hurried by the influence of upper management. Additionally, McCullough and Cunningham outlined the potential outcomes for sport organizations if they implemented environmental sustainability efforts. These outcomes include: increased fan identification, increase in goodwill perceptions, cost saving, and a competitive advantage. For the purpose of this chapter, particular attention is given to the pressures (i.e., functional, political, social) that stakeholder groups and individuals can apply to sport organizations to implement environmental sustainability efforts.

Stakeholders with a vested interest in the organization can apply pressure through various forms to break away from established and institutionalized organizational practices. One such pressure could be through political means. Political pressures refer to those pressures that arise from "performance deficiencies, the presence of conflicting interests among key stakeholder groups, pressures for organizational innovations, and altered relationships with key external agents" (McCullough and Cunningham 2010: 351).

These pressures result from shifts in the power structure of certain stakeholder groups. The conflicts can result in an individual stakeholder or group establishing more dominance within the hierarchy of stakeholders and using their position to influence change within the organization, including the incorporation of environmental sustainability efforts. For example, Paul Allen, the owner of the Seattle Seahawks, has a propensity to promote environmental sustainability through his organizations, charitable contributions, and in his ownership of the Seattle Seahawks. Due to his position as owner of the Seahawks, he clearly has influence over the daily operations of the organization. As a result, he can apply his political pressure and influence to incorporate deep levels of commitment to environmental sustainability efforts. Likewise, as mentioned earlier, citizens in Colorado launched a campaign for a special election to rescind the Olympic bid awarded to Denver. Despite the corporate influence to compile a successful bid, a citizen action group eclipsed the political power to vote to rescind the accepted Olympic bid.

Additionally, organization personnel might encounter functional pressures that result from inefficient ways of conducting daily operations within the organization. These pressures are less political in nature, but can cause a paradigm shift in operating the organization. This shift may be necessary to better compete for scarce resources (Oliver 1992). Sport organization personnel might implement environmental sustainability efforts for financial reasons. Environmental sustainability programs can save and even make money for various organizations. Stakeholder groups can influence the sport organization by applying pressure to better use fiscal resources and to ensure optimal use of scarce resources.

Lastly, social pressures applied by stakeholder groups can influence sport organizations to implement environmental sustainability efforts. Previously held beliefs or social cultures within the organization can fall to social pressures from internal or external stakeholders. These pressures can be influenced by legal mandates, changes in organizational culture, and social movements within the external organizational environment (Dacin et al. 2002; Oliver 1992; Scott 2001). These pressures can delegitimize traditionally held business practices and lead to new organizational forms and procedures (Cunningham 2002). Likewise, external stakeholders, like customers, can apply pressure through expectations of certain organizational behaviors (i.e., environmental sustainability) and ultimately change the way organizational practices are conducted in regard to various issues of concern to stakeholders.

Beyond this conceptual framework, other perspectives can be useful in understanding the influence of stakeholders on the implementation of the environmental sustainability efforts of sport organizations. Another perspective that is appropriate for the topic of this chapter focuses on the role of environmental sustainability efforts within corporate social responsibility approaches among sport organizations. Babiak and Trendafilova (2011) conducted a study that examined the motives and pressures to implement environmental sustainability as experienced by sport industry executives.

Babiak and Trendafilova (2011)

Babiak and Trendafilova (2011) examined the pressures and motives to engage in environmental sustainability within the sport industry from a corporate social responsibility lens. They noted that much attention has been given to CSR within the literature but little attention has been directed towards determining the motives and pressures for engaging in such behaviors. In order to balance the day-to-day operations and the demands of society, organizations have resorted to socially responsible behaviors (Campbell 2007). Based on institutional theory (Campbell 2007; Matten and Moon 2008; Scott 2008), organizations will adhere to socially acceptable practices in order to develop or maintain organizational legitimacy. That is, by implementing programs or organizational procedures that are "approved" among stakeholders or are used by other respected organizations, legitimacy can be created (Schumann 1995).

In this study, Babiak and Trendafilova (2011) found that sport executives were motivated to incorporate environmental sustainability efforts because it was a society norm and they believed their organization would be perceived as a good citizen. The authors also concluded that sport organization personnel are increasingly becoming aware of their environmental impact and proactively, yet strategically, implementing environmental sustainability initiatives. This proactive approach is used to avoid legal ramifications, save money, and build relationships with stakeholders (i.e., customers, fans, local communities, local, state, and federal governments, and corporate partners) (Babiak and Trendafilova 2011).

Their findings are consistent with the conceptual framework of McCullough and Cunningham (2010). Babiak and Trendafilova (2011) empirically demonstrated that sport organizations do in fact receive pressure to engage in environmental sustainability efforts and that these organizations deem these efforts worthwhile and valuable to their respective organization. Further, sport organizations realize the importance of furthering relationships with external stakeholders in specific regards to environmental sustainability issues. In the following section, other historical examples are provided to demonstrate the influence stakeholder groups have on sport organizations and their environmental sustainability efforts.

Examples of stakeholder influence

As outlined above, stakeholder groups or individuals take on various forms. The operating definition used for the purposes of this chapter follows Freeman: "any group or individual who can affect or is affecting the achievement of the firm's objectives" (Freeman 2010: 25). Additionally, the environment is not treated as a sole stakeholder but rather through the concerns of traditional stakeholder groups (Starik 1995) in particular suppliers, investors or owners, governments, political groups, customers/fans, communities, employees, trade associations, and the organization itself. The subsections below highlight a few of these stakeholder groups and the influence they have had on the sport industry or organizations and environmental sustainability efforts.

Environmental groups

Heading into the 2000 Summer Olympic Games in Sydney, Australia, the International Olympic Committee (IOC) amended its charter in 1991 so that future games would demonstrate environmental responsibility (Lenskyj 2000). The 1994 Winter Games in Lillehammer provided the best example, to that point, of how to run an environmentally sustainable mega-event. The 2000 Summer Games in Australia would present additional challenges than the Winter Games simply due to the amount of attendees and participants. However, the 2000 Summer Games would be the first Olympiad to be held after the bidding process for the Games required environmental sustainability considerations. During this Olympiad, the Sydney Planning Committee implemented many environmental initiatives, primarily focusing on waste management and energy consumption.

Along with the Olympic movement to implement environmental sustainability in the bidding process and into the Games itself, Greenpeace, an environmental group, launched a campaign to ensure that mega-events like the Olympics that were claiming they were environmentally conscientious were in fact following through on those claims. Greenpeace is an international environmental activist organization whose primary purpose is to be defenders of "the natural world and promote peace by investigating, exposing and confronting environmental abuse, and championing environmentally responsible solutions" (Greenpeace 2013: n.p.). With particular concentration on sport, Greenpeace has focused on the environmental impact of mega-events like the Olympic Games. Greenpeace, in conjunction with the United Nations Environmental Programme (UNEP) and the IOC, provides an environmental report card of each Olympiad to evaluate their environmental initiatives.

As preparations were being made before the 2000 Summer Games in Sydney, Greenpeace started placing pressure not only on the Sydney Olympic Planning Committee but also launched campaigns targeted at major Olympic sponsors to ensure their role and involvement with the Games helped to minimize the environmental impact. The organization created a website for Greenpeace's Green

Olympics Campaign. This campaign challenged organizations like Coca-Cola to implement higher standards for refrigeration that have less of an environmental impact. The campaigns also served to raise awareness and educate the general public on the impact of hosting a mega-event like the Olympic Games.

As a result the Sydney Planning Committee and sponsors gave into the pressures applied by Greenpeace through public awareness campaigns to implement environmental sustainability efforts. The Sydney Olympics were dubbed the Green Games for their environmental efforts. Greenpeace developed a manual on how to conduct and run a mega-event in an environmentally sustainable way. This manual thus set the standard for Greenpeace to evaluate future Olympiads and mega-events like the World Cup, Super Bowl, and the NCAA Men's Basketball Tournament. The extension that Greenpeace made into the sport industry was successful in creating credibility to evaluate the environmental impact of sport organizations and their events. This credibility extends their legitimacy as a stakeholder, representing the natural environment, and thereby continuing the pressure that they can wield on organizations as a stakeholder to further their environmental sustainability efforts.

Community members

Preceding the inclusion of sustainability as the Third Pillar of the Olympic movement, as will be discussed later, community members have applied pressure on sport organizations to influence the inclusion of environmental sustainability efforts. Local citizens have protested and provided civil demonstrations to bring awareness to the environmental impact of sport organizations, facilities, and events. This awareness of these issues has been approached from several perspectives within academic literature. Most recently environmental justice research has been focusing on the construction of sport facilities (Sze 2009) and mega-events (Tranter and Lowes 2009). However, during the rise of the environmental movement of the 1970s within the United States, the impact that sport had on the environment was front and center. The golf and ski industries were targets due to their impact on the environment while creating customized landscapes. For example, ski resorts will cut down trees along the mountainside to create various ski runs, which has a tremendous impact on the surrounding environment, increasing the likelihood of avalanches and landslides (Chivers 1994; Russo and Fouts 1997). This concern was not lost on concerned community members in Colorado.

A citizen action group called Citizens for Colorado's Future organized a protest and called for a statewide vote on the accepted Olympic bid for Denver to host the 1976 Winter Games. Citizens for Colorado's Future were concerned with the corporate focus with the promotion of the Games and in the development of the new facilities. This unbalanced focus on corporate relations ignored the impact that the Games would have on the environment. Because of the action and pressure that Citizens for Colorado's Future generated, the group was able to get enough signatures to introduce a ballot measure to reject the Olympic bid. In 1972, the people of Colorado voted to rescind state and federal funding to subsidize the Olympic Games in Colorado. Denver was forced to withdraw their bid to host the 1976 Winter Games. As a result, the Games were held in Innsbruck, Austria, on short notice.

Much can be said about how the situation was handled in Colorado and within the United States Olympic Committee (USOC) to ensure that Denver maintained state and federal funding for the Games. However, this situation ushered in instant legitimacy for citizen groups and community members as stakeholders for a sport organization or event. The ability for community groups or concerned citizens to vote and deny funding to subsidize the Winter Olympic Games in Denver should make sport organizations aware of the concerns of non-traditional stakeholder groups as aforementioned. These stakeholder groups may have no investment in the success of the event but may have valid concerns with regards to the environmental sustainability efforts or lack thereof surrounding an event or the daily operations of a sport organization.

Investors/owners

The last example focuses on a traditional stakeholder group—investors and owners. Owners, investors, and upper management hold a tremendous amount of influence within an organization because of their positions within the said organization. Upper echelon theory (Hambrick and Mason 1984) argues that upper management and owners can dictate the organization's priorities and have a tremendous amount of influence on policy and the culture within the organization. The same can be said about the attitudes of owners and upper management with concerns to environmental sustainability. For instance, the owner of the Philadelphia Eagles had a particular interest in implementing environmental sustainability efforts into the Eagles' daily operations.

In 2003, because of the leadership of the owners, the Lurie family, the Philadelphia Eagles started integrating environmental sustainability efforts into their daily operations and during their games. The influence of this stakeholder group may prove to be the most valuable because this group has the most to gain or lose by implementing these programs or not. Additionally, this group has the greatest control in influencing programs and initiatives that are introduced across the organization.

Conclusion

Stakeholder groups have a tremendous amount of influence on organizations, given the evolution of the business industry. Sport organizations must be aware of their social and environmental impact in order to maintain organizational legitimacy. Sport organization personnel must extend their conceptualization of stakeholder groups to include non-traditional stakeholder groups such as community groups and political groups to minimize the risks associated with organizational legitimacy.

While these groups may not actually consume the sport product delivered by the organization, these groups have a vested interest in the environmental impact of the organization. Building facilities, hosting events, and spectators traveling to and attending sporting events has a tremendous environmental impact (Collins et al. 2009). Due to the environmental impact of sport events and venues, community members surrounding the sport facility or team headquarters have a vested interest to maintain their surrounding natural environment. Additionally, political or environmental groups have a vested interest to ensure that sport organizations act responsibly. These stakeholder groups can use their influence to pressure sport organizations to implement or further their environmental sustainability efforts. As was demonstrated, if a sport organization does not properly address the concerns of certain stakeholder groups, the organization can run the risk of additional problems that may prevent the organization from making money or existing.

References

Babiak, K., and Trendafilova, S. (2011) 'CSR and environmental responsibility: Motives and pressures to adopt green management practices'. *Corporate Social Responsibility and Environmental Management*, 18: 11–24.

Campbell, J. L. (2007) 'Why would corporations behave in socially responsible ways? An institutional theory of corporate social responsibility'. *Academy of Management Review*, 32: 946–67.

Chappelet, J-L. (2008) 'Olympic environmental concerns as a legacy of the Winter Games'. *The International Journal of the History of Sport*, 25: 1884–902.

Chivers, J. (1994) 'Effects of skiing industry on the environment', thesis, Coventry University.

Collins, A., Jones, C., and Munday, M. (2009) 'Assessing the environmental impacts of mega sporting events: Two options?' *Tourism Management*, 30: 828–37.

Cunningham, G. B. (2002) 'Removing the blinders: Toward an integrative model of organizational change in sport and physical activity'. *Quest*, 54: 276–91.

Dacin, T., Goldstein, J., and Scott, W. R. (2002) 'Institutional theory and institutional change: Introduction to the special research forum'. *Academy of Management Journal*, 45: 45–56.

Donaldson, T., and Preston, L. E. (1995) 'The stakeholder theory of the corporation: Concepts, evidence, and implications'. *Academy of Management Review*, 20: 65–91.

Freeman, R. E. (2010) *Strategic Management: A stakeholder approach*. Cambridge, UK: Cambridge University Press.

Frooman, J. (1999) 'Stakeholder influence strategies'. *Academy of Management Review*, 24: 191–205.

Greening, D. W., and Turban, D. B. (2000) 'Corporate social performance as a competitive advantage in attracting a quality workforce'. *Business & Society*, 39: 254–80.

Greenpeace. (2013) 'What we do'. Available from: www.greenpeace.org/usa/en/campaigns

Guest, D. E. (2002) 'Perspectives on the study of work–life balance'. *Social Science Information*, 41: 255–79.

Hambrick, D. C., and Mason, P. A. (1984) 'Upper echelons: The organization as a reflection of its top managers'. *Academy of Management Review*, 9: 193–206.

Jacobs, M. (1997) 'The environment as stakeholder'. *Business Strategy Review*, 8: 25–8.

Kearins, K., and Pavlovich, K. (2002) 'The role of stakeholders in Sydney's green games'. *Corporate Social Responsibility and Environmental Management*, 9: 157–69.

Lenskyj, H. (2000) *The Best Olympics Ever? Social impacts of Sydney 2000*. Buffalo, NY: SUNY Press.

Mallen, C., and Chard, C. (2011) 'A framework for debating the future of environmental sustainability in the sport academy'. *Sport Management Review*, 14: 424–33.

Matten, D., and Moon, J. (2008) '"Implicit" and "explicit" CSR: A conceptual framework for a comparative understanding of corporate social responsibility'. *Academy of Management Review*, 33: 404–24.

McCullough, B. P., and Cunningham, G. B. (2010) 'A conceptual model to understand the impetus to engage in and the expected organizational outcomes of green initiatives'. *Quest*, 62: 348–63.

Oliver, C. (1992) 'The antecedents of deinstitutionalization'. *Organization Studies*, 13: 563–88.

Orlitzky, M., Siegel, D. S., and Waldman, D. A. (2011) 'Strategic corporate social responsibility and environmental sustainability'. *Business & Society*, 50: 6–27.

Orts, E. W. and Strudler, A. (2002) 'The ethical and environmental limits of stakeholder theory'. *Business Ethic Quarterly*, 12: 215–33.

Phillips, R. A., and Reichart, J. (2000) 'The environment as a stakeholder? A fairness-based approach'. *Journal of Business Ethics*, 23: 185–97.

Reed, M. S. (2008) 'Stakeholder participation for environmental management: A literature review'. *Biological Conservation*, 141: 2417–31.

Russo, M. V., and Fouts, P. A. (1997) 'A resource-based perspective on corporate environmental performance and profitability'. *Academy of Management Journal*, 40: 534–59.

Schumann, M. C. (1995) 'Managing legitimacy: Strategic and institutional approaches'. *Academy of Management Review*, 20: 571–610.

Scott, S. G., and Lane, V. R. (2000) 'A stakeholder approach to organizational identity'. *Academy of Management Review*, 25: 43–62.

Scott, W. R. (2001) *Institutions and Organizations*. Thousand Oaks, CA: SAGE.

Scott, W. R. (2008) 'Approaching adulthood: The maturing of institutional theory'. *Theory and Society*, 37: 427–42.

Smith, W. J., Wokutch, R. E., Harrington, K. V., and Dennis, B. S. (2001) 'An examination of the influence of diversity and stakeholder role on corporate social orientation'. *Business & Society*, 40: 266–94.

Starik, M. (1995) 'Should trees have managerial standing? Toward stakeholder status for non-human nature'. *Journal of Business Ethics*, 14: 207–17.

Sydney Olympics 2000 Bid Ltd (SOBL). (1993) 'Olympic guidelines for the Summer Olympic Games'. Sydney: SOBL.

Sze, J. (2009) 'Sports and environmental justice: "Games" of race, place, nostalgia, and power in neoliberal New York City'. *Journal of Sport & Social Issues*, 33: 111–29.

Tranter, P. J., and Lowes, M. (2009) 'Life in the fast lane: Environmental, economic, and public health outcomes of motorsport spectacles in Australia'. *Journal of Sport & Social Issues*, 33: 150–68.

9

EVALUATION AND ANALYSIS OF ENVIRONMENTAL ACTIONS

Kyle Bunds and Jonathan M. Casper

The purpose of this chapter is to present ways in which environmental efforts are evaluated and analyzed. In this chapter we provide reasons for why environmentally sustainable programs need evaluation metrics. Additionally, specific metrics for evaluation and analysis are explained. After providing key metrics considered in business more generally, we examine the connection with sport organization and leagues before detailing two case studies to show an example of the process from the environmental planning stage to the evaluation of efforts in both a sports team and in sport business.

Strategic planning: the importance of evaluation and measurement

As businessmen and women have begun paying attention to the fact that environmental degradation threatens business sustainability (Steg & Vlek, 2009), there has been an increased interest in creating sustainable practices from both the business industry and consumers (Bohdanowicz, 2006). Research has shown that individuals will participate in pro-environmental actions when such actions are convenient and when the individuals have a working knowledge of the importance and repercussions of their own environmental actions (Saphores et al., 2012). For example, Domina and Koch (2002) found that individuals are more likely to participate in recycling activities if the recycling program is convenient, such as programs that have curbside pickup instead of a drop-off location for recycling materials. Additionally, Scott (1999) found that those with knowledge of a local recycling scheme were more likely to participate in recycling.

Each of the research projects above indicates the necessity of careful planning and implementation strategies. Indeed, implementing sustainability programs takes an incredible amount of vision and action. Sustainability program coordinators must fully understand and cultivate directives from the stages of creating the vision, educating key stakeholders, and collecting detailed information about conservation measures. These programs can range from small-scale campaigns to raise awareness about energy consumption, to city-wide recycling programs, to large-scale initiatives such as building "green" facilities (Robertson, 2014).

While having a vision for these programs and taking the appropriate action for implementation are crucial, those with the vision to implement sustainable programs must be able to set up concrete goals and articulate those goals to fellow employees (Blackburn, 2008). Additionally, these goals must be communicated effectively so that organizational members understand the program goals and are able to fully participate in the implementation and execution of these program goals. Crucially, these goals must be measurable in order to understand the effectiveness of the program (Blackburn, 2008). Acquiring data and information about sustainability programs is the key to evaluating outcomes, which is critical to the organization's profit and the environment (Bohdanowicz & Martinac, 2007).

Evaluation and measurement of sustainability program goals are fundamental and necessary elements of sustainability work. Because a great deal of time, effort, and resources go into sustainability projects from the planning stage through implementation, reporting of successes (or failures) are essential (Robertson, 2014). That is, it is essential for managers to be able to connect goals with outcomes (Robertson, 2014). Without appropriate evaluation and measurement techniques, organizations are unable to understand whether or not the implemented program is effective and whether or not these goals have been met. However, not just any evaluation or measurement technique will work. Indeed, it is important to consider the ways that program goals are evaluated and measured.

Blackburn (2008) indicated that measurements must be valid and applicable to the program goals or they run the risk of failing to truly assess the outcomes, which could lead to continued future failings. Providing 11 examples, Blackburn explained the connection between failing to reach the program goals and faulty measurement; paraphrasing, these are: (1) the measures might not be credible with intended data users—this includes lack of reliable data, unclear meaning, lack of trained researchers to assess measurement, etcetera; (2) the use of the measures isn't readily visible or management is not interested in the results; (3) there are too many measures or they are reported too frequently; (4) results are reported too infrequently; (5) there are too few measures and the context is not understood; (6) goals are too short term; (7) no accountability; (8) unrealistic target goals; (9) goals drive the wrong performance; (10) unclear result reporting; and (11) results are not used to make business decisions. Failing to appropriately assess these goals could result in a waste of time and effort.

Appropriately implementing sustainability practices as a part of the larger push for social responsibility has become fully integrated into business models in the 2000s (Moura & Padgett, 2011). Recently there has been a push in both commercial enterprise and sport apparel for developing metrics that monetize natural capital (KPMG, 2014). As Daly explained, "Natural capital is the stock that yields the flow of natural resources—the population of fish in the ocean that regenerates the flow of caught fish that go to market; the standing forest that regenerates the flow of cut timber; the petroleum deposits in the ground where liquidation yields the flow of pumped crude oil" (Daly, 1994: 486). This example represents two kinds of natural capital. The fish and trees represent renewable natural capital, and the petroleum represents non-renewable (Daly, 1994). Large multinational corporations are beginning to see the necessity of understanding natural capital and measuring environmental impact.

Measuring sustainability outcomes and projecting the future profit and loss of natural capital is critical for businesses, governments, and non-profit organizations (Utilyx, 2013). Likewise, sport organizations, leagues, and sport apparel companies have also pushed toward appropriately evaluating and measuring sustainable practices with the help of organizations such as the Natural Resources Defense Council (NRDC) and Trucost. Councils such as this have helped sport organizations and leagues establish the key metrics for evaluating sport environmental efforts. The sport industry is at the forefront of implementing sustainable practices through work conducted with the NRDC and the Green Sports Alliance and understands the importance of both profits and the environment. As of the September 2012 NRDC report, *Game Changer: How the Sports Industry is Saving the Environment*, over 100 sport teams and facilities representing 13 sport leagues had representatives on the Green Sports Alliance. This partnership allows for the collection of data on stadium operations, one small example of the work that sport leagues are conducting (NRDC, 2012). Like any organization or program aimed at increasing environmental sustainability, programs in sport must contain detailed evaluation and measures that allow leagues and teams to save costs and strengthen community ties. We turn to these key metrics in the following section.

Key metrics for evaluating sport environmental efforts

The term "metric" is often interchangeably used with the term "indicator" to reference the creation of measurement tools and the actual measurement of sustainable practices (Tanzil & Beloff, 2006). However, "metrics" are solely quantitative measures, while "indicators" can also include narrative descriptions (Tanzil & Beloff, 2006). In referring to the importance of metrics and indicators in environmental sustainability work, Tanzil and Beloff (2006) invoked the adage "only what gets measured gets managed" (Tanzil & Beloff, 2006: 41) to portray the relationship between developing sound metrics and creating environmentally sustainable development. Within environmental sustainability, there is generally a concern for looking at indicators that impact three main areas: economic, environmental, and societal (Martins et al., 2007) (Figure 9.1). These three areas are considered important by industry standards. Indeed, "The WCED [World Commission on Environment and Development] treatise on sustainability centers on global conditions of ecology (i.e., environment), economic development (i.e., by technologies), and societal equity" (Sikdar, 2003: 1929). Each of these has its own measurements.

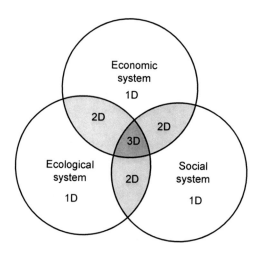

FIGURE 9.1 Schematic depiction of the three dimensions of sustainability

Source: Martins et al. (2007: 2963).

Martins and colleagues (2007) called economic, environmental, and societal considerations the three dimensions of sustainability. The authors divided the metrics that measure each dimension into three categories: 1D, 2D, and 3D. 1D metrics measure information from only one of the three areas. Therefore, metrics will be developed and utilized to measure one dimension of sustainability. For example, gross domestic product (GDP) would be a 1D indicator because it only measures economic sustainability. 2D metrics measure two dimensions of sustainability. For example, measuring waste generation would represent both a societal and economic dimension. Organizations can choose to measure 1D and 2D in a variety of ways. One popular way which focuses primarily on the economic considerations is true cost accounting, which takes into account both the fixed and variable costs of a given program's sustainability effort (Martins et al., 2007). 3D metrics are slightly more complicated given the nature of attempting to account for all three dimensions. "Examples of 3D metrics are 'energy intensity' and 'material intensity,' which account for the use of resources required for economic growth and could have a significant ecological and societal impact, because their use usually creates wastes that can affect the environment and create health effects" (Martins et al., 2007: 2963).

As Martins and colleagues (2007) point out, it is important for each individual organization or environmental sustainability campaign to carefully choose which metrics to utilize that best fit what the organization is attempting to accomplish. Although each industry, business, or organization can have its own metrics, generally there are five basic indicators:

- material intensity—mass of raw materials input to the process minus the mass of product and saleable co-products;
- energy intensity—net fuel-energy consumed to provide heat and power requirements;
- water consumption—gallons of water, excluding rainwater, consumed per unit output;
- toxic emissions—chemicals listed by the Environmental Protection Agency (EPA) as toxic. Toxic emissions are expressed as pounds of toxic material emitted per unit output;
- pollutant emissions—pounds of pollutants emitted per unit output.

(Schwarz et al., 2002: 58–60)

In the following section, we examine metrics that are specifically designed for and by sport industry constituencies.

Key metrics in the sport industry

Working alongside the National Hockey League (NHL) and Major League Baseball (MLB), the NRDC (2014) has been instrumental in creating metrics for the leagues to evaluate implemented sustainability programs. The NRDC specifically attempts to help the leagues create metrics that help them build sustainable stadia and implement sustainable practices in existing stadia. The organization does so by developing baseline operation guides to track the performance of environmentally sustainable stadia improvements and other initiatives such as waste disposal, energy usage, and water use. The aim is not only to help the organizations develop innovative ways for developing sustainable programs, but to be able to help employees create ways to help the organization save money and resources.

Additionally, the NRDC has created a league-wide data collection system. The following categories underline the environmental initiatives, particularly of stadia and facilities, that the NRDC (2014) has created in metrics for evaluation and makes available online at http://nhl.greensports.org/tracking-your-progress/sustainabilitymetrics. The following information is adapted from this website.

Energy use

Stadia use a tremendous amount of energy. The NRDC offers myriad ways that organizations can monitor energy usage. The organization recommends tracking energy consumption through close data collection of utility bills, energy meters, and advanced Energy Star management systems that help track consumption data. They recommend using the following metrics:

- total electricity consumed—in kilowatt-hours (kWh) and dollars ($) [Note: if possible obtain info about which facilities measured, time period measured];

- renewable energy proportion purchased (kWh and/or percent of total energy consumed, and $)
  [Note: if possible obtain info about type of energy provided (e.g., solar, wind)];
- energy generated through on-site renewable installations (kWh);
- energy generated through on-site fossil fuel installations (kWh);
- offsets purchased (in MWs and converted into lbs/tons of CO_2 equivalent offset, $)
  [Note: type of offset (e.g., solar, wind) and contact info of offset provider];
- other energy consumed (e.g., generator diesel)—in gallons or appropriate quantity;
- energy efficiency benefits achieved, if available: data of quantified energy savings through efficiency measures (kWh, $).

Waste generation and diversion

Organizations can work with their trash haulers to track the amount of waste at the stadium. The NRDC recommends using the EPA's waste tracking system to input and track waste diversion data, and recommend the following metrics:

- total solid waste produced (in lbs/tons);
- cost per ton of garbage disposed ($);
- percent and tonnage of each component of waste stream recycled (plastics, metals, paper, cardboard, cooking oil, etc.) (in lbs/tons);
- percent and tonnage of waste stream composted (in lbs/tons).

Water use

This can be tracked similarly as energy by utilizing an Energy Star tracking system and the following metrics:

- total water use (in cubic feet or gallons);
- cost of water acquisition ($ per $feet^3$ or m^3 or gallon);
- cost of water disposal/sewage ($ per $feet^3$ or m^3 or gallon);
- any available data of quantified water savings through efficiency measures (e.g., waterless urinals);
- any available data on greywater use.

Paper purchasing

Paper purchasing data should be readily available through business operations. Additionally, there are resources available through the NRDC website that can link organizations to tools that help them estimate the cost of switching to recycled paper. The following metrics can be utilized to track paper usage:

- restrooms/offices: total tissue paper (towels, napkins, tissue) consumed (percent of recycled content, percent of postconsumer content, in lbs/tons, per event or per year);
- office: total copier paper consumed (percent of recycled content, percent of postconsumer content, in lbs/tons, per event or per year);
- programs, yearbooks, media guides (percent of recycled content, percent of postconsumer content of all paper consumed, in lbs/tons);
- if available, other grades of paper consumed, e.g., coated paper, cardboard (percent of recycled content, percent of postconsumer content of all paper consumed, in lbs/tons);
- if available, total paper consumed that is FSC-certified.

The previous metrics by the NRDC provide a general outline for how stadium managers and sport organizations more generally can track the environmental sustainability of the organization. In the following, we turn to two specific examples to show sustainability programs in action and the metrics that are utilized by a National Basketball Association (NBA) team and a leading sport apparel manufacturer.

Case studies

Portland Trail Blazers: Moda Center

In 2010, the Portland Trail Blazers became the first professional sports organization in the world to have a LEED certified stadium, an important goal for the organization (NRDC, 2012). Depending upon the focus of the project, becoming LEED certified involves meeting standards of the U.S. Green Building Council (USGBC) in building design and construction, interior design and construction, building operations and maintenance, neighborhood development, or home development. As evidence of the dedication to becoming an organization with an environmentally sustainable stadium, the Trail Blazers achieved the USGBC's Existing Building Standard by overhauling the then 15-year-old arena. Similar to the metrics the NRDC supplied as recommendations for sustainable stadium metrics, LEED's certification of existing buildings involves meeting standards of water efficiency, energy and atmosphere, materials and resources, and environmental quality (LEED, 2014).

At the time of the NRDC (2012) report, the Trail Blazers had achieved savings in energy, water, and waste allowing them to accrue almost $500,000 in profit above and beyond the initial costs of the green investment. This took a tremendous amount of time and effort and is ultimately able to be evaluated based on the appropriateness of the evaluative metrics utilized by the organization. Additionally, the organization had to monitor and continue to evaluate the metrics laid out by LEED's certification. This took multiple years to implement and is an ongoing initiative.

To begin, Portland organized a sustainability team that developed obtainable and measurable goals for the stadium. To develop their team, they solicited interested individuals from multiple departments (NRDC, 2012). They decided to also expand their team to include outside partners and even hired a consultancy group to help them determine the best courses of action and the most obtainable goals. As explained by the director of sustainability and planning, the Trail Blazers hired "a local, nationally recognized sustainability consultant, Green Building Services, to accurately measure our current carbon footprint and provide us with a road map toward making significant reductions to these impacts" (NRDC, 2012: 62). The organization chose to focus on scope 3 emissions analysis to help them measure their carbon footprint.

The EPA provides three "scopes" of greenhouse gas (GHG) emissions. Scope 1 emissions are directly related to sources controlled onsite, such as burned fossil fuels. This can be emission created by onsite landfills and wastewater treatment, for example (EPA, 2014). Scope 2 emission is indirect emissions caused by things such as the generation of electricity and heating or cooling. Scope 3 emissions are from sources "not owned or directly controlled by the entity but related to the entity's activities…losses associated with purchased electricity, employee travel and commuting, contracted solid waste disposal, and contracted wastewater treatment" (EPA, 2014). Importantly, elements in Scopes 1 and 2 are owned and operated by the entity in focus. Scope 3 applies to the Moda Center and the Trail Blazers because they do not directly own the source of electricity, but they do use electricity, for example. Therefore, they can rely on contracted information from waste disposal contracts to measure their waste, or monitor and evaluate their electricity cost and usage to evaluate their energy usage.

For the Trail Blazers, tracking, measuring, and constant evaluation was critical. Therefore, the organization hired Green Building Services to track their activities (NRDC, 2012). Additionally, they implemented an extensive carbon footprint monitoring initiative. The team reports that they were able to achieve incremental results within the first year by implementing new recycling and composting procedures, for example (NRDC, 2012). They measure this by monitoring usage rates. As seen in Figure 9.2, they have improved every year since first implementing their sustainability programs.

Some highlights of the improvements include achieving an 80 percent diversion rate of waste, meaning that trash is recycled rather than taken to landfills; the Trail Blazers' fans and workers have increasingly utilized public transportation; water usage has been cut by 17 percent; and there is 100 percent usage of recyclable trash can liners (NRDC, 2012). All of this has been accomplished by the sustainability team creating clearly defined goals and constantly evaluating them through creation of indicators and metrics analyzed internally and by outside consultancy firms. Together, these groups have allowed the Trail Blazers to become a model organization for sustainable stadia.

PUMA: environmental profit and loss

In a move foreign to merchandising conglomerates, in 2010 PUMA set out to create measures that placed an economic focus on sustainable manufacturing practices.

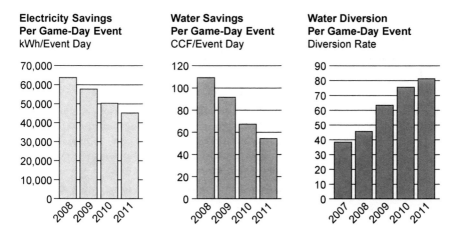

**Electricity Savings
Per Game-Day Event**
kWh/Event Day

**Water Savings
Per Game-Day Event**
CCF/Event Day

**Water Diversion
Per Game-Day Event**
Diversion Rate

FIGURE 9.2 Portland Trail Blazers' energy savings and diversion rate

Source: NRDC (2012).

Although natural capital has been discussed for over two decades as an important element for understanding the current and future global market place (e.g. Daly, 1994), corporations have just recently begun to consider natural capital and the environmental toll manufacturing practices take on both global climate and potential future profit. PUMA wanted to be at the forefront of creating practices intent on creating profit while also creating quantifiable metrics for examining potential loss of natural capital.

Initially, the project started as an attempt to reduce CO_2 emissions, energy, waste, and water usage at PUMA's plants, offices, stores, and warehouses (PUMA, 2011). Chief Sustainability Officer Jochen Zeitz reported that he had a vision in 2009 to create a program that considered the toll of PUMA's business on nature and the environment. Zeitz realized "that never before had a company accounted for and integrated the immense value—the true cost—of these services provided by nature such as fresh water, clean air, healthy biodiversity and productive land—which all businesses depend on" (PUMA, 2011). The idea was to understand how much nature would have to be paid if PUMA were to pay the environment for the services and materials it provided. Zeitz asked, "If our planet was a business, how much would it ask to be paid for the services it provides to a company in order to operate?" (PUMA, 2011). They began by determining the key definitions of what they wanted to research (see Table 9.1).

Initial findings indicated that the organization and its supply chain would owe the environment hundreds of millions of dollars. Placing this monetary value on the environment helped the organization discuss the importance of environmental sustainability with key stakeholders (PUMA, 2011). This was a way for the company to develop metrics that recognized the importance of natural capital in

TABLE 9.1 PUMA's environmental profit and loss account

Term	Definition
Profit	Activities that benefit the environment
Loss	Activities that adversely impact the environment
Environmental impact	A change in the make-up, functioning, or appearance of the environment. For example, GHGs contribute to climate change, which is associated with a range of environmental impacts such as reduced crop yields, changes in water availability, and increases in extreme weather.
Ecosystem services	Ecosystem services are the benefits that people and businesses derive from nature, like fiber, fuel, regulation of climate, assimilation of waste, opportunities for recreation, protection from extreme events, and cultural and spiritual enrichment
Monetary value	The economic value to society of the profits/losses
Entire supply chain	From production of raw materials to transport to stores, the total impact of bringing products to market

Source: PUMA (2011).

decision-making. To determine exactly what to measure and create a valuation of, the organization first had to consider what encompassed environmental impact for PUMA. Because PUMA outsources the majority of its manufacturing, they had to determine supply chain tiers (see Figure 9.3).

Utilizing these tiers, PUMA then calculates water use, GHG emissions, land use, other air pollution, and waste for each process in the supply chain. This allows the organization to determine what sources impact the total environmental profit and loss the most. Water usage is measured in cubic meters, GHGs in tons of CO_2, land use in hectares, and other pollution and waste in tons (PUMA, 2011). Specifically, PUMA collected data from each office and suppliers. Some Tier 1 suppliers were closely engaged to allow for more data to be collected. They monitored GHG emissions other than CO_2, including, for example, methane, nitrous oxide, carbon monoxide, sulphur dioxide, and nitrogen oxide. All emissions are measured in tons. Only 30 percent of GHG emissions, 11 percent of air pollution, 1 percent of water, and 55 percent of total waste was actually observed and collected from suppliers. The remainder was modeled based on the available data. PUMA further divided the information into regional analysis, segments (i.e., footwear, apparel, and accessories), and material intensity. These measures helped determine the environmental impact of producing and selling sport apparel.

By effectively implementing natural capital measures that take into account the environmental profit and loss of the company, PUMA was able to place a monetary value on its environmental impact. Since this initial report, the company

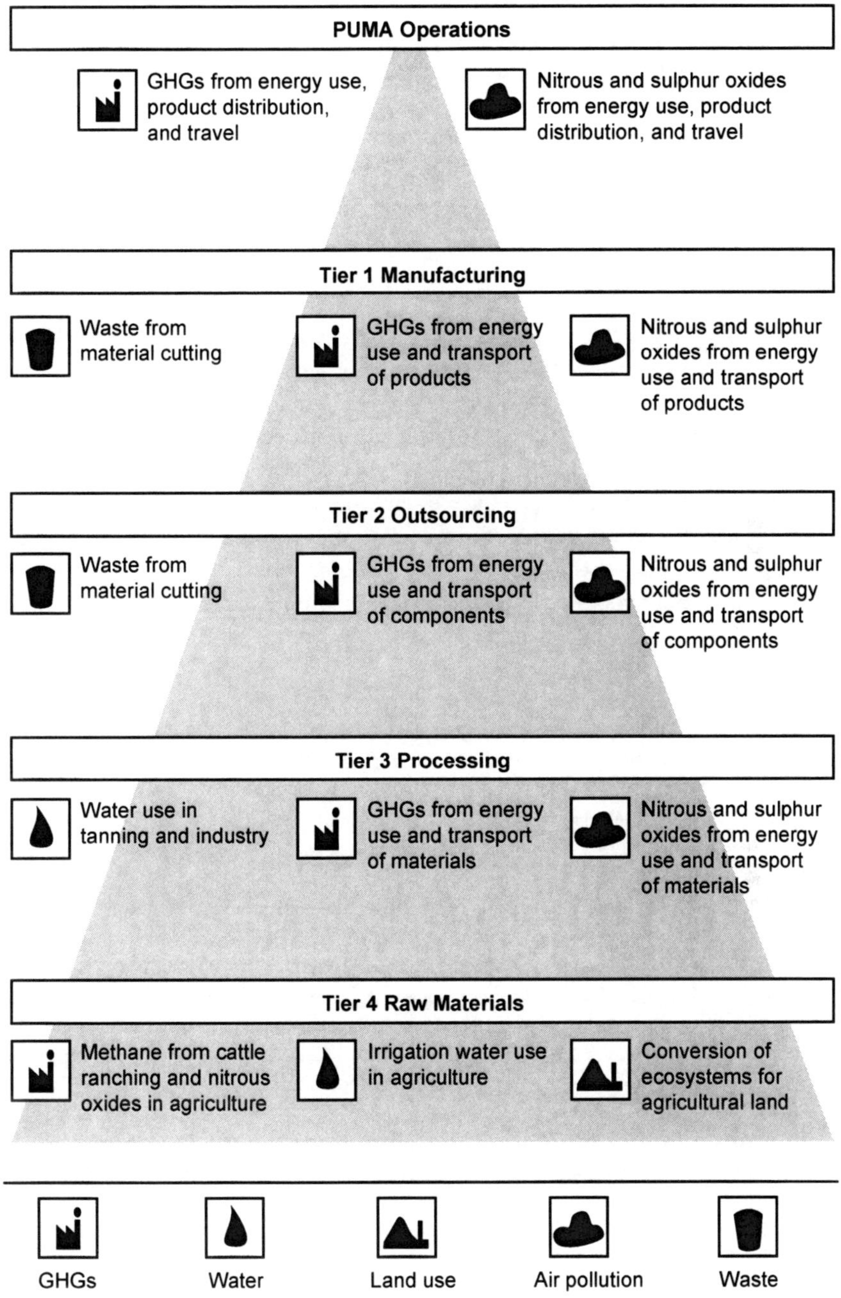

PUMA Operations

 GHGs from energy use, product distribution, and travel

 Nitrous and sulphur oxides from energy use, product distribution, and travel

Tier 1 Manufacturing

 Waste from material cutting

 GHGs from energy use and transport of products

 Nitrous and sulphur oxides from energy use and transport of products

Tier 2 Outsourcing

 Waste from material cutting

 GHGs from energy use and transport of components

 Nitrous and sulphur oxides from energy use and transport of components

Tier 3 Processing

 Water use in tanning and industry

 GHGs from energy use and transport of materials

 Nitrous and sulphur oxides from energy use and transport of materials

Tier 4 Raw Materials

 Methane from cattle ranching and nitrous oxides in agriculture

 Irrigation water use in agriculture

 Conversion of ecosystems for agricultural land

 GHGs

 Water

 Land use

 Air pollution

 Waste

FIGURE 9.3 PUMA's supply chain tiers

Source: PUMA (2011).

has continued to alter and reassess their impact on the environment. Without appropriate measures, the organization would not have been able to effectively determine its impact, and the time and effort spent on creating this model would have been detrimental to PUMA. The environmental profit and loss analysis created by a sport apparel company has been influential throughout the general business industry and is yet another example of how sport organizations, leagues, and manufacturers are at the forefront of environmental sustainability.

Conclusion

Implementing sustainable practices is a difficult process. As indicated in the above examples, it takes a tremendous amount of planning, patience, and effort from multiple constituencies. Without proper evaluation and metrics, there is no real way for an organization to determine if the implemented programs have been successful or have failed. In this chapter we have shown how sport leagues, teams, and apparel companies are at the precipice of environmental sustainability innovation. Through creating new systems of knowledge and creating an industry built on strong partnerships, sport organizations and apparel companies have the ability to continue the push toward creating metrics for environmental stewardship.

References

Blackburn, W. R. (2008). *The Sustainability Handbook*, Washington D.C.: Earthscan.

Bohdanowicz, P. (2006). 'Environmental awareness and initiatives in the Swedish and Polish hotel industries—survey results', *Hospitality Management*, 25: 662–82.

Bohdanowicz, P., & Martinac, I. (2007). 'Determinants and benchmarking of resource consumption in hotels—Case study of Hilton International and Scandic in Europe', *Energy and Buildings*, 39: 82–95.

Daly, H. E. (1994). 'Operationalising sustainable development by investing in natural capital'. In N. C. Sahu & A. K. Choudhury (eds.) *Dimensions of Environmental and Ecological Economics* (pp. 481–94). Himayatnagar, Hyderabad, India: Universities Press.

Domina, T., & Koch, K. (2002). 'Convenience and frequency of recycling: Implications for including textiles in curbside recycling programs', *Environment and Behavior*, 34: 216–38.

Environmental Protection Agency (EPA) (2014). 'EPA's greenhouse gas emission reductions'. Available online at www.epa.gov/greeningepa/ghg (accessed 2 October 2014).

KPMG (2014). 'Natural capital'. Available online at www.kpmg.com/uk/en/services/audit/sustainability/pages/natural-capital.aspx (accessed 24 September 2014).

LEED (2014). 'LEED v4 for building operations and maintenance'. Available online at www.usgbc.org/sites/default/files/LEED%20v4%20EBOM_10.01.14_current.pdf (accessed 5 October 2014).

Martins, A. A., Mata, T. M., Costa, C. A. V., & Sikdar, S. K. (2007). 'Framework for sustainability metrics', *Industrial & Engineering Chemistry Research*, 46: 2962–73.

Moura, R. C., & Padgett, R. C. (2011). 'Historical background of corporate social responsibility', *Social Responsibility Journal*, 7: 528–39.

Natural Resources Defense Council (NRDC) (2012). 'Game changer: How the sports industry is saving the environment'. Available online at www.nrdc.org/greenbusiness/guides/sports/files/Game-Changer-report.pdf (accessed 16 April 2014).

Natural Resources Defense Council (NRDC) (2014). 'Tracking your progress—Sustainability metrics'. Available online at http://nhl.greensports.org/tracking-your-progress/sustainabilitymetrics (accessed 9 September 2014).

PUMA (2011). 'PUMA's environmental profit and loss account for the year ended 31 December 2010'. Available online at http://about.puma.com/damfiles/default/sustainability/environment/e-p-l/EPL080212final-3cdfc1bdca0821c6ec1cf4b89935bb5f.pdf (accessed 28 August 2014).

Robertson, M. (2014). *Sustainability Principles and Practice*. New York: Routledge.

Saphores, J. D. M., Ogunseitan, O. A., & Shapiro, A. A. (2012). 'Willingness to engage in a pro-environment behavior: An analysis of e-waste recycling based on a national survey of U.S. households', *Resources, Conservation and Recycling*, 60: 49–63.

Schwarz, J., Beloff, B., & Beaver, E. (2002). 'Use sustainability metrics to guide decision-making', *Chemical Engineering Progress Magazine*, June: 58–63.

Scott, D. (1999). 'Equal opportunity, unequal results: Determinants of household recycling intensity', *Environment and Behavior*, 31: 267–90.

Sikdar, S. K. (2003). 'Sustainable development and sustainability metrics', *AIChE Journal*, 49: 1928–32.

Steg, L., & Vlek, C. (2009). 'Encouraging pro-environmental behavior: An integrative review and research agenda', *Journal of Environmental Psychology*, 29: 309–17.

Tanzil, D., & Beloff, B. R. (2006). 'Assessing impacts: Overview on sustainability indicators and metrics', *Environmental Quality Management*, 15: 41–56.

Utilyx (2013). 'Monetising natural capital through environmental profit & loss for decentralised energy assets: Summary report November 2013'. Available online at www.utilyx.com/documents/pdf/natural-capital-report.pdf (accessed 18 September 2014).

SECTION III

Marketing and communications

10

SUSTAINABILITY MARKETING

How to Effectively Speak *Greening* in the Sport Industry

Sheila Nguyen

Overview

At its very core, marketing is purely a conversation. Marketing is a process focused on an exchange of value (the conversation) between two parties (namely product/ service provider and consumer), whereby elements of the process are coordinated in a systematic and well-aligned manner. The process is designed, supported, executed, and evaluated for its ability to achieve outcomes (e.g., affective, cognitive, behavioral). What affects the communication process (e.g., channels, audience, positioning, etc.) is as critical as the message itself and, further, the impact it has on the awareness, knowledge, and behaviors of the involved parties interests marketing efforts. Outcomes are measured on the ability of the process to coordinate an exchange that ends in value for both parties. The marketing outcomes are evaluated against the answers of questions such as: Has the conversation's message been acknowledged and received? Has the conversation been effective in reinforcing or changing perceptions and consequently influencing behaviors such as developing loyal fans, creating vocal ambassadors, or growing an army of supportive participants? In summary, marketing is a process centered on effective communication and exchange of value with outcomes that include cognitive, affective, and behavioral outcomes. In sport, we have an opportunity to do this, with a focus on our environmental sustainability engagement, through speaking *greening*.

The sport industry has embarked on the journey of *greening* in devising the right strategies, activating the relevant ideas, and measuring how effective the marketing process has been in positioning the sport industry as a critical actor in the environmental protection movement. The methods, strategies, and outcomes of the marketing process in the sport industry, focused on speaking *greening*, will be addressed throughout this chapter. Moreover, several examples will be provided to illustrate the range of ways in which sport can include environmental sustainability as part of their messaging, positioning, and equity building through their marketing strategies and activation. The link between environment and sport will be discussed alongside the resultant opportunities, the marketing efforts engendered, and the role of the other side of the conversation, namely fans, in ultimately lifting the sport industry into the hall of fame for industry environmental stewards.

The link: marketing–sport–natural environment

The natural environment–the sport industry: where's the link?

There is often silence in response to the somewhat grandiose question: "How can sport save the planet?" Before the establishment of high-profile partnerships between the sport industry with environmentally minded partners (e.g., Indian Premier League, United Nations Environmental Programme, National Basketball Association, Natural Resources Defense Council, etc.), the consideration of the environment was barely on the radar and, for some in the industry, environmental action and protection was considered someone else's responsibility; the formation of alliances has shown its effectiveness in the environmental movement (Parise and Casher 2003; Thibault 2009). Prior to the well-known good work of these partnerships, the long-standing prioritized focus of sport was mainly directed towards the marketing benefits of on-field success and financial viability, and over time the positioning impacts of efforts made to address a handful of social issues such as community education and health and wellbeing.

Fast-forward to the present day and a sneak peek into the future, there is a strong groundswell of interest and action on the part of the sport industry, mainly in North America, where environmental stewardship for most is considered a means for business sustainability by being responsive to market changes, and for some a point of competitive advantage as an industry leader (see Natural Resources Defense Council 2012 for a comprehensive review of examples in North America). Often couched under the corporate social responsibility (CSR) banner (Babiak and Trendafilova 2011; Godfrey 2009; Trendafilova et al. 2013), commitment to the environment is the latest wave of interest, and the sport industry is slowly and steadily climbing the learning curves of integrating the needs of environmental management in their daily and strategic business. As Babiak and Trendafilova (2011) explained, professional sport organizations adopt environmental business practices due to both strategic and institutional pressures, and this is further reinforced by the notion that sport business entities are perceived to be in a unique position to impact society (Godfrey 2009; Smith and Westerbeek 2007).

Mainly seen through operational execution (e.g., grounds management, facility maintenance, etc.), sport organizations are extracting the business benefits through cost savings in better facility and venue design and management and are building brand equity through savvy marketing strategies. In a Deloitte Report, it was found that the intangible assets (e.g., environmental reputation, social responsibility, etc.)

were estimated to contribute upwards of 81 percent of the components of S&P 500 market valuation (Hespenheide and Koehler 2011). The equity in being environmentally conscious is being capitalized on, as seen by sport organizations being able to attract commercial partners with the addition and integration of the developed eco-conscious brand attribute. This was highlighted with the American Airlines Arena, the home of the Miami Heat, where they were able to attract $1 million in new corporate partners due to their greening efforts and eco-conscious brand image (NRDC 2012). The management group noted that "being environmentally conscious improves our brand's image so that we now talk with companies that never would have approached us before, such as Johnson & Johnson and Georgia Pacific" (NRDC 2012: 44). Through these gains, the gap between sport and the environment is narrowing, and there are certainly sport leaders that are at the core of this wave capitalizing on the emblazoned opportunities to improve their marketing communication and enhancing their position in the marketplace as such.

The opportunities in sport

Similar to other goods and services, the sport industry has a supply chain and network of partners, technical and non-technical suppliers, and other stakeholders (e.g., government, customers) who are part of the creation and delivery of its offerings. Considering the value of and reach of the sport industry, there are a number of opportunities where environmental sustainability could be integrated, heralded, and provide a return on investment. Sport is offered as both participation and entertainment goods and services, with a number of stakeholders that assist in its delivery.

In sport events, there are a number of direct stakeholders such as athletes, sponsors, volunteers, event managers, operational and medical staff, and other like individuals (Emery 2010; Parent 2008). Indirectly, you have those who manufactured the equipment and apparel that are used by the athletes, those who designed and built the facility and the components that outfit the venue, and the utility providers that supply resources and support the operation and delivery of such an event. Beyond high-performance settings, sport participation occurs in recreational and leisure settings, which also has its own specific supply chain and stakeholder networks. Evidenced by the complexity of the web of relationships in sport, there are diverse and enumerate opportunities to speak *greening* and through which to achieve marketing goals.

The above-referred stakeholders only name those involved at the tip of the sport industry iceberg; further consider those involved with the industry inputs, the process, and output of such production, delivery, and respective collaboration that form the body of the industry (Chelladurai 2006; Mallen and Adams 2008). Across the spectrum of sport delivery, the marketing opportunities to speak *greening* are founded on the basis of aims focused on three general areas: *Being a Good Corporate Citizen, Building and Contributing to Brand Equity*, and *Leading to Ensure a Sustainable Future* (discussed later in this chapter).

Regardless of the focus of the marketing process, there are frameworks in how we design, evaluate, and measure its outcomes. With the connection between sport and the natural environment established and the opportunities highlighted, the rest of the chapter will be dedicated to delineating the elements of the process, identifying the impact of the context, and emphasizing the importance of all parties who are engaged in the marketing conversation on *greening*. The marketing process is implemented with the aim of assisting an organization in achieving its strategic objectives, both for financial (e.g., sales, growth, etc.) or non-tangible benefit (e.g., brand equity, reputation, etc.). The marketing *greening*'s overall effort is centered on converting the groundswell into an effective movement and conversation which everyone can understand and contribute to.

The marketing strategy: speaking *greening* to save our planet

Objectives, the strategy's compass

A marketing strategy frames the conversation had among the sport industry network. Developing a marketing strategy involves intimately understanding the market, product, and the marketing process. The marketing process is based on an exchange of benefits between provider and consumer. In sport, there are a number of goods and services that are offered in the market dependent on the demands and interests to satisfy the particular needs of the sport consumer (Mullin et al. 2014; Smith and Zook 2011). In order to maximize the exchange (conversation), identification of the strategy's objectives will help develop a plan that integrates the most appropriate resources, actions, and methods to ensure success (e.g., controls, alignment) and to best evaluate its outcomes (see Figure 10.1 and Case Study 10.1).

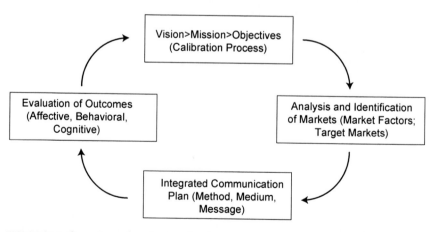

FIGURE 10.1 Overview of marketing development strategy

Source: author.

CASE STUDY 10.1: *GREENING* OF THE SYDNEY OLYMPIC GAMES—GOING FOR GREEN

The marketing strategy is driven by a clear set of objectives (see Figure 10.1). An example of objectives that linked resources, methods, and actions occurred during the 2000 Sydney Olympic Games, which was considered the *Green Games* for its environmental remedial process and ongoing commitment to protecting the environment. Their endearing title as the *Green Games* was attributed to its primary goal, that of a public commitment to improving the environmental health of the Games' site and focus on leaving a sustainability-centered legacy. While not the first and only *Green Games* (consider the first at Lillehammer in 1994 and at London in 2012), Sydney's Games established and reinforced their ongoing recognition as one that values and considers its environmental footprint well after the Games were finished (Kearins and Pavlovich 2002).

In support of the primary goal noted above, the Sydney Olympic precinct continues to maintain two of their four environmental objectives:

- any new development complies with best practice environmental and town planning standards, and
- the natural heritage of the Parklands is protected and enhanced.

(SOPA 2013)

The Sydney Olympics' objectives were established to reinforce their position in the Australian and global markets as an environmental sustainability leader with tactics driven by the objectives described above. This positioning and reinforcement was communicated clearly to the other Sydney Olympic Park precinct neighbors, such as retailers, restaurants, hotels, and other businesses, resulting in their adoption of similar eco-conscious practices. For example, through various programs and associations (e.g., Sydney Olympic Park Business Association, Office of Environment and Heritage, etc.), the Sydney Olympic Park precinct community benefits from education, infrastructure and building development, and engagement aimed at minimizing the impact they have on their natural environment. The objectives drive the strategy and are calibrated to ensure that it matches the vision, mission, and ongoing evaluation of previous actions and outcomes.

Limitations and delimitations of market context

The foundation of the markets in which conversations take place and with whom we speak *greening* are based on established objectives. While objectives direct the marketing efforts, there are a number of market factors that may limit and delimit the outcomes of our marketing efforts and strategy. Context (place) has an immense impact on how your message is effectively exchanged to the extent that it can facilitate or hinder clear and effective communication. In the U.S., regional legislation and market needs and subsequent demands vary and influence the way in which we communicate environmental stewardship. Historically, the Midwest relied heavily on coal as a source of power. In the latest American Council on Renewable Energy *Renewable Energy in the 50 States* report (ACORE 2013), there has been a reported move towards equivalence in wind energy. However, in the short term, recycling in the Midwest has been associated with greater upfront costs compared to that of sending materials to landfill which challenges the incentive markets. In contrast, West Coast legislation has been comparatively faster and progressive; it was cited by the Clean Air Council that Seattle, Washington, Portland, Oregon, Westchester, Berkeley, and Malibu have all banned Styrofoam foodware, and Laguna Beach and Santa Monica have banned all polystyrene (#6) foodware (Clean Air 2013). In other markets, and in comparison to the U.S., Australia has a stronger governance emphasis on environmental issues. The Australian federal government developed an energy efficiency program that sets minimum energy performance requirements for new buildings and major refurbishment (Australian Government Department of Industry 2014).

As evidenced by change in ability and opportunity due to market factors, they are understood to influence what are critical elements to the marketing message and reflect how best to navigate the market conditions (e.g., legal challenges, market readiness, geographical and environmental demands, etc.). These are the context challenges in designing a marketing strategy that makes sense for communicating the *greening* messages within the marketing strategy and process. For example, Arizona is best known for its desert geography and climate, and for its vast access to sunny conditions. Thus, the installation of a 1,100-panel solar array atop the US Airways Center's parking garage was a suitable and market-appropriate choice (NRDC 2012). The solar panel addition in an Arizona market can readily be communicated in accordance with local conditions and audiences in an effective and logical manner (minimizing cognitive dissonance) (Cialdini 2003; Schultz et al. 2011).

The audience in the exchange process

While context is a critical consideration, so is the audience for which the message is intended (Cheng et al. 2011; Cialdini 2003; Gilg et al. 2005; McKenzie-Mohr 2002; Milfont and Duckitt 2010). The match between appropriate audiences and effective messaging (e.g., content, framing, medium, etc.) determines how successful you can be in the *greening marketing strategy*. In exploring appropriate audiences, a survey of the U.S. adult population identified approximately 40 million individuals that are attracted to a "marketplace for goods and services focused on health, the environment, social justice, personal development and sustainable living" (LOHAS 2014a) known as the Lifestyles of Health and Sustainability (LOHAS) market, and is estimated to be worth $290 billion, with more than half of its value derived directly from the environmentally focused sectors (e.g., green building, eco tourism, etc.). Within the LOHAS market, there were five target market segments identified based on attitudinal, behavioral, and cognitive profiles (LOHAS 2014b). Further, and specific to environmental worldviews, Earth Justice created the Ecological Roadmap which identified ten segment groups to segment and better understand the types of attitudes that are clustered in the marketplace (Ecological Roadmap 2014) (see Figure 10.2).

The sport industry environmental efforts to identify and initiate their strategy and conversation with a targeted approach is nascent and unsubstantial, but over time and in line with the evolution of the industry becoming more sophisticated, strategies will include more involved segmentation and targeting of audiences. Consumer segmentation and worldviews specific to the sport industry are opportunities for exploration and initiation across our industry to improve our marketing decisions and impact.

LOHAS consumer segments	Ecological Roadmap worldviews
LOHAS consumers have strong attitudes regarding personal and planetary health, which are widely reflected in their behavior. They are heavy users of green products and exude a strong influence over others. Hence, LOHAS consumers can be a prime target for companies marketing green, socially responsible, or healthy products, as often their buy-in is fundamental to reaching other consumer segments.	Greenest Americans believe that everything is connected, and our daily actions have an impact on the environment.
	Idealists think that green lifestyles are part of a new way of thinking.
	Caretakers believe healthy families need a healthy environment.
NATURALITES are interested in protecting the environment and is mainly a byproduct of their internalized personal drive to be healthy and is namely reflected in their consumption of green products and services.	Traditionalists believe that religion and morality dictate actions in a world where humans are superior to nature.
	Driven Independents think protecting the earth is fine as long as it doesn't get in the way of success.
DRIFTERS have a shifting commitment to many issues, including sustainability. As the youngest segment, DRIFTERS are steered by the latest trend and more likely to view price as a roadblock to green living. However, while sustainability remains a trendy issue, this group is a prime target.	Murky Middles are indifferent to mostly everything, including the environment.
	Fatalists believe meeting material and status needs on a daily basis trumps worries about the planet.
CONVENTIONALS are not particularly environmentally conscious in attitude, though their behaviors sometimes indicate otherwise—they are practical consumers whose energy-conservation and recycling efforts can make them a viable target for some marketers.	Materialists say little can be done to protect the environment, so why not get a piece of the pie?
	Cruel Worlders think that resentment and isolation leave no room for environmental concerns.
	UnGreens believe environmental degradation and pollution are inevitable parts of America's prosperity.

FIGURE 10.2 LOHAS and Ecological Roadmap consumer segments

Sources: LOHAS (2014b); Makower (2009).

Promoting greening

Identifying the targets and markets that are in line with the set objectives should then coalesce with the choices of the methods, mediums, and messages used in speaking *greening*. Integrating environmental stewardship within the marketing process can achieve key marketing outcomes gained (e.g., positioning, stakeholder response, brand equity, etc.) if done in a well-directed manner. Currently, and in the main, the sport industry leaders have taken a mass marketing approach with the aim of using in-stadium actions, advertising campaigns, and some experiential mediums as their effort to educating stakeholders about the link between sport and its impact on the environment.

For most North American professional and university sport venues, and other sport entities, environmental Public Service Announcements (PSAs) are a primary marketing action as they serve to expose greater numbers of individuals to a message that makes the audience more aware of the connection between the actions taken in sport and its impact on the environment. PSAs contribute to the objective of educating the sport community on the degrading conditions of our natural environment and the opportunities to be part of the stewardship movement. Another awareness and education mechanisms example across the industry is Major League Baseball's Washington Nationals, who are partnered with the EPA to provide "green tours of our facility as an educational tool and to promote the good work we're doing at Nationals Park," says Bryan Minniti, Assistant GM (personal communication, 3 December 2013). Nationals Park is the nation's first major professional stadium to become LEED Silver Certified by the U.S. Green Building Council (NRDC 2012).

The evolution of the greening *marketing efforts*

As the industry efforts progress and the integration of environmental stewardship deepens, changing attitudes and mobilizing behaviors will be broached as a reflection of the advances along the lifecycle stages in marketing engagement (see Figure 10.3). Considering where the organization is, who is part of the conversation, what is being said, and what can be achieved as a result of the discussion can help dictate the appropriate marketing choices for product, pricing, place, and promotion in an integrated and appropriately effective manner (Lee and Edwards 2013; Smith and Zook 2011). For example, an organization that is starting to consider the natural environment in their strategy (e.g., *Introduction* stage), but is limited by various reasons (e.g., internal expertise, a champion, funding, local legislation, market conditions, etc.), may make more *low hanging fruit decisions*, such as recycling and green promotion, when compared to an organization that may have executive support and cultural and organizational buy-in, and can undertake actions and efforts more readily (*Mature* stage). The sport industry's involvement in environmental stewardship is a burgeoning movement; speaking *greening* in the sport industry is at the *Introduction* or *Growth* stages, where their efforts are focused

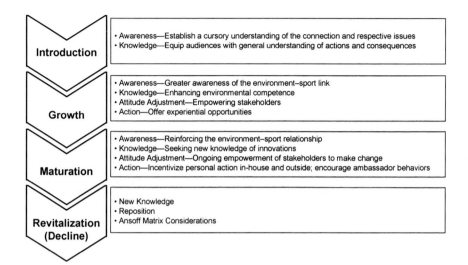

Introduction
- Awareness—Establish a cursory understanding of the connection and respective issues
- Knowledge—Equip audiences with general understanding of actions and consequences

Growth
- Awareness—Greater awareness of the environment–sport link
- Knowledge—Enhancing environmental competence
- Attitude Adjustment—Empowering stakeholders
- Action—Offer experiential opportunities

Maturation
- Awareness—Reinforcing the environment–sport relationship
- Knowledge—Seeking new knowledge of innovations
- Attitude Adjustment—Ongoing empowerment of stakeholders to make change
- Action—Incentivize personal action in-house and outside; encourage ambassador behaviors

Revitalization (Decline)
- New Knowledge
- Reposition
- Ansoff Matrix Considerations

FIGURE 10.3 Lifecycle approach and marketing objective matching

Source: author.

on building awareness and trying to educate their networks on the obvious links and relevant opportunities in addressing environmental challenges.

While objective setting, market analyses, segmentation and targeting, and a robust marketing action plan make up the majority of the marketing strategy, the key in ensuring that the plan is effective is through measurement and evaluation. Particularly in the environmental sustainability space, a large part of effective marketing is built on the use of facts and figures in the messaging. Sport community stakeholders want to know about the progress, the changes, and the improvements made from the sport organization's involvement with environmental sustainability, all of which can be measured and evaluated. In the marketing process, measurement acts as the feedback that is provided to reinforce and clarify its key messages and to illustrate the marketing outcomes and impact of such efforts. As earlier noted, Major League Baseball (MLB) in partnership with the NRDC, created an analytical tool to monitor and evaluate their environmental efforts, which have resulted in better understanding of best practices that are league specific and practically valuable for the clubs (NRDC 2012). When energy, materials, waste, and resources are measured, the strength of the link between sport and its environmental impact is more clearly communicated (e.g., energy for all home games, 90 percent waste diversion, recycled shoes can be used to create X new basketball courts, etc.). Being able to assess and to evaluate improvement provides organization personnel with the ability to tell the story of their environmental involvement, and every time there is progress, the conversation continues with objectives for education, corporate social responsibility, and equity more readily achievable.

The marketing mix

The marketing strategy materializes in the form of the marketing mix elements (product, price, place, and promotion) (see marketing texts for a further review of the marketing mix: Mullin et al. 2014; Shilbury et al. 2014). The *greening* conversation is most effective when all the components are aligned, appropriate, and seamlessly integrated, with evidence of success when objectives are achieved. In sustainability sport marketing conversations, the two key driving elements are promotion and place. In particular, the most salient components of speaking *greening* are based on how we build awareness and knowledge and encourage behavior through communication related to the marketing mix, and the way in which place (venue and facility features) creates an optimal environment for our exchange of value. The following highlights these key marketing mix elements for speaking *greening* effectively through promotion and place.

It's not easy being green…what's in it for me?

Promotion is focused on informing, reminding, and persuading others through communication related to the goods and/or service (Cialdini 2007; Clow and Baack 2007); promotion is contingent on identifying the benefits of the goods and/or service—in other words, your product. The way in which you communicate (promotion) what you're offering (product) and how to position yourself relative to your good/service in the marketplace is through delivering on the bundle of benefits derived from engagement. A clear understanding of what you are and what you're offering assists promotion efforts aimed at answering the question "What's in it for me?" from both internal and external audiences. Answering the question "What's in it for me?" is based on three possible messages:

- *Being an Environmental Steward is Being a Good Corporate Citizen*: As stated by National Basketball Association Commissioner David Stern, "All corporations have a social responsibility to contribute to the health, welfare and advancement of communities in which they operate, but professional sports leagues carry a special obligation [which] empowers them to effect change" (Wilner 2008: 21). Speaking *greening* is part of being a socially responsible entity and community member (Sharma and Mehta 2012).
- *Being an Environmental Steward Builds and Contributes to Brand Equity*: Brand equity is heavily reliant on the intangible assets such as reputation (Hespenheide and Koehler 2011). Through engagement with environmental sustainability initiatives, sport organizations can build equity that comes with respective commercial and community opportunities (see Contractor 2001; Keller 2013).
- *Being an Environmental Steward is Acting as a Leader to Ensure a Sustainable Future*: Sport has long been a vehicle for social movements and conversations (Smith and Westerbeek 2007), and the environmental movement is being

heralded by the sport industry, paving a path for innovation and adoption of eco-consciousness across its communities. Sport is taking a leadership role as a means to accommodate the expected environmental changes; survival and sustainability are key outcomes of environmental consideration (Shallcross and Robinson 2006).

Internal marketing efforts emphasize the public praise and recognition effects of being a good corporate citizen and leader within the sustainability space, with consideration of its impact on outcomes such as satisfaction and desire to work above and beyond what is expected (Carrico and Riemer 2011; Greaves et al. 2013; Handgraaf et al. 2013; Van de Velde et al. 2010). The internal marketing efforts are aimed at building strong ambassadors to speak *greening* on behalf of the sport organization which enhance the marketing efforts overall. Externally, the conversation is based on positioning *greening* efforts as opportunities; sport organizations' external stakeholders (e.g., fans, partners, etc.) have an opportunity to gain membership to the *loyal and elite* leadership group. In communication both internally and externally, sport organizations have relied on the effectiveness of social identity theory tenets (Davis et al. 2011; Dono et al. 2010; Scott and Lane 2000; Stephenson et al. 2010; Tajfel and Turner 1979) to assist in developing and framing the conversation and in implementing a sustainability culture that reinforces the good and casts out those who don't tow the loyal group line (creating *otherness*) (see seminal *Social Identity Theory* research for further exploration: Melnick 1993; Scott and Lane 2000; Tajfel and Turner 1979). Informing, reminding, and persuading stakeholders to engage in the conversation is based on the optimal interplay of personal characteristics, appropriate messages, and contextual influences. The built environment (venues and facilities) plays a significant role in contextual influences in this interplay.

The built environment: the place built for a conversation about being green

Building green, being green

Place has been extensively explored as a key factor in building attachment and impacting behaviors (Halpenny 2010; Ramkissoon et al. 2012); this understanding of the role of place is a significant opportunity for sport venues and facilities. The *greening* conversation can be designed flawlessly, with clear objectives, robust marketing actions, and an evaluation process to provide the necessary feedback, but as in the standard communication models, the context (built environment) must be able to support clear communication (e.g., minimized white noise, conducive context, etc.) and induce engagement in speaking *greening* (Halpenny 2010; Smith and Zook 2011). Imagine you are conversing (marketing) and you want to convince your audience that you are an environmental sustainability leader, all the while standing in the middle of a facility that has no recycling bins and hosts highly intensive resource usage features (e.g., waterfall using potable water, video screen powered using conventional light bulbs, etc.); the message may not be communicated authentically and the conversation will be ineffective in positioning your organization accordingly. The built environment plays an important part in signaling various messages to your audiences; it acts as a moderator for your conversation, enhancing or minimizing the effect of the message (Connelly et al. 2011).

The opportunities for building green in communicating *greening* efforts are found in various forms. Certification or acknowledgement by external parties to verify and accredit the facility or the organization signals to the audience that the efforts are genuine and effective. Other signals are found in the physical evidence of environmental sustainability such as using innovations in sustainable sites such as green roofs, native landscaping, and energy-generation solutions (e.g., wind generators, solar panels, etc.). All of these efforts provide signals, which may influence attitudinal, behavioral, and cognitive responses from the conversing parties within the marketing exchange (Connelly et al. 2011). The Philadelphia Eagles' (National Football League [NFL]) personnel integrated their facility's sustainability features (e.g., solar panels and wind generators) into their conversation about being green, and it helps that green is one of their team colors to maintain consistency and salience across the conversation.

It's been built; will they come?

As seen in the lifecycle approach to actions and marketing efforts (Figure 10.3), the aims and outcomes of a conversation about *greening* evolve over time. While the investments in building standards, features, and facility management practices may change and improve, the conversation requires an active engagement by both parties. Within the sport industry, there are a number of identified stakeholders that can facilitate and challenge the discussion on *greening*, and the sport industry in general has been fortunate to have a number of allies to effectively achieve its marketing objectives. As previously identified, the NRDC, the EPA, and the United Nations Environment Programme, among many others, have actively partnered with sport organizations and leagues to lead a movement on a large scale and with national and international exposure and impact. Sponsors, government, and non-government agencies have become friends of the sport industry and are actively advising, asking questions, and supporting the environmental stewardship movement. Several of the new facilities are being supported by government funding, and commercial partners are investing in capital costs for major infrastructure projects such as those seen at Lincoln Financial Field (Philadelphia, Pennsylvania, USA), and in 2011 Metricon Stadium (Gold Coast, Queensland, Australia) was built with support from Stadiums QLD, Gold Coast City Council, the Australian Football League, and the Australian Federal Government.

The active involvement of such a motley crowd of stakeholders is a result of each party seeing the environmental stewardship movement through sport as an effective vehicle for a number of marketing outcomes. With Lincoln Financial

Field, NRG (the Eagles' official energy provider) supplied the upfront capital costs of $30 million and in return they committed to a long-term power purchase agreement (PPA). For Metricon Stadium, the Queensland Government's Department of Clean Energy and the Gold Coast City Council provided the financial and political support to finalize its construction with the hopes that the solar panel arrays would serve as an educational vehicle alongside being a clean energy offset of the facility's operations.

Developing the content of the conversation and constructing a place which stakeholders can attach to and where speaking *greening* can take place with a range of stakeholders engenders engagement that would contribute to the awareness, education, and activation for a collective environmental stewardship effort. The activation and leveraging of marketing strategic plans and partnerships have led to marketing outcomes such as brand positioning, preference, associations, commercial opportunities, and the education of the sport industry community, and a development of better-equipped ambassadors for the environmental stewardship movement.

The future of the environment as a marketing strategy consideration

In this chapter, the link between sport and the natural environment was established with a review of how the marketing (*conversation*) of *greening* efforts are communicated within the sport industry. There are many sport industry leaders with equally committed partners in the conversation and the environmental stewardship movement, as evidenced in the examples given. While the sport industry's marketing efforts are nascent, it will only develop over its lifecycle, and the innovations in built environment advancements and stakeholder engagement strategies will exponentially increase and, over time, refine and improve its effectiveness in influencing attitudinal, cognitive, and behavioral responses. One of the considerations is of social media and other methods for maximizing the partnership between sport and environmental sustainability (e.g., gamification, alliances, partnerships, etc.). In particular, eco-gamification has been acknowledged as a solution to driving sustainability through successful stakeholder engagement (Owen 2013). Regardless of the medium and changing trends for places to speak *greening* (e.g., social media, gamification, etc.), sustainability marketing efforts will always be most effective using an integrated, considered, well-aligned, and evaluated strategy using traditional and new platforms leveraging the advantages of networks (e.g., industry associations, etc.) and the impact of incentive models (e.g., gamification, etc.). In developing the marketing (conversation) details, the respective efforts will facilitate effective step changes to support the noted groundswell into a wave that will change the face of the sport industry in a manner where environmental stewardship is inculcated to the degree it becomes *business as usual* and to speak *greening* is equivalent to operating in a deft fashion to ensure the sustainability of sport goods and service delivery.

References

American Council on Renewable Energy (ACORE) (2013) Renewable energy in the 50 states: Midwestern region. Available online at www.acore.org/images/documents/Midwestern_Region_Report.pdf (accessed 10 February 2014).

Australian Government Department of Industry (2014) Non-residential buildings. Available online at www.industry.gov.au/ENERGY/ENERGYEFFICIENCY/NON-RESIDENTIALBUILDINGS/Pages/default.aspx (accessed 14 January 2014).

Babiak, K. and Trendafilova, S. (2011) 'CSR and environmental responsibility: Motives and pressures to adopt sustainable management practices', *Journal of CSR and Environmental Management*, 18: 11–24.

Carrico, A. and Riemer, M. (2011) 'Motivating energy conservation in the workplace: An evaluation of the use of group-level feedback and peer education', *Journal of Environmental Psychology*, 31: 1–13.

Chelladurai, P. (2006) *Human Resource Management in Sport and Recreation*, Champaign, IL: Human Kinetics.

Cheng, T., Woon, D.K., and Lynes, J.K. (2011) 'Message framing in the promotion of environmentally sustainable behaviors', *Social Marketing Quarterly*, 17: 48–62.

Cialdini, R.B. (2003) 'Crafting normative messages to protect the environment', *Current Directions in Psychological Science*, 12: 105–9.

Cialdini, R.B. (2007) *Influence: The Psychology of Persuasion*, New York: Collins.

Clean Air (2013) Waste facts. Available online at www.cleanair.org/Waste (accessed 26 October 2013).

Clow, K. and Baack, D. (2007) *Integrated Advertising, Promotion and Marketing Communications*, Upper Saddle River, NJ: Pearson Prentice.

Connelly, B.L., Certo, S.T., Ireland, R.D., and Reutzel, C.R. (2011) 'Signalling theory: A review and assessment', *Journal of Management*, 37: 39–67.

Contractor, F.J. (2001) *Valuation of Intangible Assets in Global Operations*, Westport, CT: Quorum.

Davis, J., Coy, A., and Le, B. (2011) 'Building a model of commitment to the natural environment to predict ecological behavior and willingness to sacrifice', *Journal of Environmental Psychology*, 31: 257–65.

Dono, J., Webb, J., and Richardson, B. (2010) 'The relationship between environmental activism, pro-environmental behaviour and social identity', *Journal of Environmental Psychology*, 30: 178–86.

Ecological Roadmap (2014) Available online at www.climateaccess.org/sites/default/files/ReGreen%20The%20Ecological%20Roadmap.pdf (accessed 20 February 2014).

Emery, P.P. (2010) 'Past, present, future major sport event management practice: The practitioner perspective', *Sport Management Review*, 13: 158–70.

Gilg, A., Barr, S., and Ford, N. (2005) 'Green consumption or sustainable lifestyles? Identifying the sustainable consumer', *Futures*, 37: 481–504.

Godfrey, P. (2009) 'Corporate social responsibility in sport: An overview and key issues', *Journal of Sport Management*, 23: 698–716.

Greaves, M., Zibarras, L., and Stride, C. (2013) 'Using the theory of planned behavior to explore environmental behavioral intentions in the workplace', *Journal of Environmental Psychology*, 34: 109–20.

Halpenny, E.A. (2010) 'Pro-environmental behaviours and park visitors: The effect of place attachment', *Journal of Environmental Psychology*, 30: 409–21.

Handgraaf, M., Van Lidth de Jeude, M., and Appelt, K. (2013) 'Public praise vs. private pay: Effects of rewards on energy conservation in the workplace', *Ecological Economics*, 86: 86–92.

Hespenheide, E. and Koehler, D. (2011) Disclosure of long-term business value: What matters? Available online at www.corpgov.deloitte.com/binary/com.epicentric.contentmanagement.servlet.ContentDeliveryServlet/USEng/Documents/Board%20Governance/Short-%20and%20Long-termism/Long%20term%20Business%20value_September2013.pdf (accessed 22 August 2012).

Kearins, K., and Pavlovich, K. (2002) 'The role of stakeholders in Sydney's green games'. *Corporate Social Responsibility and Environmental Management*, 9: 157–69.

Keller, K. (2013) *Strategic Brand Management: Building, Measuring, and Managing Brand Equity*, Harlow, UK: Harlow Pearson.

Lee, A. and Edwards, M. (2013) *Marketing Strategy: A Life-Cycle Approach*, Cambridge: Cambridge University Press.

LOHAS (2014a) About. Available online at www.lohas.com/about (accessed 11 March 2014).

LOHAS (2014b) Consumers. Available online at www.lohas.com/sites/default/files/lohasconsumers.pdf (accessed 11 March 2014).

Makower, J. (2009) *Strategies for a Green Economy*, New York: McGraw Hill.

Mallen, C. and Adams, L. (2008) *Sport, Recreation, and Tourism Event Management: Theoretical and Practical Dimensions*, Burlington, MA: Elsevier/Butterworth-Heinemann.

McKenzie-Mohr, D. (2002) 'The next revolution: Sustainability'. In P. Schmuck and P.W. Schultz (eds), *Psychology of Sustainable Development*, Norwell, MA: Kluwer, pp. 19–36.

Melnick, M.J. (1993) 'Searching for sociability in the stands: A theory of sports spectating', *Journal of Sport Management*, 7: 44–60.

Milfont, T.L. and Duckitt, J. (2010) 'The environmental attitudes inventory: A valid and reliable measure to assess the structure of environmental attitudes', *Journal of Environmental Psychology*, 30: 80–94.

Mullin, B., Hardy, S., and Sutton, W. (2014) *Sport Marketing*, 3rd edn, Champaign, IL: Human Kinetics.

Natural Resources Defense Council (2012) NRDC Report, Game Changer: How the sports industry is saving the environment. Available online at www.nrdc.org/greenbusiness/guides/sports/files/Game-Changer-report.pdf (accessed 23 October 2012).

Owen, P. (2013) *How Gamification Can Help Your Business Engage in Sustainability*, Oxford, UK: Do Sustainability.

Parent, M.M. (2008) 'Evolution and issue patterns for major-sport-event organizing committees and their stakeholders', *Journal of Sport Management*, 22: 135–64.

Parise, S. and Casher, A. (2003) 'Alliance portfolios: Designing and managing your network of business partner relationships', *Academy of Management Executive*, 17: 25–39.

Ramkissoon, H., Weiler, B., and Smith, L. (2012) 'Place attachment and pro-environmental behaviour in national parks: The development of a conceptual framework', *Journal of Sustainable Tourism*, 20: 257–76.

Schultz, F., Utz, S., and Goritz, A. (2011) 'Is the medium the message? Perceptions of and reactions to crisis communication via Twitter, blogs, and traditional media', *Public Relations Review*, 37: 20–7.

Scott, S.G. and Lane, V.R. (2000) 'A stakeholder approach to organizational identity', *Academy of Management*, 25: 43–62.

Shallcross, T. and Robinson, J. (2006) *Global Citizenship and Environmental Justice*, Amsterdam: Rodopi.

Sharma, S. and Mehta, S. (2012) 'Where do we go from here? Viewing corporate social responsibility through a sustainability lens', *Journal of Contemporary Management Research*, 6: 69–76.

Shilbury, D., Westerbeek, H.M., Quick, S., Funk, D., and Karg, A. (2014) *Strategic Sport Marketing*, 4th edn, Sydney: Allen and Unwin.

Smith, A. and Westerbeek, H. (2007) 'Sport as a vehicle for deploying corporate social responsibility', *The Journal of Corporate Citizenship*, 25: 43–54.

Smith, P.R. and Zook, Z. (2011) *Marketing Communications: An Integrated Approach*, 5th edn, London, UK: Kogan Page Limited.

Stephenson, J., Barton, B., Carrington, G., Gnoth, D., Lawson, R., and Thorsnes, P. (2010) 'Energy cultures: A framework for understanding energy behaviours', *Energy Policy*, 38: 6120–9.

Sydney Olympic Park Authority (SOPA) (2013) Legacy. Available online at www.sopa. nsw.gov.au/our_park/legacy (accessed 22 November 2013).

Tajfel, H. and Turner, J.C. (1979) 'An integrative theory of intergroup conflict'. In W.G. Austin and S. Worchel (eds), *The Social Psychology of Intergroup Relations*, Monterey, CA: Brooks/Cole, pp. 33–47.

Thibault, L. (2009) 'Globalization of sport: An inconvenient truth', *Journal of Sport Management*, 23: 1–20.

Trendafilova, S., Babiak, K., and Heinze, K. (2013) 'Corporate social responsibility and environmental sustainability: Why professional sport is greening the playing field', *Sport Management Review*, 16: 298–313.

Van de Velde, L., Verbeke, W., Popp, M., and Van Huylenbroeck, G. (2010) 'The importance of message framing for providing information about sustainability and environmental aspects of energy', *Energy Policy*, 38: 5541–9.

Wilner, B. (2008, 1 February) 'Brand of happiness', *Sport Business International*, 131: 20–1.

11

THE NECESSITY OF STAKEHOLDER *BUY IN* OF ENVIRONMENTAL SUSTAINABILITY EFFORTS

An overview

Brian P. McCullough

Introduction

As sport organization personnel begin to implement environmental sustainability efforts across the organization and game day experiences, it is imperative for stakeholders to be on board with these initiatives. Stakeholders can have a tremendous amount of influence in applying pressures for sport organizations to implement environmental sustainability efforts (McCullough and Cunningham 2010). Additionally, these stakeholder groups can legitimize these programs, validating their environmental authenticity. However, there is a gap between environmental thought and action (Blake 1999) known as the value action gap. As stakeholders desire sport organizations to implement environmental sustainability efforts, how do these organizations get stakeholders to *buy in* to help the sport organization reach its environmental sustainability goals?

Stakeholder groups can contribute to the overall impact of the sport organization and/or event (Friedman et al. 2004). Since each stakeholder group contributes to the overall environmental impact of the organization, these groups can also help minimize their contribution to this impact. Ultimately, the sport organization can engage and influence the various stakeholder groups to utilize more environmentally friendly products or engage in more environmentally friendly behaviors.

Due to the nature of the industry, sport organizations have a tremendous amount of influence on spectators and society (Coakley and Pike 1998). Sport organizations can use this influence to promote social causes and influence the prestige of being associated with the sport organization to influence sponsors or suppliers (Green Sports Alliance n.d.). One area that sport organizations can influence outside stakeholders is in the area of environmental sustainability efforts. Additionally, sport organizations can use the fan identification of spectators to engage in environmental sustainability efforts. This chapter outlines how sport organizations engage stakeholders to further sport organizations' environmental sustainability efforts.

Stakeholders

Stakeholders have a unique role within the sport industry compared to other industries. Within the sport industry, stakeholders help co-produce the sport product. A collection of stakeholders from suppliers, contractors, concessionaires, vendors, merchandisers, spectators, broadcasters, and tertiary events all contribute to the overall experience of the consumable sport product or experience of a sporting event. The more popular the event, the more spectators will attend the main and surrounding events.

Additionally, sport organizations are in a unique position to influence various stakeholder groups to incorporate environmental sustainability efforts to further reduce the sport organization and event's environmental impact (Casper et al. 2012; McCullough and Cunningham 2010). Sport organization personnel can use the high identification of fans to influence individual and collective fan behaviors. Fan identification can be used to influence this specific stakeholder group. Other groups that have business-oriented relationships with the sport organization may need to be *sold* on environmental sustainability in other ways. One such way that sport organizations have operationalized this tactic is through cause-related marketing and sponsorship (Irwin et al. 2003). This method emerged to address the increased expectation and pressure from stakeholders for organizations to engage in corporate social responsibility. For example, sport teams may feature a Green Game where pro-environmental behaviors are promoted and encouraged. These events can also feature the environmental efforts of sponsors who have a relationship with the sport team (Casper et al. 2014).

Opposite to the pressures discussed in Chapter 8, sport organization personnel can apply their own pressure to various stakeholder groups to implement more environmentally friendly efforts. As sport organizations encourage stakeholder groups to *buy in* to environmental sustainability efforts that the organization wishes to achieve, benefits for each stakeholder group need to outweigh the challenges that these groups may encounter when they are asked to be more environmentally friendly (McCullough 2013).

While sport organizations might encounter the pressures that stakeholder groups can apply to sport organizations to implement environmental sustainability efforts into their daily operations and event management, as discussed in Chapter 8, these pressures can influence organizations to become more environmentally conscientious (McCullough and Cunningham 2010). Not all stakeholder groups might apply pressure on the organization to implement environmental sustainability. In fact, various stakeholder groups may have differing agendas and priorities to achieve within the organization (e.g., Greenpeace, Natural Resources Defense Council, Green Sports Alliance). Once organizational personnel decide to implement environmental sustainability efforts, the organization still faces challenges to appease stakeholder groups.

(Co)production of environmental processes

The functional processes that help minimize the environmental impact of the organization can be updated, revised, or reconfigured to continually minimize the impact on the organization (McCullough and Cunningham 2010). By way of finding new functional processes, sport organizations can use their invested stakeholders and those groups associated with the organization to help co-produce the sport product and/ or event. Sport organization personnel can collaborate with these stakeholders to minimize their environmental impact by incorporating new environmental sustainability efforts, reducing the overall impact of the sport organization and/or event. This *buy in* is key to all parties to ensure the success of the environmental initiatives. Ultimately a win–win situation has to be understood by both stakeholders and the sport organization. In the following sections, examples are provided to demonstrate how sport organizations have already collaborated with stakeholders to forward the environmental sustainability efforts of the sport organization.

The collaborative process is necessary to lend certain expertise and legitimacy to the environmental sustainability efforts of the sport organization. Ideally, sport organization personnel will start the process of implementing various initiatives to decrease the environmental impact of the organization (Pfahl 2011). Through this process, organizational personnel will reach out and partner with environmental organizations that have experience in implementing environmental sustainability programs (Poncelet 2002). Several organizations are currently collaborating with professional and collegiate teams in the United States. These organizations include: the Natural Resources Defense Council (NRDC), Environmental Protection Agency (EPA), Audubon International, Green Sports Alliance (The Alliance), Greenpeace, and individual college or university sustainability offices (Pfahl et al. 2015). These organizations can be classified as non-traditional stakeholders since they represent the needs of the environment.

Additionally, when organizations partner with outside organizations, like those with an expertise in environmental sustainability, the environmental initiatives carry more legitimacy than if the sport organization simply tried to implement these initiatives autonomously (Barringer and Harrison 2000). Environmental groups like the NRDC, The Alliance, EPA, Greenpeace, Leadership in Energy and Environmental Design (LEED), and Audubon International can provide specific guidelines on how to minimize the environmental impact of sport organizations and events. Additionally, these organizations can provide personnel support to ensure that the sport organization personnel follow these procedures and recommendations (Bäckstrand 2006).

An additional benefit comes through association between the sport and environmental organization. Both organizations gain legitimacy of their environmental purpose by associating with one another (Barringer and Harrison 2000). The sport organization gains legitimacy by having the endorsement through the partnership with an environmental organization (e.g., NRDC, LEED). Additionally, partnering environmental organizations gain legitimacy for assisting and being associated with a sport organization, thereby positively presenting the environmental organization to new populations (i.e., sport spectators).

Applied examples

As previously mentioned, sport organizations gain legitimacy for their environmental sustainability efforts by partnering or being certified by outside environmental organizations (Bäckstrand 2006; Barringer and Harrison 2000). Three primary organizations that have been increasing their collaboration between sport organizations and leagues are the NRDC, EPA, and The Alliance. While higher education institutions can keep their collaborations in house between university sustainability offices and intercollegiate athletic departments, outside organizations are also available to further provide expertise to advance the sport organization's environmental sustainability efforts. These collaborations have come to fruition at the Collegiate Sports Sustainability Summit, which is a helpful outlet to further environmental sustainability efforts within collegiate sport.

These organizations help bridge the gaps and assist the efforts of sport organization personnel to minimize their environmental impacts and jump start and further their environmental sustainability efforts. Agencies like the NRDC use the non-threatening, non-politicized setting to engage people regarding environmental sustainability (DeLuca 2005). The NRDC has helped many sport leagues and individual organizations to develop and strategically plan their environmental sustainability efforts (Pfahl 2011). The NRDC not only promotes the environmental benefits but also makes the business case, indicating the financial benefits of greening the organization. Additionally, the NRDC offers services to help organizations (i.e., sport organizations) reduce the environmental impact of operations and events. These resources are available for the public and can be found on their website (see www.nrdc.org/enterprise/greeningadvisor).

The EPA has started to become more involved with the construction of sport facilities. The EPA initially developed a scale to evaluate the environmental sustainability levels of sport facilities. Currently, the EPA offers a range of programs and provides a scorecard for the various aspects of environmental sustainability efforts. These areas include: increasing energy efficiency, renewable energy, water conservation, reducing waste, using safer chemicals, and increasing environmental awareness (Perciasepe 2013). The agency even offers a Green Sports Scorecard for these various initiatives (see www2.epa.gov/green-sports/green-sports-scoreboard). Through these initiatives the EPA can engage the sport community, including teams and fans, to increase their environmental awareness and to decrease behaviors which impact on the environment.

As the sport industry moves towards deeper commitments to environmental sustainability, various teams have created a collective association of teams already engaged in environmental sustainability efforts. The Alliance was formed to "help sport teams, venues, and leagues enhance their environmental performance" (Green Sports Alliance n.d.). The Alliance's membership includes over 200 sport teams and venues representing 16 different sport leagues. The Alliance hosts an annual conference to bring together academics and sport and environmental professionals to share their experiences and to further the environmental sustainability efforts across the sport industry (for examples see Pfahl 2013).

The examples that follow are based on practical examples of how sport organizations have collaborated with various stakeholder groups to further environmental sustainability efforts. The examples provided are not exhaustive of all the possibilities for collaborations between sport organizations and external stakeholders. In fact, the more notable partnerships provided below are from international, professional, and collegiate sport contexts. There are many other possibilities that should be examined among government (e.g., city government, state government) and non-government organizations (e.g., interscholastic and recreational levels of sport, civic groups).

Collegiate sport

Collegiate sporting events draw millions of sport fans every year to campuses across the country. Former and current students, boosters, and casual fans all attend collegiate sporting events including some of the more highly attended college sports: football, men's and women's basketball, and baseball. These spectators have a propensity to make a day out of the sporting event, tailgating before and after the game. The more spectators attend a sporting event, the greater the environmental impact. While some college campuses have implemented environmental sustainability across academic units, athletic departments have been removed from these efforts. As a result, some university stakeholders have approached the athletic department to implement environmental sustainability efforts into the game day management of college athletics.

Initial research indicates that college campuses were engaging in some but not extensive environmental sustainability efforts despite the response that 72 percent of respondents said such efforts were a priority (Casper et al. 2012). One way to further these initiatives is through an increase in collaboration between institutional departments such as the athletic department and the campus sustainability office (Casper et al. 2012; McCullough 2013). There are substantial benefits if college athletic departments, or sport teams for that matter, incorporate and promote pro-environmental behavior. Inoue and Kent (2012) found that sport teams positively influence sport spectator (i.e., consumer) perceptions towards the team's environmental efforts where they support these initiatives by participating (behavior) in them and incorporate these behaviors into their daily lives.

Further, Pfahl and colleagues (2015) examined the collaborative relationship between stakeholder groups—college sustainability offices and intercollegiate athletic departments. They found that the sustainability office generally initiated these relationships to collaborate and initiate environmental sustainability efforts. Athletic departments in this study were generally motivated to make initial steps to implement a recycling program surrounding tailgating activities and within athletic venues. Data from this study indicated that sustainability offices take the brunt of the planning, execution, measurement, and post-event follow up. However, these initial collaborations did lead to more formalized relationships.

By way of creating the initial collaboration, sustainability officers were able to meet formally with college athletic department staff. Although the athletic departments commonly had the final say on what initiatives could move forward, members of these groups include faculty and sustainability office staff who have expertise in a wide array of environmental sustainability issues (Pfahl et al. 2015). These communication lines have been demonstrated to be rather important to the success of the collaboration.

Pfahl and colleagues (2015) also found that, although the communications from the upper echelons of the university were indirect, the sustainability office and athletic departments were left to cultivate and sustain their collaboration. These collaborations were sustained through consistent contact whether on a daily basis or on an event-by-event basis. Initial trust was founded through easy steps like establishing a recycling program, and then once the trust was reputable sustainability offices would take the next step to propose more impactful environmental sustainability efforts. Ultimately, the university and athletic director's commitment to environmental sustainability issues drove or inhibited this relationship and environmental sustainability efforts.

As trust can be further established between the athletic department and sustainability office, further programming and efforts can be developed and implemented into the game day experience. Campus-wide recycling and composting programs are becoming more popular across college campuses during game days. Further, Ohio State University initiated a zero-waste campaign in Ohio Stadium (Pfahl 2013). Additionally, college athletic departments have collaborated with various stakeholders to host Green Games.

Green Games are a non-threatening way to educate sport spectators on various environmental sustainability efforts. These games also provide an opportunity for the college athletic department to collaborate with the sponsors and vendors of the athletic department to demonstrate their environmental sustainability efforts and products. Green Games can educate spectators on various issues like recycling, composting, responsible *green* tailgating, carpooling, and everyday behaviors.

One such study conducted by Casper et al. (2014) examined the effectiveness of a Green Game at a NCAA Division I intercollegiate football game. The results of this study indicate that spectators with higher levels of environmental values expect that the athletic department incorporate environmental sustainability initiatives into their daily operations and strategic planning. Further, spectators with higher levels of environmental values were more likely to engage in environmental sustainability efforts while attending the Green Game and in their everyday lives. Nearly 77 percent of spectators responded that they recycled while tailgating and attending the game, which is well over the national recovery rates of recyclable materials of 50 percent (Consumer Reports n.d.).

These environmental sustainability efforts are encouraging given the educational value of Green Games. By way of these Green Games, educating sport spectators on how to conduct tailgates in more environmentally friendly ways and to increase spectator environmental values will further the success of the environmental sustainability efforts of the sport organization. The more spectators increase their environmental values, the more successful other programs will be in the future. Trust, by way of collaboration established between sustainability offices and college athletic departments, is needed between the college athletic department and their spectators. Green Games are a strategic step in the effort to decrease the environmental impact of the organization, but also a gateway to further environmental sustainability efforts and initiatives.

Professional sport

The Seattle Mariners are located in a rather progressive area concerning environmental sustainability. Considering their location and easy *buy in* from spectators and surrounding industry, the Seattle Mariners had a perfect opportunity to make tremendous steps in bolstering their environmental sustainability efforts and further reduce their environmental impact. Despite these advantages, the Mariners had a diversion rate of 12 percent and daily utility costs of $4,000 (i.e., gas, electric, water) before 2006. Fortunately for the Mariners, in 2006 then Director of Stadium Operations, Scott Jenkins—former Chair of the Green Sports Alliance—led the charge to incorporate environmental sustainability into the Mariners' daily operations (Natural Resources Defense Council 2012). He now serves as the Stadium General Manager for the Atlanta Falcons.

Initially, Jenkins ordered a carbon footprint analysis to identify the largest areas of potential improvement across the organization, which included fan travel and utility consumption. From there Jenkins and the Mariners staff identified the areas that they had the most control over—the first being utility consumption. Jenkins worked closely with internal stakeholders (i.e., ballpark operations and engineers) to further reduce the daily costs of energy and water consumption throughout the organization and the ballpark. By targeting easy changes, the Mariners reduced their energy consumption by 25 percent in the first year, exceeding the benchmark financial savings goal of $100,000 and saving $275,000 (Natural Resources Defense Council 2012).

Once the initial attempt to start the *greening* process was underway, further financial investments by the organization were made to further their utility savings. Additionally, the focus expanded to other ways that the organization could reduce their environmental impact and increase bottom-line savings. Another area that Jenkins and the Mariners wanted to target was waste diversion. Other organizations within Major League Baseball had success with these programs. For example, the San Francisco Giants have a very high rate of diversion of stadium waste and saved nearly $250,000 in the first year of their recycling and composting program at AT&T Park (King 2008). Initially the Mariners offered fans three options to dispose of the waste generated during games at Safeco Park (i.e., recycle, compost, landfill). However, each category had to be hand sorted after each game, which was a dramatic labor cost for the organization.

Through innovation and working with external stakeholders, concessioners, and vendors, the Mariners were able to eliminate landfill waste receptacles. By eliminating this option, fans were left with choosing to compost or to recycle their waste. This strategy also minimizes the involvement of another stakeholder group—the spectator. By simplifying their choices to dispose of their waste, the likelihood of disposing waste improperly decreases. This strategy also decreases the dependence on sorting the waste after each game, which decreases labor costs for the organization.

Further, it was important that the Mariners worked with vendors to ensure that the products that were used in concession distribution were biodegradable. With these initial changes and with working with external stakeholders, the Mariners were able to increase their diversion rate from 12 percent in 2006 to a diversion rate of 81 percent in 2011 (Natural Resources Defense Council 2012). The Mariners still work with vendors to increase their diversion rates and meet their target goal of 90 percent (Natural Resources Defense Council 2012). The Mariners and vendors are working creatively to redesign packaging for products such as candy wrappers, condiment packets, and other pre-packaged items, which currently contaminate their compost.

The Mariners also have been engaging their fans in efforts to further bolster their waste diversion program. In 2012, the Mariners initiated a zero-waste campaign. This campaign initially started with an educational program to inform fans of all ages about the zero-waste initiative. Most notably, the Mariners also share the fruits of the spectators' and organization's labors. In a partnership with Cedar Grove Composting, the Mariners give away free compost for fans to use in their own gardens. The compost was generated from the compost waste disposed of at previous Mariners games (Broom 2011).

National tournaments

The US Open is one of the largest tennis tournaments in the world, attracting nearly 700,000 fans over two weeks. A large environmental impact is created given the amount of people that converge on the Billie Jean King National Tennis Center in New York. Billie Jean King approached the NRDC sport greening team in 2008 to help the Billie Jean King Tennis Center and the US Open, which is held at the tennis center, continue their commitment to environmental stewardship. Through this collaboration with the NRDC, the United States Tennis Association (USTA) and the Billie Jean King Tennis Center began with a water bottle and recycling program. Since then the facility has increased its environmental sustainability efforts.

Surrounding the facility, the USTA added individual temperature control to reduce the amount of energy consumed by the facility. This addition reduced the carbon emissions generated by 70 metric tons and saved the facility nearly $34,000 (Natural Resources Defense Council 2012). Additionally, the NRDC assisted the US Open to identify new suppliers to produce a recyclable tennis ball can. Given their expertise in the area, the NRDC is able to connect sport organizations with outside suppliers that can help sport organizations in their environmental sustainability efforts. Further, the NRDC identified other areas where the USTA and the Billie Jean King Tennis Center can further reduce their environmental impact.

These areas included consolidating the website server space provided by IBM, which reduced energy and cooling demand. The Tennis Center started a one-to-one recycling to trash receptacle program. The recycling bins were provided by Evian, which gives the bottled water company goodwill for participating in the efforts. Used tennis balls are now distributed to community and youth organizations instead of being deposited in landfills. Paper used in the production of game day draw sheets used 100 percent post-consumer product, while all other paper products within the facility use at least 30 percent post-consumer content (Natural Resources Defense Council 2012).

The Tennis Center also partnered with food vendor Levy Restaurants to offer healthier local food options. Additionally all the service items for food were compostable, further increasing the landfill diversion rates of the tournament. Lastly, the USTA encouraged fans to use public transportation when traveling to and from the event. Using eSurance as a sponsor, the USTA offered over 2,000 metro cards to attendees to encourage the use of public transportation (US Open 2013). The USTA saw dramatic increases in the use of public transportation from 32 percent in 2006 to 60 percent in 2011 (Natural Resources Defense Council 2012).

The US Open hosted by the USTA at the Billie Jean King Tennis Center serves as a strong example of the potential partnerships and potential sponsorships that can arise from moving toward an environmentally sustainable organization. The examples provided above from the US Open clearly demonstrate the wide array of areas that environmental sustainability efforts can be used within the organization or event. Further, these efforts can be subsidized through sponsorships, which can ultimately lead to furthering the environmental sustainability efforts of both organizations involved in the newly established collaboration.

International mega-events

Mega-events like the Olympics have a tremendous environmental impact. Consider all the construction of facilities before the Games and the total number of events, athletes, and spectators that will converge on one city for two weeks. As mentioned in Chapter 8 with the Concerned Citizens for Colorado, the pressures that stakeholders have put on the International Olympic Committee (IOC) and various host sites demonstrate the investment stakeholders have in the environmental sustainability of the Olympic Games. In response to these pressures, the

IOC added sustainability, including environmental sustainability, as the third pillar of the Olympic Movement (Paquette et al. 2011). Bidding cities now have to include an environmental impact assessment and outline ways in which the potential host committee will counter the environmental impact of hosting the Games.

One of the benchmark Olympiads to incorporate environmental sustainability efforts was the 2000 Summer Games in Sydney, Australia. The Sydney Organising Committee partnered with various sponsors of the Olympic Games to incorporate environmental sustainability efforts to make the 2000 Summer Games the Green Games. "The staging of the Olympic Games became a showcase for environmental efforts and for the way in which technology and innovation of Olympic sponsors can further the environmental agenda" (Olympic Sponsorship Overview 2000: 56).

The Sydney Organising Committee partnered with their sponsors to incorporate environmental sustainability efforts into the 2000 Games. The Organising Committee encouraged sponsors to take a proactive role to minimize the environmental impact of the Olympic Village and the overall 2000 Summer Games. Sponsors were active to ensure that waste was properly disposed of. More importantly, sponsors were conscientious of the life cycle of their operations and products that were brought to the Olympic Village. For example, Xerox used recycled paper for official documents. Coca-Cola was pressured by Greenpeace to update their refrigeration technologies during the 2000 Summer Games in Sydney (Greenpeace 2009). The environmental impact of HFC refrigeration technology is rather substantial. Refrigeration units use direct energy to operate the machine, increasing the electric consumption of the Olympic Park. Additionally the chemicals used to produce the insulation foam for the machine commonly use HFC. Lastly, the refrigerant gases used in the cooling system can have a detrimental impact on the environment if disposed of improperly. With the number of coolers and vending machines Coca-Cola has in place around the world, it is no surprise Greenpeace targeted Coca-Cola in regards to the environmental impact of their refrigeration units at such a high-profile event.

The pressure from Greenpeace encouraged Coca-Cola to implement more environmentally friendly products at the Olympic Games. Coca-Cola used the opportunity and exposure from being a major Olympic sponsor to introduce the new refrigeration technologies in the Sydney Olympic Park. All the equipment supplied for the 2000 Summer Games utilized HFC-free (i.e., hydrofluorocarbon-free) refrigeration technologies. These new technologies included two different solutions. One option featured hydrocarbon refrigeration for small equipment and carbon dioxide refrigeration for larger equipment.

The collaboration between Greenpeace, Coca-Cola, and the International Olympic Games is ongoing. Greenpeace and Coca-Cola collectively are finding new cost-effective and environmentally sustainable refrigeration technologies. To date, Coca-Cola has further reduced the impact of their refrigeration equipment by eliminating their green house emissions by 99 percent compared to the traditional equipment used before the Sydney Games (Greenpeace 2009). The 2000 Summer Games still stands as the Green Games. The lasting collaborations between various stakeholder groups are a further testament to the legacy of the environmental sustainability efforts of the 2000 Summer Games and the International Olympic Committee.

Conclusion

As sport organizations incorporate environmentally sustainable efforts into their daily operations, it is imperative that stakeholder groups *buy in* to these efforts. Stakeholder groups can dramatically help these efforts to further reduce the sport organization's impact on the natural environment. Additionally, as the examples in this chapter have demonstrated, the collaborations with various external and internal stakeholder groups can be very valuable to the organization. As relationships are developed with various stakeholder groups, trust will emerge and the *buy in* for additional environmental sustainability efforts will be easier.

The relationships developed through collaboration can help with the innovation of functional operations to continue the greening process. Further, environmental sustainability efforts open the door to new sponsorship inventory, providing not only a corporate social responsibility or goodwill benefit (Babiak and Trendafilova 2011; McCullough and Cunningham 2010), but also a financial benefit for the sport organization. Sport organizations are in a unique position where external stakeholder groups co-produce the sport product and the environmental impact. Thus, *buy in* from stakeholder groups is critical for the success of any sport organization's environmental sustainability efforts.

References

Babiak, K., and Trendafilova, S. (2011) 'CSR and environmental responsibility: Motives and pressures to adopt green management practices'. *Corporate Social Responsibility and Environmental Management*, 18: 11–24.

Bäckstrand, K. (2006) 'Multi-stakeholder partnerships for sustainable development: Rethinking legitimacy, accountability and effectiveness'. *European Environment*, 16: 290–306.

Barringer, B. R., and Harrison, J. S. (2000) 'Walking a tightrope: Creating value through interorganizational relationships'. *Journal of Management*, 26: 367–403.

Blake, J. (1999) 'Overcoming the "value–action gap" in environmental policy: Tensions between national policy and local experience'. *Local Environment*, 4: 257–78.

Broom, J. (2011) 'Like bobbleheads, Seattle sport fans? Try free compost night'. *Seattle Times*. Available online at http://seattletimes.com/html/localnews/2014563757_greenteams22m.html (accessed 1 December 2013).

Casper, J., Pfahl, M., and McCullough, B. P. (2014) 'Intercollegiate sport and the environment: Examining fan engagement based on athletics department sustainability efforts'. *Journal of Issues in Intercollegiate Athletics*, 7: 65–91.

Casper, J., Pfahl, M., and McSherry, M. (2012) 'Athletics department awareness and action regarding the environment: A study of NCAA athletics department sustainability practices'. *Journal of Sport Management*, 26: 11–29.

Coakley, J. J., and Pike, E. (1998) *Sport in Society: Issues and Controversies* (pp. 438–45). Boston, MA: Irwin/McGraw-Hill.

Consumer Reports (n.d.) 'Plastic recycling'. Available online at www.greenerchoices.org/home.cfm (accessed 18 October 2013).

DeLuca, K. (2005) 'Thinking with Heidegger: Rethinking environmental theory and practice'. *Ethics & the Environment*, 10: 67–87.

Friedman, M. T., Parent, M. M., and Mason, D. S. (2004) 'Building a framework for issues management in sport through stakeholder theory'. *European Sport Management Quarterly*, 4: 170–90.

Green Sports Alliance (n.d.) 'The Green Sports Alliance'. Available online at http://greensportsalliance.org (accessed 3 October 2013).

Greenpeace (2009) 'Coca-Cola commits to climate-friendly refrigeration through engagement with Greenpeace'. Press release, 3 December 2009. Available online at www.greenpeace.org/usa/en/media-center/news-releases/coca-cola-commits-to-climate-f (accessed 20 November 2013).

Inoue, Y., and Kent, A. (2012) 'Sport teams as promoters of pro-environmental behavior: An empirical study'. *Journal of Sport Management*, 26: 417–32.

Irwin, R. L., Lachowetz, T., Cornwell, T. B., and Clark, J. S. (2003) 'Cause-related sport sponsorship: An assessment of spectator beliefs, attitudes, and behavioral intentions'. *Sport Marketing Quarterly*, 12: 131–9.

King, B. (2008) 'Finding growth in green: Seeds of opportunity'. *Sports Business Journal*, 10 November.

McCullough, B. P. (2013) 'Identifying the influences on sport spectator recycling behaviours using the theory of planned behaviour'. *International Journal of Sport Management and Marketing*, 14: 146–68.

McCullough, B. P., and Cunningham, G. B. (2010) 'A conceptual model to understand the impetus to engage in and the expected organizational outcomes of green initiatives'. *Quest*, 62: 348–63.

Natural Resources Defense Council (2012) 'Game changer: How the sports industry is saving the environment'. Available online at www.nrdc.org (accessed 20 March 2013).

Olympic Sponsorship Overview (2000) 'Sydney 2000 sponsorship'. Available online at www.olympic.org/Documents/Reports/EN/en_report_253.pdf (accessed 8 December 2013).

Paquette, J., Stevens, J., and Mallen, C. (2011) 'The interpretation of environmental sustainability by the International Olympic Committee and Organizing Committees of the Olympic Games from 1994 to 2008'. *Sport in Society*, 14: 355–69.

Perciasepe, B. (2013) 'Green sports to combat climate change'. EPA Connect. Available online at http://blog.epa.gov/epaconnect/2013/08/greensportsalliance (accessed 30 November 2013).

Pfahl, M. (2011) 'Strategic issues associated with the development of internal sustainability teams in sport and recreation organizations: A framework for action and sustainable environmental performance'. *International Journal of Sport Management, Recreation & Tourism*, 6: 37–61.

Pfahl, M. (2013) 'The environmental awakening in sport'. *Solutions*, 4: 67–76.

Pfahl, M., Casper, J., Trendafilova, S., McCullough, B. P., and Nguyen, S. N. (2015) 'Crossing boundaries: An examination of sustainability department and athletics department collaboration regarding environmental issues'. *Communication & Sport*, 3(1): 27–56.

Poncelet, E. C. (2002) 'In search of the 'win–win', partnership and leadership'. *Eco-Efficiency in Industry and Science*, 8: 41–59.

US Open (2013) 'Green initiatives'. Available online at http://2013.usopen.org/en_US/about/green_initiatives.html (accessed 10 October 2013).

12

COMMUNICATING THE
GREEN IN SPORT

Michael E. Pfahl and Austin Stahl

For years, sport provided fans with data and information about games, events, players, etc. Data drives sport and is as much a part of the games as playing them. Data and information in sport has taken tremendous leaps forward in terms of access, amount, and style since the emergence of the Internet. Digital spaces occupy a complex place in sport fandom as news, information, opinion, and speculation coalesce in ways that individuals can customize to their desire. For sport personnel, using these spaces means there is no single way to communicate environmental activities to stakeholders because a particular sport organization's environmental goals and objectives will vary in both content and conduct over time (Chiou et al. 2010; Isenmann 2004; Isenmann et al. 2007; Rikhardsson et al. 2002; Shepherd et al. 2001). Thus, when sport organization personnel make the decision to utilize digital options to disseminate information about environmental issues and/or initiatives (e.g., website, social media), the efforts should be grounded in goals and objectives that are identified clearly and in line with environmental strategy and broader organizational strategic plans.

This chapter examines how sport personnel use the digital space in relation to their environmental efforts. To do this, the chapter will make a brief overview of the current state of the digital space and sport. Then, the emphasis will shift to examinations of tactics used by sport personnel to share environmental information through digital spaces. Finally, it will conclude with an examination of *better* practices and future ideas for sport personnel to consider when developing digital strategies for environmental information and activities.

Sport and the digital space

No one should be surprised the digital space is a popular place for sport discussion, information, revenue generation, viewership, and many other aspects of the sport experience. We see this in everything from fantasy sport to marketing opportunities (Dwyer and Drayer 2010; Gillentine and Shulz 2001; Mahan 2011; Mahan and McDaniel 2006; Pfahl et al. 2012; Ruihley and Hardin 2011a, 2011b; Schultz and Sheffer 2008).

First, a common digital platform used by sport personnel is that of websites (Caskey and Delpy 1999; Evans and Smith 2004; Jae Seo et al. 2007). By their nature, websites are excellent archival resources and provide useful areas to disseminate and store information, including audio and video content (Anderson 2008; Anderson and Wolff 2010).

Second, recent years have seen the rise of engaging digital platforms that allow individuals to share a variety of information with each other and are broadly known as social media (Newman et al. 2013; Safko and Brake 2009). These include Twitter (closed system, text communication), Facebook (closed system text and video communication), Foursquare (open and closed system, location-based communication), Instagram (open and closed system, image communication), and probably a dozen more that are in the process of becoming popular at this very moment, as well as a few that were just invented a moment ago. Social media comes in many forms (Table 12.1) and provides useful engagement opportunities that facilitate other actions (e.g., revenue generation). The strengths of the social media platforms are that they are in near real time/real time, they allow open and closed systems to be developed, and they are functional with each other. However, they do not all have to be used in the same way or for the same purpose.

Third, alongside the rise in social media is the rise in demand for content in the digital space (Cohen 2013; *The Economist* 2012; Hutchins 2008; Maffesoli 1996). Increasingly, individuals are seeking visual content away from television at their discretion. For the first time in twenty years, the Nielsen Company (2012) reported data that showed a decrease of about one million homes in the United States with at least a single television and a cable, satellite, or other content provider. Other data also shows a decrease in television viewing or numbers of hours viewed, a trend not just confined to the United States (Eurodata 2013; Magid 2011; Niemeyer 2013; TelecomAsia 2011). Sport personnel use the digital space for revenue generation and other marketing opportunities, and can now do so to disseminate news and information about their environmental activities.

A strategic approach to the digital space

This section of the chapter is an examination of the current tactics used by sport personnel to share environmental information through digital spaces. As noted earlier, the digital space offers a variety of platforms (e.g., Facebook) and levels (e.g., individual, community) through which sport personnel can disseminate content and information about their environmental efforts or environmental news and information in general. Reporting of environmental information comes in a variety of forms (Adams 2004; Kolk et al. 2001; Pfahl 2011). Reports can be made through one, all, or some combination of press releases, audit reports, news stories (developed

TABLE 12.1 Social media forms

Format	Example	Key characteristics
Publishing Services		
	Blog	News and information provided with reader comments
	Forum	Community centered on topics; users exchange information under control of monitors
	Wiki	Collaborative website to generate and to link pages related to various topics
Media Sharing Services		
	Social news websites	Rate news story links
	Social bookmarking websites	Save and review links to news and other content
	Video-sharing sites	Upload and share user-generated content
	Photograph-sharing sites	Upload and share user-generated content
	Audio-sharing sites	Upload and share user-generated content
	Presentation and document sharing sites	Upload and share user-generated content
	Live streaming sites	Live video feeds
Networking Services		
	Social networking sites	Interest-based social engagement
	Real-time micro blogging platforms	Limited text updates of news and information
	Opinion and review sites	Share opinions and reviews related to products and services
	Social shopping sites	Provides access to limited-time purchase deals with a buyer-number requirement
	Crowdsourcing sites	Gathering-point website to contribute ideas, resources, and expertise to a common goal

Sources: Newman et al. (2013); Safko and Brake (2009).

internally and externally), full environmental reports of activities, part of an annual report, website content, et cetera. This chapter focuses on the digital space because it is a central point for communication today, a good resource to store data and information, and to disseminate and to store content of all kinds (Jones and Walton 1999; Jose and Lee 2007; Pfahl 2011; Shepherd et al. 2001; van Staden and Hooks 2007).

Sport scholars are beginning to examine what and how digital platforms are used, but also in terms of what frequency and strategic combination (Clavio 2011; Moore and Carlson 2013; O'Shea and Alonso 2012; Wallace et al. 2011). Sport personnel use these channels for many purposes (e.g., news, information, marketing, ticket sales). With the advent of corporate social responsibility and other reasons for addressing environmental issues, sport personnel are using digital platforms to disseminate information about their environmental activities as well as engaging with fans and other stakeholders about the issues. Space constraints make it impossible to cover all possibilities for sport personnel to use digital platforms in this manner (Bruhn et al. 2012; Hennig-Thurau et al. 2010; Libai et al. 2010; Van Doorn et al. 2010). Websites, Facebook, and Twitter will be discussed here as a sample of the possibilities and also because of their high levels of use comparatively speaking among social media users.

Websites

Websites are a common method of distributing information about environmental information due to their ability to archive data easily and to incorporate graphics, video, text, and links to other internal and external sources (Jones and Walton 1999; Jose and Lee 2007; Shepherd et al. 2001). The ways data and information can be delivered across this platform is another reason why it is attractive. For example, different stakeholders can have data and information aggregated in different forms that best fit the audience (e.g., school children, scientists), but the same access platform can be used (Isenmann and Lenz 2001).

Research into the corporate reporting of environmental information via websites has shown a focus on several key elements: environmental policy, environmental philosophy, strategic focus, strategic drivers (external and internal), environmental planning processes, commitment by different levels of organizational members, integration across organizational units, audits, disclosure, stakeholder engagement, and many other factors (Hart 1995; Hart and Milstein 2003; Jose and Lee 2007; Kolk 1999, 2004, 2008; Pfahl 2011). While sport marketing and fan usage of sport organization websites revealed much about how this platform can be used for engagement, marketing, and other aspects of sport business (Brown 2003; Hur et al. 2011; Jae Seo et al. 2007), little emphasis has been given to environmental reporting in the sport website context. Many sport organizations do not have publicly available financial reports such as those from a publicly traded corporation. Further, many, if not most, do not have self-reported data or third-party verified data consolidated into an environmental report (Death 2011; Girginov 2012; Jose and Lee 2007; Mol 2010; Samuel and Stubbs 2013; Unerman 2000).

Recycling, energy conservation, and water conservation are common tactics used to achieve team environmental goals and are some of the most visible efforts from which team personnel can use to communicate environmental activities (Casper et al. 2012; Natural Resources Defense Council 2012). To better understand how environmental issues are communicated, the content of sport organization websites was studied for evidence of six key categories related to information presented on them (Tables 12.2–12.6) (Fried and Pfahl 2010). Across the leagues, team websites were examined for content related to primary areas of concern: site sustainability (e.g., efforts undertaken to make the stadium area sustainable), water conservation, energy efficiency, recycling efforts, transportation (e.g., information about fan programs of car pooling), and food conservation (e.g., donation of food not eaten at a game to a local food bank). Additional research sought to identify related areas including material sources (e.g., use of Green Seal certified cleaning products in a venue), green fan education (e.g., outreach programs to educate fans about environmental issues or organization green efforts), giveaways (e.g., an environmentally themed premium), and green ticketing programs (e.g., discounts for using public transportation to a game) (Fried and Pfahl 2010). In addition, surveys were sent to team personnel to verify the accuracy of the content analysis, but received a response rate of 8.57 percent.

Another survey of website content was conducted in 2013 (Stahl and Pfahl 2013). It focused on all MLB, NFL, NBA, NHL, and MLS team websites and the types of information found on it that related to environmental efforts. The review noted the following categories: green operations, fan and community engagement, environmental mission statement, environmental vision statement, environmental goals, evidence of front office commitment, evidence of manager or coach commitment, evidence of player commitment, advocacy for league efforts, evidence of sharing best practices, evidence of organizational values, evidence of external collaboration, evidence of supporting environmental groups, evidence of environmentally oriented partnerships/sponsorships, and evidence of environmentally oriented activation with partners/sponsors. This information does not indicate the full extent of environmental activities within or commitment to environmental issues. Rather, it shows what information sport personnel provide to external stakeholders via a website. This is a passive marketing communication activity, but one that does provide valuable information to stakeholders. The results reported in Table 12.7 illustrate selected categories with the most information provided and is organized by the top teams within each league based on quantity of information provided. The data shows that team personnel are promoting and marketing their environmental efforts, but what they are touting varies by team. However, it is important to note that simply not having information on a website does not mean a sport organization is not doing anything related to the environment. It does mean, though, that individual teams are making conscious decisions to inform external stakeholders of the actions team personnel are taking in relation to the environment. The content for these teams, and those not shown, will most certainly change as time goes on.

TABLE 12.2 MLB sustainability content analyses data (2010)★

Team	Site sustainability	Water conservation	Energy efficiency	Recycling	Transportation	Food conservation	Materials resources	Education	Giveaways	Tickets
Boston Red Sox	X		X	X						
Chicago Cubs				X	X					
Chicago White Sox		X	X	X	X					
Cincinnati Reds				X			X	X		
Cleveland Indians			X	X						
Colorado Rockies			X							
Detroit Tigers			X	X		X	X			
Houston Astros	X	X	X	X			X	X		
Los Angeles Dodgers	X	X	X	X						
Minnesota Twins	X	X	X	X	X	X	X	X		
New York Mets	X	X	X	X	X	X	X	X		

Team	Site sustainability	Water conservation	Energy efficiency	Recycling	Transportation	Food conservation	Materials resources	Education	Giveaways	Tickets
New York Yankees	X		X	X	X	X		X		
Oakland As				X						
Philadelphia Phillies			X	X		X		X		
Pittsburgh Pirates			X	X		X		X		
San Diego Padres	X	X	X	X	X	X		X		
San Francisco Giants			X		X	X		X		
St. Louis Cardinals			X	X		X	X			
Tampa Bay Rays	X	X	X	X	X	X	X	X		
Toronto Blue Jays			X	X		X				
Washington Nationals	X	X	X	X						

* Only teams with publicly available digital information in 2010 reported shown in table

Source: Fried and Pfahl (2010).

TABLE 12.3 NBA sustainability content analyses data (2010)⋆

Team	Site sustainability	Water conservation	Energy efficiency	Recycling	Transportation	Food conservation	Materials resources	Education	Giveaways	Tickets
Charlotte Bobcats	X	X	X	X		X	X			
Cleveland Cavaliers			X	X			X	X		
Dallas Mavericks				X	X			X		
Denver Nuggets	X	X	X	X	X	X	X	X		
Houston Rockets	X		X	X			X	X		
Los Angeles Clippers	X	X	X	X						
Los Angeles Lakers	X	X	X	X						
Miami Heat	X	X								
New Jersey Nets⋆⋆	X					X		X		
Oklahoma City Thunder								X		
Orlando Magic	X		X	X		X	X			

Team	Site sustainability	Water conservation	Energy efficiency	Recycling	Transportation	Food conservation	Materials resources	Education	Giveaways	Tickets
Philadelphia 76ers			X	X				X		
Phoenix Suns			X	X	X		X	X		
Portland Trail Blazers	X	X	X	X	X	X	X	X		
San Antonio Spurs	X	X		X				X		
Toronto Raptors		X	X	X		X	X			

* Only teams with publicly available digital information in 2010 reported shown in table
** Now Brooklyn Nets

Source: Fried and Pfahl (2010).

TABLE 12.4 NFL sustainability content analyses data (2010)*

Team	Site sustainability	Water conservation	Energy efficiency	Recycling	Transportation	Food conservation	Materials resources	Education	Giveaways	Tickets
Arizona Cardinals			X	X	X					
Atlanta Falcons	X	X	X	X	X	X	X	X		
Baltimore Ravens	X	X	X	X	X	X	X	X		
Chicago Bears				X				X		
Dallas Cowboys	X			X		X	X			
Denver Broncos			X	X				X		
Green Bay Packers	X	X	X	X			X	X		
Houston Texans			X	X			X			
Indianapolis Colts				X						
Miami Dolphins	X			X				X		
Minnesota Vikings				X				X		

Team	Site sustainability	Water conservation	Energy efficiency	Recycling	Transportation	Food conservation	Materials resources	Education	Giveaways	Tickets
New England Patriots			X							
New Orleans Saints				X						
Oakland Raiders			X	X						
Philadelphia Eagles			X	X	X	X	X	X		
Seattle Seahawks	X	X	X	X	X	X	X	X		
St. Louis Rams			X	X						
Tennessee Titans				X						

* Only teams with publicly available digital information in 2010 reported shown in table

Source: Fried and Pfahl (2010).

TABLE 12.5 NHL sustainability content analyses data (2010)⋆

Team	Site sustainability	Water conservation	Energy efficiency	Recycling	Transportation	Food conservation	Materials resources	Education	Giveaways	Tickets
Anaheim Ducks				X						
Atlanta Thrashers								X		
Boston Bruins		X	X	X	X	X		X		
Buffalo Sabres			X	X			X	X		
Colorado Avalanche	X		X	X			X			
Columbus Blue Jackets		X	X	X		X	X	X		
Florida Panthers				X		X	X			
Los Angeles Kings	X	X	X	X	X					
Minnesota Wild	X	X	X	X	X	X	X	X		
Ottawa Senators	X			X				X		
Philadelphia Flyers			X	X				X		

Team	Site sustainability	Water conservation	Energy efficiency	Recycling	Transportation	Food conservation	Materials resources	Education	Giveaways	Tickets
Phoenix Coyotes						X		X		
Pittsburgh Penguins	X									
San Jose Sharks			X					X		
Toronto Maple Leaves		X	X	X		X	X	X		

★ Only teams with publicly available digital information in 2010 reported shown in table

Source: Fried and Pfahl (2010).

TABLE 12.6 MLS sustainability content analyses data (2010)*

Team**	Site sustainability	Water conservation	Energy efficiency	Recycling	Transportation	Food conservation	Materials resources	Education	Giveaways	Tickets
Chicago Fire				X					X	X
Colorado Rapids		X	X	X	X			X	X	X
Columbus Crew				X						
F.C. Dallas								X		
Houston Dynamo				X						X
Los Angeles Galaxy								X		
San Jose Earthquakes	X		X					X	X	X
Seattle Sounders	X		X							
Toronto F.C.				X	X					

* Only teams with publicly available digital information in 2010 reported shown in table

** Teams in Portland and Vancouver entered the MLS in 2011

Source: Fried and Pfahl (2010).

TABLE 12.7 Environmental information on sport team websites (United States) (abridged)

	Green opers.	Fan and community engagement	Green mission statement	Green vision statement	Green goals	Evidence of front office commitment	Advocacy for league efforts	Evidence of external collaboration	Evidence of environmentally oriented partnerships and sponsorships	Total environmentally oriented information on website
NBA										
LA Lakers	1	2	0	0	0	1	0	1	0	7
Memphis Grizzlies	0	3	0	0	0	0	0	2	1	8
New Orleans Hornets	0	1	0	0	1	0	0	1	1	8
New York Knicks	0	0	0	0	0	0	0	1	0	2
Portland Trail Blazers	3	2	3	3	3	3	3	3	3	41
MLB										
Boston Red Sox	2	0	0	1	0	1	0	2	1	10
Cleveland Indians	3	1	2	1	0	1	0	2	1	15
Minnesota Twins	3	0	3	3	0	1	0	2	0	17
New York Yankees	3	0	0	0	0	1	0	2	1	10
Pittsburgh Pirates	3	2	1	0	0	3	0	3	2	18
San Diego Padres	3	3	2	0	0	0	0	3	3	19

continued

TABLE 12.7 Environmental information on sport team websites (United States) (abridged), *continued*

	Green opers.	Fan and community engagement	Green mission statement	Green vision statement	Green goals	Evidence of front office commitment	Advocacy for league efforts	Evidence of external collaboration	Evidence of environmentally oriented partnerships and sponsorships	Total environmentally oriented information on website
NFL										
Atlanta Falcons	3	2	3	0	1	3	0	2	2	23
Chicago Bears	3	2	3	0	0	0	0	2	2	21
Indianapolis Colts	0	2	0	0	0	0	0	1	2	8
Philadelphia Eagles	3	2	2	3	0	1	1	3	2	25
St. Louis Rams	3	2	3	0	0	0	0	1	3	17
MLS										
Houston Dynamo	2	0	0	0	0	0	0	2	0	6
LA Galaxy	0	2	0	0	0	0	0	0	0	3
Portland Timbers	2	0	0	0	0	0	0	0	0	4
NHL										
Buffalo Sabres	0	3	3	0	0	0	0	2	0	10
Montreal Canadiens	3	1	2	0	0	0	0	0	0	12
Philadelphia Flyers	2	0	0	0	0	0	0	3	2	10
Pittsburgh Penguins	3	0	0	0	0	0	0	3	2	10
San Jose Sharks	3	2	0	0	0	0	0	2	2	14

Note: Not all leagues had five rankable teams.

Source: Stahl and Pfahl (2013).

Facebook

Facebook is becoming a popular place for posting news and information about green activities in sport because it is becoming a more popular platform for interactions between organizational personnel and stakeholders (Hennig-Thurau et al. 2010; Lin and Lu 2011; Vorvoreanu 2009). While team personnel can utilize the platform in this manner, it is being used effectively by organizations such as the Green Sports Alliance (the Alliance) and the Natural Resources Defense Council (NRDC) (for their sport work). Facebook allows for images, videos, and links to additional sources, but more importantly, sharing of information among stakeholders and other interested parties.

The viral nature of Facebook helps the Alliance, for example, communicate information from the sport organizations with which they work. An example of how the Alliance uses Facebook occurred on 6 August 2013:

> @Atlanta_Falcons announce new #recyclingcampaign to engage fans in #greensports initiatives at the @GeorgiaDom http://ow.ly/nFTUC
> (Green Sports Alliance 2013a)

Another example of one of their posts occurred on 9 August 2013:

> In 2008, the Boston Red Sox became the first MLB team to install a solar thermal system at their ballpark. Fenway Park features 28 solar panels used to heat the ballpark's water.
> (Green Sports Alliance 2013b)

Additionally, the 8 August post included a link to a featured story on the Alliance's website about the recently launched National Women's Soccer League (NWSL) and the Portland Thorns' environmental efforts, along with those of the personnel of the JELD-WEN Field where they play. Demonstration of efforts leads to more interest and more perceived value of the sport organization. It also shows how teams benefit from having additional publicity and a platform to engage fans and potential fans alike through environmental work. This type of engagement creates a moment between the Alliance and fans, although the reactions/actions based upon the update can range from ignore/missed it to passing it along to others. On the positive side, this effort by the Alliance personnel cost little and can act as a departure point for a variety of actions. Facebook, as a platform, is seeing changes in usage patterns among different communities. Most prominent is a decrease in use among younger people (e.g., teens) (Bercovici 2013).

Twitter

The short message service, Twitter, has drawn praise and scorn since its inception (Hargittai and Litt 2011; Marwick 2011). While this is not the proper place to discuss its value to society, it is a place to discuss how it is used to disseminate environmental information by sport organizations. While the service is constrained by design (i.e., 140 characters per Tweet), the ability for a person to send a message to a wide variety of contacts is important. Further, Twitter is becoming increasingly more adept at handling photograph and video links, making it more dynamic than ever. Twitter, then, was seemingly made for sport, especially engagement opportunities between fans and athletes (Hambrick et al. 2010). Twitter allows for digital content to be sent to a wide variety of followers of a particular person or organization. As with Facebook (and email), news and information can be disseminated about environmental activities at relatively low cost.

As an example of Twitter usage, the Alliance utilizes it to publicize its own efforts as well as those of member organizations. Below are just a few examples.

> College Sports Follow the Lead of #NHLGreen. Via @NRDCGreenSports http://ow.ly/qv13c #GreenSports #sportsbiz
>
> (Green Sports Alliance 2013c)

> 2014 #GreenSports Summit Early-Bird Registration is LIVE! Sign up for a steal today! http://ow.ly/qyDpn
>
> (Green Sports Alliance 2013d)

> Alliance Members go head to head tonight in #StanfordOregon. Check out more on Collegiate #GreenSports via @NRDC http://ow.ly/qAikA
>
> (Green Sports Alliance 2013e)

> @NHL #StanleyCup contender @LAKings are #GreenSports leaders w/ 1,727 #solar panels on their home @STAPLESCenter. #NHLGreen @ AEG1EARTH
>
> (Green Sports Alliance 2014)

The use of Twitter in conjunction with other digital platforms, including those discussed in this chapter, makes information dissemination an important part of environmental strategy for sports personnel.

In sum, using these three platforms (plus other desired ones) means that sport organization personnel can strategically plan for their communication efforts. Key to these efforts are the goals and objectives developed and the tactics that will be used to place action on the ground. If awareness of an event is desired, then messages can be created accordingly, with response rates tracked either digitally or by RSVP. Given that most environmental activities are non-revenue generating, defining objectives to reach goals and to develop tactics is critical, especially as many objectives will be awareness or action oriented (e.g., do something, visit somewhere). Careful strategic planning is needed to address environmental communication and marketing, as would be expected of ticket sales plans or marketing campaigns.

Key elements for providing and disseminating environmental information

This chapter concludes with a brief examination of *better* practices and future ideas for sport personnel to consider when developing digital strategies for environmental information and activities. A few simple tips are provided here to make the most of efforts to disseminate information about the environmental strategies and operations of a sport organization. It is important to note that this information does not constitute a set of standards. It is important to make sure the information is contextualized, informative in different ways (e.g., mixture of graphics and text), and easy to understand (i.e., language, amount).

Contextualized information

Tables 12.2–12.7 showed different categories of information that are commonly reported by sport personnel on team websites. It is important to remember that the information provided should support the organization's goals and objectives related to its environmental strategy. Sport personnel cannot always report all of the environmental undertakings with great depth and breadth, but should work to provide the most salient and understandable information they can. Wherever information is presented, it needs to be explained through the lens of a team or event's environmental strategy. Without context, the information risks being seen as disjointed and not strategic or a part of the organization's cultural practices. Charges of greenwashing or insincerity can arise from such situations. Value statements, mission statements, and strategic points of emphasis should be included with other environmental information in text or video form.

For example, the Cleveland Indians provide a limited amount of information about their green efforts under the tagline of Our Tribe Is Green. However, what they do provide is clearly organized in a scroll-down manner with a set of links at the top of the page that take a visitor directly to the story/ information desired on the page (versus scrolling). In addition, there is an interesting video of the team installing a wind turbine, but the information is not contextualized with an explanation as to what the video is about nor does it provide more information on the initiative itself. There is a story about the wind power initiative included in the information provided, but it is not connected to the video. Doing so would tighten the message and tactics used to illustrate the message that otherwise hold together well. The Minnesota Twins follow a similar contextualized approach under the auspices of Go Twins Go Green. The information is organized into neat categories that are accompanied by headlines in bold. As information is presented, it needs to appear in a variety of forms to enhance its explanatory power.

Informative in different ways

The overwhelming majority of teams provide information in text format. While this is good for explanation, it can lead to large amounts of information being placed on web pages that require a user to scroll again and again down the page. Graphical representation of data can help to alleviate this issue. Graphical representations make the data more accessible by putting it into an alternative format that helps many users digest the data quickly. The St. Louis Cardinals do this well as they have three easy-to-understand graphics related to aspects of their environmental work at Busch Stadium located in the center of their green webpage (4 A Greener Game). This information represents tons of compost and recycling collected since the inception of their program in 2008, total dollar value of food donations for the same period, and a current diversion rate of recyclable and compostable items out of the trash stream. There is an introductory paragraph for these graphics, adding a contextualization element. Further, the team has a green mission statement (white on a green background) and provides a series of strategic environmental operations areas in a table that is tabbed by content area for easy access and viewing. Areas include: the green team, the ballpark experience, accomplishments of the team, environmental objectives, the Green Path (in conjunction with Delaware Northern), solar power information, news, and partners with whom the team personnel work. The information is neat and clean, and each tab offers clear and understandable information.

In another example, the Philadelphia Eagles, long a leader in environmental issues, also have an informative green webpage. The website builds on the contextual principles by segmenting each idea to its own graphically represented area of the site. The Eagles have applications that show real-time data about environmental actions at the Novacare Complex (training facility) and shows data in a variety of graphic forms (e.g., sortable graph). A second application for similar information about Lincoln Financial Field (main stadium) is also available. Both are good resources for explaining environmental information to fans. Additionally, the graphical nature and real-time elements in it make this particular approach to data presentation accessible for stakeholders to use (e.g., teachers in the classroom).

Easy to understand

While intuitive, it is important to remember that too much data can be overwhelming. The same can be said for too many news stories or information items about environmental work. The same care that goes into developing the back office hierarchy of a website for ticket sales or team news needs to be applied to the environmental page. The University of Colorado exemplifies a straightforward, simple approach. The Environmental Center of the university provides an easy-to-navigate website that organizes key aspects of its operations into webpages that all exist above the *fold* or bottom of a screen. Tabs then take a visitor to various other resources, reports, or in-depth stories about activities around campus or initiatives undertaken. The website uses a consistent graphical package and embedded hyperlinks to related stories or resources. The Greening CU portal link takes visitors deeper into the environmental actions at the university. Compared to the professional-level sites, university websites, from progressive institutions around the country (e.g., Yale University, Ohio University, Ohio State University, University of Florida), have broad and deep platforms that organize information well and provide a large amount of information in manageable ways for visitors.

Conclusion

As noted previously, there is no single way to approach information dissemination. This chapter provided context within which environmental information dissemination via digital means can be undertaken. It provided a brief overview of the current state of the digital space and sport. Then, it explored tactics used by sport personnel to share environmental information through digital spaces. Finally, it provided a set of *better* practices and future ideas for sport personnel to consider when developing digital strategies for environmental information and activities. While this chapter examined key digital outlets for information dissemination, on-site events and other community outreach programs can build awareness and action through face-to-face interaction.

References

Adams, C. (2004) 'The ethical, social and environmental reporting–performance portrayal gap'. *Accounting, Auditing & Accountability Journal*, 17: 731–57.

Anderson, C. (2008) *The Longer Long Tail: Why the future of business is selling less of more*. New York: Hyperion.

Anderson, C. and Wolff, M. (2010) 'The web is dead. Long live the Internet'. *Wired*. Available online at www.wired.com/magazine/2010/08/ff_webrip (accessed 16 July 2013).

Bercovici, J. (2013) 'Facebook admits it's seen a drop in usage among teens'. *Forbes*. Available online at www.forbes.com/sites/jeffbercovici/2013/10/30/facebook-admits-its-seen-a-drop-in-usage-among-teens (accessed 7 November 2013).

Brown, M. (2003) 'An analysis on online marketing in the sport industry: User activity, communication objectives, and perceived benefits'. *Sport Marketing Quarterly*, 12: 48–55.

Bruhn, M., Schoenmueller, V., and Schäfer, D. (2012) 'Are social media replacing traditional media in terms of brand equity creation?' *Management Research Review*, 35: 770–90.

Caskey, R. and Delpy, L. (1999) 'An examination of sport websites and the opinion of web employees toward the use and viability of the World Wide Web as a profitable sports marketing tool'. *Sport Marketing Quarterly*, 8: 13–24.

Casper, J., Pfahl, M., and McSherry, M. (2012) 'Athletics department awareness and action regarding the environment: A study of NCAA athletics department sustainability practices'. *Journal of Sport Management*, 26: 11–29.

Chiou, W., Lin, C., and Perng, C. (2010) 'A strategic framework for website evaluation based on a review of the literature from 1995–2006'. *Information & Management*, 47: 282–90.

Clavio, G. (2011) 'Social media and the college football audience'. *Journal of Issues in Intercollegiate Athletics*, 4: 309–25.

Cohen, N. (2013) 'The growth of digital advertising and branded content is gaining pace'. *The Guardian*. Available online at www.guardian.co.uk/media-network/media-network-blog/2013/jun/25/growth-digital-advertising-branded-content (accessed 16 July 2013).

Death, C. (2011) '"Greening" the 2010 FIFA World Cup: Environmental sustainability and the mega-event in South Africa'. *Journal of Environmental Policy & Planning*, 13: 99–117.

Dwyer, B. and Drayer, J. (2010) 'Fantasy sport consumer segmentation: An investigation into the differing consumption modes of fantasy football participants'. *Sport Marketing Quarterly*, 19: 207–16.

Eurodata. (2013) 'One TV year in the world: 2012 or the multiple TV experience'. Available online at www.mediametrie.com/eurodatatv/solutions/one-television-year-in-the-world.php?id=57 (accessed 4 July 2013).

Evans, D. and Smith, A. (2004) 'The internet and competitive advantage: A study of Australia's four premier professional sporting leagues'. *Sport Management Review*, 7: 27–56.

Fried, G. and Pfahl, M. (2010) 'Professors examine green initiatives at professional sport teams'. *Sports Litigation Alert*, 7: 1–8.

Gillentine, A. and Shulz, J. (2001) 'Marketing the fantasy football league: Utilization of simulation to enhance sport marketing concepts'. *Journal of Marketing Education*, 23: 178–86.

Girginov, V. (2012) 'Governance of the London 2012 Olympic Games legacy'. *International Review for the Sociology of Sport*, 47: 543–58.

Green Sports Alliance. (2013a) Facebook post. Available online at https://facebook.com (accessed 6 August 2013).

Green Sports Alliance. (2013b) Facebook post. Available online at https://facebook.com (accessed 9 August 2013).

Green Sports Alliance. (2013c) Twitter feed. Available online at https://twitter.com/sportsalliance (accessed 4 November 2013).

Green Sports Alliance. (2013d) Twitter feed. Available online at https://twitter.com/sportsalliance (accessed 6 November 2013).

Green Sports Alliance. (2013e) Twitter feed. Available online at https://twitter.com/sportsalliance (accessed 7 November 2013).

Green Sports Alliance. (2014) Twitter feed. Available online at https://twitter.com/sportsalliance (accessed 7 May 2014).

Hambrick, M., Simmons, J., Greenhalgh, G., and Greenwell, T. (2010) 'Understanding professional athletes' use of Twitter: A content analysis of athlete tweets'. *International Journal of Sport Communication*, 3: 454–71.

Hargittai, E. and Litt, E. (2011) 'The tweet smell of celebrity success: Explaining variation in Twitter adoption among a diverse group of young adults'. *New Media & Society*, 13: 824–42.

Hart, S. (1995) 'A natural-resource-based view of the firm'. *The Academy of Management Review*, 20: 986–1014.

Hart, S. and Milstein, M. (2003) 'Creating sustainable value'. *The Academy of Management Executive*, 17: 56–67.

Hennig-Thurau, T., Malthouse, E., Friege, C., Gensler, S., Lobschat, L., Rangaswamy, A., and Skiera, B. (2010) 'The impact of new media on customer relationships'. *Journal of Service Research*, 13: 311–30.

Hur, Y., Ko, Y. J., and Valacich, J. (2011) 'A structural model of the relationships between sport website quality, e-satisfaction, and e-loyalty'. *Journal of Sport Management*, 25: 458–73.

Hutchins, B. (2008) 'Signs of meta-change in second modernity: The growth of e-sport and the World Cyber Games'. *New Media & Society*, 10: 851–69.

Isenmann, R. (2004) 'Internet-based sustainability reporting'. *International Journal of Environment and Sustainable Development*, 3: 145–67.

Isenmann, R., Bey, C., and Welter, M. (2007) 'Online reporting for sustainability issues'. *Business Strategy and the Environment*, 16: 487–501.

Isenmann, R. and Lenz, C. (2001) 'Customized corporate environmental reporting by internet-based push and pull technologies'. *Eco-Management and Auditing*, 8: 100–10.

Jae Seo, W., Christine Green, B., Jae Ko, Y., Lee, S., and Schenewark, J. (2007) 'The effect of web cohesion, web commitment, and attitude toward the website on intentions to use NFL teams' websites'. *Sport Management Review*, 10: 231–52.

Jones, K. and Walton, J. (1999) 'Internet-based environmental reporting'. *Sustainable Measures: Evaluation and Reporting of Environmental and Social Performance*, 1: 412–74.

Jose, A. and Lee, S. (2007) 'Environmental reporting of global corporations: A content analysis based on website disclosures'. *Journal of Business Ethics*, 72: 307–21.

Kolk, A. (1999) 'Evaluating corporate environmental reporting'. *Business Strategy and the Environment*, 8: 225–37.

Kolk, A. (2004) 'A decade of sustainability reporting: Developments and significance'. *International Journal of Environment and Sustainable Development*, 3: 51–64.

Kolk, A. (2008) 'Sustainability, accountability and corporate governance: Exploring multinationals' reporting practices'. *Business Strategy and the Environment*, 17(1): 1–15.

Kolk, A., Walhain, S., and Van de Wateringen, S. (2001) 'Environmental reporting by the Fortune Global 250: Exploring the influence of nationality and sector'. *Business Strategy and the Environment*, 10: 15–28.

Libai, B., Bolton, R., Bügel, M., de Ruyter, K., Götz, O., Risselada, H., and Stephen, A. (2010) 'Customer-to-customer interactions: Broadening the scope of word of mouth research'. *Journal of Service Research*, 13: 267–82.

Lin, K. and Lu, H. (2011) 'Intention to continue using Facebook fan pages from the perspective of social capital theory'. *Cyberpsychology, Behavior, and Social Networking*, 14: 565–70.

Maffesoli, M. (1996) *The Time of the Tribes: The decline of individualism in mass society.* Thousand Oaks: SAGE.

Magid, L. (2011, 1 March) 'Tech and the decline of traditional TV'. *Huffington Post*. Available online at www.huffingtonpost.com/larry-magid/tech-and-the-decline-of-t_b_829738.html (accessed 4 July 2013).

Mahan, J. (2011) 'Examining the predictors of consumer response to sport marketing via digital social media'. *International Journal of Sport Management and Marketing*, 9: 254–67.

Mahan, J. and McDaniel, S. (2006) 'The new online arena: Sport, marketing, and media converge in cyberspace'. In A. Raney and J. Bryant (eds), *Handbook of Sports and Media* (443–69). New York: Lawrence Erlbaum Associates.

Marwick, A. (2011) 'I tweet honestly, I tweet passionately: Twitter users, context collapse, and the imagined audience'. *New Media & Society*, 13: 114–33.

Mol, A. (2010) 'Sustainability as global attractor: The greening of the 2008 Beijing Olympics'. *Global Networks*, 10: 510–28.

Moore, J. and Carlson, A. (2013) 'Reaching the audience: New communication technology practices in college sports public relations'. *Journal of Global Scholars of Marketing Science*, 23: 109–26.

Natural Resources Defense Council. (2012) *Game Changer: How the sports industry is saving the environment*. New York: National Resources Defense Council.

Newman, T., Frederick Peck, J., Harris, C., and Wilhide, B. (2013) *Social Media in Sport Marketing*. Scottsdale, Arizona: Holcombe Hathaway Publishers.

Nielsen Company. (2012) 'The cross-platform report: A look across screens'. Available online at www.nielsen.com/us/en/reports/2013/the-cross-platform-report--a-look-across-screens.html (accessed 4 July 2013).

Niemeyer, B. (2013) 'Latest Nielsen data confirms a decline in TV consumption is underway'. Available online at http://tdgresearch.com/latest-nielsen-data-confirms-a-decline-in-tv-consumption-is-underway (accessed 4 July 2013).

O'Shea, M. and Alonso, A. (2012) 'Opportunity or obstacle? A preliminary study of professional sport organisations in the age of social media'. *International Journal of Sport Management and Marketing*, 10: 196–212.

Pfahl, M. (2011) *Sport and the Natural Environment: A strategic guide*. Dubuque, Iowa: Kendall Hunt Publishing Company.

Pfahl, M., Kreutzer, A., Maleski, M., Ryznar, J., and Lillibridge, J. (2012) 'If you build it, will they come? A case study of virtual spaces and brand in the NBA'. *Sport Management Review*, 15: 518–37.

Rikhardsson, P., Andersen, R., Jacob, A., and Bang, H. (2002) 'Sustainability reporting on the Internet'. *Greener Management International*, 40: 57–75.

Ruihley, B. and Hardin, R. (2011a) 'Beyond touchdowns, homeruns, and three-pointers: An examination of fantasy sport participation motivation'. *International Journal of Sport Management and Marketing*, 10: 232–56.

Ruihley, B. and Hardin, R. (2011b) 'Message boards and the fantasy sport experience'. *International Journal of Sport Communication*, 4: 233–52.

Safko, L. and Brake, D. (2009) *The Social Media Bible: Tactics, tools, and strategies for business success*. New York: Wiley.

Samuel, S. and Stubbs, W. (2013) 'Green Olympics, green legacies? An exploration of the environmental legacies of the Olympic Games'. *International Review for the Sociology of Sport*, 48: 485–504.

Schultz, B. and Sheffer, M. (2008) 'Left behind: Local television and the community of sport'. *Western Journal of Communication*, 72: 180–95.

Shepherd, K., Abkowitz, M., and Cohen, M. (2001) 'Online corporate environmental reporting: Improvements and innovation to enhance stakeholder value'. *Corporate Environmental Strategy*, 8: 307–15.

Stahl, A. and Pfahl, M. (2013) 'Behind the green curtain: An analysis of professional sport team environmental information provided on team websites'. Unpublished manuscript.

TelecomAsia. (2011) 'Social media changing TV viewing habits'. Available online at www.telecomasia.net/content/social-media-changing-tv-viewing-habits (accessed 4 July 2013).

The Economist. (2012, Technology Quarter 3) 'Lost in cyberspace'. Available online at www.economist.com/node/21560992 (accessed 16 July 2013).

Unerman, J. (2000) 'Methodological issues—Reflections on quantification in corporate social reporting content analysis'. *Accounting, Auditing & Accountability Journal*, 13: 667–81.

Van Doorn, J., Lemon, K., Mittal, V., Nass, S., Pick, D., Pirner, P., and Verhoef, P. (2010) 'Customer engagement behavior: Theoretical foundations and research directions'. *Journal of Service Research*, 13: 253–66.

van Staden, C. and Hooks, J. (2007) 'A comprehensive comparison of corporate environmental reporting and responsiveness'. *The British Accounting Review*, 39: 197–210.

Vorvoreanu, M. (2009) 'Perceptions of corporations on Facebook: An analysis of Facebook social norms'. *Journal of New Communications Research*, 4: 67–86.

Wallace, L., Wilson, J., and Miloch, K. (2011) 'Sporting Facebook: A content analysis of NCAA organizational sport pages and Big 12 Conference Athletic Department pages'. *International Journal of Sport Communication*, 4: 422–44.

SECTION IV
Finance and sponsorship

13

THE FINANCIAL DRIVERS FOR EMBEDDING SUSTAINABILITY INTO A SPORTS ORGANIZATION

Colleen Theron and Larissa Prevett

This chapter will explore the key development questions about the financial aspects of incorporating the natural environment into sport organization operations. It will also answer the following questions specifically by using supporting case studies relevant to the sports sector:

- What elements comprise a sustainability strategy?
- What is the return on investment in the sustainability context?
- What role can standards play in adding value for organizations?
- What are the financial drivers, barriers and costs of embedding sustainability?
- How and to what extent has the sports sector demonstrated financial returns on sustainability initiatives?

Setting the scene

Increasingly, sport organization personnel, as with their counterparts in the corporate world, are beginning to focus on a sustainable approach to operating their business (Kirwan 2013). The expectation for organization personnel to demonstrate their corporate responsibility has never been greater. The spotlights on climate change, use of natural resources, employee well-being, value chains and the global economic crises have all led to increased pressure to manage the impacts of business activity on all stakeholders and contribute to sustainable industries (Chartered Institute for Personnel Development 2013). This demand for greater transparency and the continued desire by companies to increase profits at all costs provides a challenge for companies considering implementing sustainability principles. The challenge is, first, understanding why. And, second, understanding how. Many organizations are realizing the impact of sustainability issues on their core business, including resource constraints, climate change, labour issues and poverty.

In the context of this external scrutiny, more companies are reviewing their sustainability approach to determine what changes may be required. In a report carried out by Ernst & Young (2010), the participants described a three-stage journey that companies go through when they decide to embed sustainability in their corporate cultures. The three stages are as follows:

- ensuring they are in compliance with regulations;
- focusing on and reporting on economic benefits;
- integrating sustainability into the core strategy and culture.

In the case of a company adopting a framework under an ISO standard, the first step is planning what is required for the sustainable management system (International Organization for Standardization 2014). These issues are no different for sporting organizations.

Common concepts

Interviews from the pilot study described in Case Study 13.8 of this chapter demonstrated that those implementing sustainability in sports organizations mainly view it as *being green* and also costly (Whistler 2020 2011). Willard refers to the executive mindset having to evolve from seeing early sustainability initiatives – that is, those labelled 'green', 'environmental' and 'sustainable' – as an expensive and bureaucratic impediment to success (Willard 2012: 20). However, from an organizational perspective, sustainability covers more than environmental measures. It is about an organization being able to withstand the test of time profitably and understanding the strengths and weaknesses of your business, according to the views of those who can influence it and are influenced by it. It's almost like an organizational 360 appraisal.

The long-term financial viability of organizations, and more broadly the economy, is central to sustainability. The *United Nations 2005 World Summit Outcome Document* refers to the 'interdependent and mutually reinforcing pillars' of sustainable development, which are:

- economic development;
- social development; and
- environmental protection.

(World Health Organization 2014: 12)

Environmental, social and governance practices

Environmental, social and governance (ESG) practices of an organization occur in a number of different ways (e.g., Environmental Social Governance, Corporate Social Responsibility and Sustainability). Although strictly speaking they do not all mean the same thing, some argue that there is sufficient overlap and that they adequately capture the essence of sustainability (Willard 2012). However, others argue that the use of the term *sustainability* provides a more comprehensive approach to addressing all three elements (Savitz 2013). In this chapter, sustainability is the preferred umbrella term for the three key dimensions of responsible organizations.

The triple bottom line

Frequently mentioned under the auspices of sustainability is the concept of the *triple bottom line*. It was originally proposed by John Elkington (1998), who suggested that businesses should measure their success notionally by the traditional bottom line of financial performance (most often expressed in terms of profits, return on investment (ROI) or shareholder value) as well as by their impact on the broader economy, the environment and the society in which they operate.

Sustainability strategy and SROI

Embedding sustainability strategically can add value to and realize benefits for organizations, including sports organizations. Sustainability strategies may include either isolated or multiple coordinated measures. Thus, it refers to an organizational process or group of initiatives that aim to enhance social welfare or reduce environmental impacts. Implementing a standard or an environmental or sustainable management system is an integrated and systematic approach, which allows sustainability to form part of core business decisions.

ROI in this case refers to the financial benefits derived from a sustainability initiative for a particular period compared with the cost of implementing the measure. In contrast, Sustainable Return on Investment (SROI) integrates the ability to measure the social, economic and environmental returns on sustainability initiatives (Earthshift 2011). Whilst the environmental benefits of sustainability are widely accepted, the business case for implementing a sustainability management system or strategy is still in its infancy. Do sustainability strategies tend to cover solely those measures where it is easier to predict the financial benefits and costs? If so, would organizations be more likely to focus on a broader set of sustainability measures if ROI figures were more readily available for those measures? Understanding the return on investment of improving environmental and social practices in organizations is largely under-researched, including in the sports sector. This is largely due to the difficulty of quantifying the financial gains accurately or accounting for sustainability activities within traditional accounting systems (Larrinaga-Gonzalez and Bebbington 2001; Mathews 1997). These aspects of sustainability demonstrate the importance of embedding sustainability issues within organizational strategy.

Embedding sustainability

The Star Model, developed by Jay Galbraith (1995, 2014), is one way of focusing on a number of elements in an organization and how they factor into sustainability planning (Figure 13.1). The framework has five elements (strategy, structure,

CASE STUDY 13.1: FACTS AND FIGURES

Wembley Stadium, London, and Millennium Stadium, Cardiff, have both reported significant savings as a result of their environmental sustainability strategies. As expected, this area is where most organizations are more readily able to provide percentage ROI figures or at least a total amount of savings over a given period. The success rates for energy management efforts for sporting venues is notable. The Millennium Stadium stated that simply by removing water heaters they were able to save £217,000 pa, amounting to an ROI of 130.9 per cent. Moreover, replacing the venue's lighting system has reduced lighting costs by 70 per cent pa.

Wembley Stadium claims that through their sustainability measures over the past five years, including putting in place 100 per cent renewable energy, they have saved an average of nearly £¾ million pa. Their waste-management initiative is another major achievement, which provides them with a return of £5 per tonne of recycled waste.

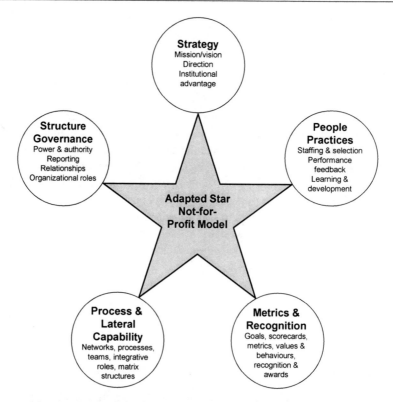

FIGURE 13.1 Star Model adapted to social change organizations

Source: adapted from Galbraith (1995).

processes, people and rewards) essential to changing the culture of an organization (Galbraith 2014; Network for Business Sustainability n.d.). For organization personnel committed to embedding sustainability into their strategy, it is key to know what is on the boardroom agenda.

What's on the boardroom agenda?

In many instances, sustainability initiatives might be pushed for by the operations managers rather than top management. A key question for any person wanting to look at embedding sustainability in an organization, where it is not being led from the top, is to ask: What is on the boardroom agenda? Is compliance linked to sustainability? What about revenue generation? Are directors aware of their personal liability?

The business case for sustainability is growing. Measuring return on investment is essential for any company. When considering what is on the boardroom agenda, using language that the CFO or CEO is familiar with is necessary to obtain *buy in* and support, especially when undertaking standardization practices and processes.

Standards

Codes and standards play an important role in encouraging companies to adopt sustainable practices, as they can provide a common understanding of CSR issues and a more uniform approach to managing environmental, social and economic risks. ISO 26000 and ISO 20121, with their emphasis on sustainable development principles, have changed the way organizations think about social and environmental impacts. Certification also informs customers that a supplier (for example, food caterers to a venue, such as Sodexho) implemented a management system conforming to certain standards. The use of standards to reduce adverse environmental impacts is established (Theron and McKenzie 2012: 24).

What is ISO 20121?

ISO 20121 is one example of a framework for the implementation of a sustainable management system and is a standard designed to help organization personnel in the events industry to improve the sustainability of their event-related activities, products and services. It is intended to integrate sustainability into the management practices of events, sports and hospitality industries – operationally and strategically. It can be applied by any organization in the events sector, including organizers, venues and suppliers.

It is based on a British predecessor from 2007, the *BS901 Specification for a Sustainability Management System for Events*, and was formally launched for the London Olympics in 2012 (Lambert 2013). The involvement of the London Organising Committee of the Olympic and Paralympic Games (LOCOG) in developing the standard means it is an important part of the London 2012 legacy (Queen Elizabeth Olympic Park 2014). A year on from the event, its proliferation

CASE STUDY 13.2: SUSTAINABILITY AS A PART OF THE GAME PLAN

The London 2012 Olympics

Sustainability was given a prominent role in the build up towards and throughout the duration of the event. In many ways, the event created a platform for promoting sustainability leadership in the sports sector by making it a priority of the Games and elevating its exposure in the public eye. The event has undoubtedly shaped the entire sporting community's attitude towards the importance of its own sustainability, but to what end and extent is not clear.

Obtaining sponsorship

Above all, the event confirmed the marketing value of sustainability strategies. In particular, the London Organising Committee of the Olympic and Paralympic Games (LOCOG) was able to use its sustainability strategy to engage with sponsors, many of whom wanted to improve their own sustainability credentials by collaborating with the Olympics and becoming associated with London 2012.

Legacy

LOCOG personnel sought to demonstrate strong sustainability leadership and did so to great effect. For many sporting organizations, the event is likely to have put sustainability on the map for the first time. However, there is also a question of whether the Olympics can be criticized for overshadowing the achievements of venues who have been pursuing a sustainability strategy for a longer term and whose practices have been developed to a higher standard than those adopted by LOCOG during London 2012.

Some context is also required. Undeniably the Olympics raised the profile of sustainability in the sport and event sector significantly, and this merits special recognition as there may be less motivation to implement a sustainability strategy when there is no long-term gain involved. Contrastingly, ensuring good sustainability credentials is easier when limited to a particular event, albeit very complex and large-scale, and for a set duration. Although desirable, it is perhaps less realistic for venues to fervently prioritize sustainability habitually and it is more interesting to see how venues used during the Olympics, such as ExCel, continue to demonstrate leadership and make sustainability core to its business on an on-going basis.

in the sporting sector began to take off. ISO 20121 requires organizational personnel to focus on the following aspects:

- economic – operating in a way that is financially viable for the organization and its customers and suppliers;
- environmental – minimizing the use of resources and reducing waste;
- social – considering the needs and expectations of those affected by the organization or event.

(International Organization for Standardization 2014)

Although it follows the same formula as other ISO standards, namely a PLAN, DO, CHECK and ACT process, it is not a tick box system or checklist. This distinguishes it from the ASTM General Meetings Standards, too (ASTM 2014). ASTM, previously known as the American Society for Testing and Materials, is an international technical standards body. Through the implementation of ISO 20121, an organization involved in the events sector can innovate, drive continuous improvement and add value. These are broader business benefits, which should translate into financial gain, as well as cultural and performance gains.

This means that ISO 20121 is not only about environmental or *green* issues, and it is not the same as ISO 14001, which is an international standard for environmental management. ISO 14001 only deals with environmental impacts, whereas ISO 20121 is a holistic standard, which requires leadership, understanding the internal and external risks to the organization, and an emphasis on communication and supply chain awareness. These are all critical elements of a comprehensive and systematic sustainability strategy (CLT envirolaw 2014a).

CASE STUDY 13.3: THE VALUE OF STANDARDS

The Aviva Stadium in Dublin, Ireland, is BS901 certified. The venue's business case (Kirwan 2013) demonstrates the broad benefits of implementing a sustainability management system, as a result of improved processes and operations. Effective waste and resources management strategies have led to the following:

- 400,000 litres of water saved annually;
- use of low-impact materials such as GGBS concrete saved approximately 4,000 t CO_2 in embodied energy;
- CO_2 savings equate to removing 1,280 vehicles from the road for one year;
- 62 per cent of all waste generated recycled in 2012;
- diesel oil generator reduced carbon emissions by 50 per cent;
- electrical usage was reduced by 26 per cent between 2010 and 2011.

The significant savings have released €100,000 to be spent on an annual community fund.

CASE STUDY 13.4: LEGAL COMPLIANCE AND BEST PRACTICE

Part of ISO 20121 is moving towards best practice and ensuring continuous improvement in the operation of the sustainability management system. A crucial stepping stone in understanding how to move beyond compliance is being able to understand what compliance requirements an organization is subject to in the first place and being able to demonstrate compliance clearly.

CLT envirolaw assisted UBM Live, an events organizer, in developing a bespoke and comprehensive register outlining all mandatory and voluntary developments in sustainability. The company was able to get a clear understanding of its legal obligations in different regions of operation and thereby minimize the risk of liability under packaging and waste regulations, for example. Arguably the ROI in some instances of non-compliance far outweighed the investment in developing the process, as the fines for non-compliance could have extended upwards of £¼ million in this particular case.

Moreover, from the register the organization was able to identify areas where moving towards best practice was feasible and realize continuous improvement.

Drivers and benefits vs barriers and costs

Drivers: return on investment

Organizational change generally occurs for two key reasons – to capture opportunities or to mitigate risks (Willard 2012: 128). Companies will approach how they want to achieve either of these objectives in different ways. The Ernst & Young report (2010) suggests that companies usually achieve embedding sustainability into their organizations in a three-step process, working from first trying to achieve compliance through to embedding cultural changes. Willard (2012) also describes a three-stage journey from pre-compliance to compliance to beyond compliance. To fully embed sustainability into its organizational strategies and operations, the organization personnel need to develop a business case. This case should include the risks of what might happen if the company does not take action as well as the benefits it can reap if it does. The gains to be made are thus all about making savings and increasing efficiency, as well as demonstrating leadership, enhancing reputation and, hopefully, acquiring a competitive advantage in the market (Kirwan 2013). Willard (2012) articulated the business case and sustainability benefits, as demonstrated in Figure 13.2.

In his book *Leading Change Toward Sustainability*, Doppelt (2009) documents that, although initial investment costs might be required, the returns on implementing sustainability measures are endless. He stated that this conclusion corresponds to

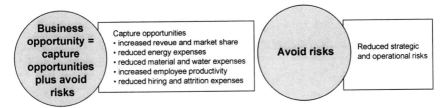

FIGURE 13.2 A business case for sustainability

Source: adapted from Willard (2012: 29).

CASE STUDY 13.5: SUSTAINABILITY SELLS

Both Wembley Stadium and Aviva Stadium have won tenders for hosting events on the back of their sustainability credentials. In Aviva Stadium's business case for sustainability, it states:

> Sustainable venue certification has enabled the stadium to successfully compete for a number of major sporting events including the Europa League Final 2011 and the Heineken Cup Final 2013, while also attracting major corporations for non-match day events such as the Nokia global conference and, more recently, the global launch of BMW's new hybrid car at an event to discuss the future of green motoring.

---

economic benefits documented by leading companies across the globe that have adopted sustainability policies. However, he pointed out that comparatively few organizations in Western society have successfully adopted these measures, leading to an important question – why don't more organization personnel adopt them where the need is perceived as urgent and the benefits potentially great? (Doppelt 2009).

Engagement and stakeholders

Whilst there is a body of research on other drivers pushing companies to work towards fully integrating sustainability into corporate strategy and culture, external stakeholders are increasingly asking companies to account for their sustainability performance. These include the following:

- client requirements;
- equity analysts are including climate change-related factors in the valuation of companies (it can impact on security of supply, for instance);
- investors are increasingly looking at ESG performance data as shareholding periods are getting longer;

- NGOs are drawing public attention to corporate environmental and human rights mishaps through effective campaigns;
- regulators and standard setters – hard and soft law are on the rise;
- banks and insurers are placing more information on building sustainability principles into their underwriting practices and preceding decisions.

(Ernst & Young 2010)

Getting comprehensive information before setting a strategy is therefore crucial. A key part of this is stakeholder engagement, yet a survey by the Chartered Institute of Personnel and Development (CIPD) (Chartered Institute of Personnel and Development 2013) found that only a third of organizations collect information from stakeholders about what responsibilities they see the organization having to the economy, society and the environment.

Decisions by current and potential customers and investors increasingly take into account non-financial information. If the customers and investors in your sector include sustainability performance in their purchasing/investment decisions, then the process of embedding sustainability, including engagement, can help organization personnel assess how to rank high in the purchasing/investment selection (Global Reporting 2011).

CASE STUDY 13.6: BETTER STAKEHOLDER RELATIONS FOSTER INNOVATION

CLT envirolaw assisted in the implementation of ISO 20121 for a global event organizer listed on the FTSE 250. During the second year of the management system's lifecycle, CLT envirolaw ran a stakeholder forum for the company to get all key suppliers involved in the strategy.

By collaborating with the suppliers, the company became more innovative. It was found that companies further down the supply chain had very creative suggestions for measures that could be implemented in the sustainability strategy. An example was the recycling of PVC banners to manufacture school bags which were then shipped by a supplier to a charity in Africa. Usually the recycling of PVC banners is a problem as they do not biodegrade and finding uses for them post an exhibition is challenging. This suggestion led to a win–win situation:

- the organization met its waste minimization objectives, and
- tied this into a community project that supported its social goals and thereby provided a tangible benefit to a community.

Organizations that are more likely to be assessed in these areas by their stakeholders are those that:

- have high brand presence;
- work in an industry currently that has high environmental or social impacts; or
- are listed on any sustainability indices (Carbon Disclosure Project 2014; Dow Jones Sustainability Indices 2014; FTSE4Good 2014).

(Globescan 2004)

Attaching the sustainability message to sport is an important opportunity (Balch 2013). By accessing and engaging with the fan base attending live games, for example, initiatives such as Pump It Up by Global Action Plan are able to spread their educational message wide (Global Action Plan 2014). The role of sport fans in assessing non-financial information is also slowly starting to emerge. Recent years have seen a small but growing interest in sporting infrastructure, such as low-carbon stadiums (Balch 2013; Casper *et al.* 2014). However, mega sporting events, such as the 2014 Winter Olympics in Sochi and the upcoming Qatar FIFA World Cup in 2022, saw a rise in civil society campaigners and trade unionists seeking to highlight a range of social and environmental concerns across the event lifecycle (Institute for Business and Human Rights 2013).

Benefits

The benefits of embracing sustainability organizationally, operationally and strategically overlap with the drivers. However, it is important to note that many organization personnel recognize, or are likely to experience, unanticipated benefits from embedding sustainability. That is to say, in addition to their original drivers, the benefits have proved far wider than original strategic goals and objectives might have predicted or hoped for. This belief is supported by the quantitative data from the sports sector study described in Case Study 13.8. Whilst the main drivers for participants were cost reduction, reputational enhancement and management of environmental impacts, the resulting benefits, which were highlighted, are as follows:

- cost reduction;
- improved brand image;
- better understanding of legal compliance issues;
- better supply chain management;
- improved stakeholder engagement.

Thus, the process of embedding sustainability properly, which incorporates stakeholder engagement, is in itself seen as valuable to organizations (i.e. the Wembley Stadium example in Case Study 13.7).

CASE STUDY 13.7: SUSTAINABILITY BONUS

According to the UK Government-sponsored engagement scheme, Engage for Success, lack of employee engagement is associated with an existing productivity gap in the UK. Improving engagement could add an estimated £25.8bn to national GDP. Research produced by Hay states that 94 per cent of the world's most admired companies believe that their efforts to engage their employees have created a competitive advantage.

Wembley Stadium, London, in particular highlights the benefits which have resulted from encouraging the active involvement of staff in their environmental initiatives and giving employees greater ownership of sustainability.

Barriers

In the pilot study discussed later on in this chapter (Case Study 13.8), the participants stated that despite socially responsible activities being a seemingly major driver towards sustainability, this has its limitations. Most interviewees complained that their venues can only implement sustainability to the extent that it is possible given a lack of:

- budget;
- stakeholder pressure; and/or
- understanding of how sustainability fits within the broader organization.

When implementing a sustainability management system in adherence to a particular framework or standard, such as ISO 20121, barriers often include:

- lack of *buy in* often due to the use of the language of the standard;
- lack of understanding about the standard;
- complexity of the law;
- a desire to treat it as a box ticking exercise as with some ISO protocols;
- seen as something that was dealt with by the operational managers.

Other general organizational barriers to adopting sustainability measures are (Chartered Institute of Personnel and Development 2013: 16):

- other business objectives take immediate priority;
- the business benefits are not obvious;
- too much focus on short-term goals;
- unwilling to make the required financial investment in corporate social responsibility;
- cynicism from the workforce;

- lack of knowledge across the organization about corporate social responsibility (Casper *et al.* 2012);
- lack of awareness of environmental or sustainability issues more broadly (Casper *et al.* 2012);
- lack of leadership support for corporate social responsibility;
- sustainability or corporate social responsibility is not in anyone's remit/job role;
- lack of capability to put corporate social responsibility into practice.

As noted earlier, top management buy-in is a fundamental starting point in embedding sustainability effectively. If the decision-makers in an organization do not understand the reason for embedding sustainability *properly*, then an organization is unable to unlock its full potential. Embedding sustainability as a strategic issue goes beyond a marketing exercise as its value lies in changing and transforming the culture and operations of an organization. Proper leadership provides direction and cohesion to the range of environmental and social activities undertaken by an organization.

Key costs

In introducing any new concept or process to an organization, or in order to innovate, time and money, to different extents, are prerequisite. This includes making sustainability habitual. Organization personnel contemplating embarking upon a sustainability journey must consider and plan for the following items:

- employee time of those responsible for managing the process (e.g. a sustainability manager);
- employee time of those employees involved in the process (e.g. capturing data and reporting back to management);
- acquiring knowledge and skills (e.g. consultancy and training);
- communications;
- quality assurance to audit performance and obtain third-party certification;
- any technological tool used in the process (e.g. bespoke software for the capturing of data).

Conclusions

The use of the ISO 20121 standard sets a framework for an organization to start its sustainability journey. Strategically, it contributes to the organization's better understanding of its business issues, as well as its environmental, social and economic context issues, as demonstrated by the case study of UBM Live within the events sector (Case Study 13.4).

As part of the process, the organization also has to understand its external environment to achieve its objectives. In the case of UBM Live, a leading

CASE STUDY 13.8: A PILOT STUDY OF THE SPORT SECTOR'S VIEWS ON SUSTAINABILITY STRATEGIES AND THEIR RETURN ON INVESTMENT BY CLT ENVIROLAW

December 2013 Executive Summary

Overview

This report is the product of a pilot study including eight sporting event venues with varying sustainability strategies. The study assessed the drivers and barriers to commencing the implementation of diverse sustainability strategies, such as ISO 20121, and the benefits and costs associated with the implementation of each. In addition to getting participants to fill out a survey questionnaire, CLT envirolaw also interviewed the organizations to assess whether the benefits and costs of the sustainability measures could be translated into financial data to provide a return on investment ('ROI') figure for each sustainability measure, as well as the overall strategy.

Key findings

In summary, the principal driver for participating organizations was achieving cost reductions through measures that could produce a more demonstrable ROI or translate easily to financial gains (e.g. energy management). Some participants noted that for other measures (e.g. stakeholder engagement) not being able to predict ROI was a barrier to implementation. However, once implemented, all participants agreed, when prompted, that the process of implementing these measures provided a wider range of benefits (e.g. improved stakeholder relationships). CLT envirolaw therefore believes that translating intangible benefits into more tangible data will assist in the selection of, and allocation of resources for, a wider range of beneficial sustainability measures, such as a reduced risk of litigation due to enhanced understanding of legal compliance issues and improved productivity between an organization and its employees, suppliers and other stakeholders. This process will require organizations to gather more detailed data. Some of the pilot study participants noted that this data could be time-consuming to gather. For this reason, CLT envirolaw hopes to research further and determine whether this data could be gathered in a more cost-efficient manner.

Overview of findings

The principal findings can be summarized as follows:

- Cost reduction was the only driver, and lack of budget the only barrier, cited by more than half the organizations in the survey.
- Sustainability measures focused on those areas with the highest potential for cost reductions, particularly in energy management. These were the same measures that some participants were able to provide ROI figures for.
- Venues that are competing for both sporting and commercial events (e.g. ExCel and Millennium Stadium) used their sustainability credentials to attract these customers. Other venues, particularly those associated with well-known brands linked to a single sport (e.g. Lord's and Emirates), did not feel this was a driver.
- Stakeholder engagement was undertaken by all venues as part of their sustainability strategies. All organizations stated that the engagement process had been beneficial.
- Finding it difficult to project direct financial returns for a measure can be a barrier to getting a budget for its implementation. This is particularly the case for social measures such as community engagement.
- The drivers and benefits for ISO 20121 for the participating venues were varied. Some saw it as a seal of approval whilst others used it as a framework for delivering other benefits. All certified or soon-to-be-certified venues believe the standard has overcome the barrier of showing how sustainability fits within the broader strategy of the organization.
- The majority of organizations stated that improved supply chain management and/or understanding of legal compliance issues were a benefit resulting from implementing a sustainability strategy. However, no participant provided ROI figures for these benefits.

Accounting for limitations of data collected

- Interviewees' views do not necessarily reflect the view of the organizations and its entire top management.
- Most participants were situated in London.
- Limited types of sports venues were involved, most of which were used for football and/or rugby.
- Majority of interviewees had a facilities and operations background, which may influence the focus of an organization's sustainability strategy.

Nonetheless, the data clearly shows that internal and external pressures will vary according to whether venues are multi-use or used predominantly for a single sport. It also provided insights on how these different pressures can influence a sustainability strategy, particularly its span and level of implementation. Moreover, there was a high degree of commonality between participants' answers during both the survey and interview stages. Whether information on ROI can be readily produced or not will be similar across all types of venues as it is more related to the nature of the sustainability measure than the type of sporting venue and its location. For instance, no participant was able to provide a figure representing the financial gains from the more intangible, but nonetheless expressly acknowledged, benefits associated with sustainability strategies.

Quantitative data taken from the survey

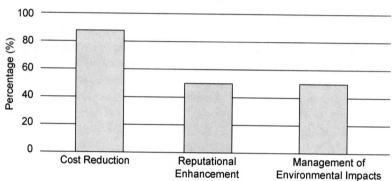

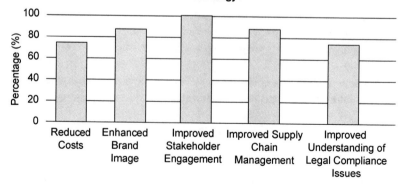

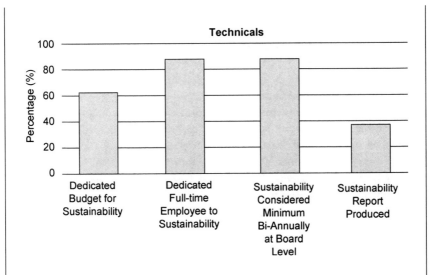

Next steps

The pilot study brought to light patterns which are worth investigating further. Additional respondents will help shed more light on these patterns as well as improve the quality of our sample and the credibility of our findings. Further respondents will help to determine whether ROI is generally included in choosing a sustainability strategy and assessing its impact, and whether there is potential to gather more specific information around the wider range of benefits, such as improved internal and external stakeholder relations, reputation enhancement and reduced staff turnover, leading to higher productivity.

If sufficient information is gathered, it may be possible to develop guidelines to help organizations project and/or determine the ROI for their sustainability strategies. Further recommendations for the following phase of this study are outlined at the end of the report. To view the full report visit www.clt-envirolaw.com/introductory-guides-research-and-reports.

business-to-business company (i.e. exhibition events), and other organizations adopting ISO 20121 (e.g. the Millennium Stadium in London), third-party certification and maintaining this certification to preserve reputation and ensure continuous improvement has meant that year on year the company's performance has grown, both in terms of maturing and measuring the impacts of the system. Critically, it has begun to show savings across operations, including those falling outside the scope of the system, making ROI a key feature of its worth. For example, UBM Live saved €15,000 in printing costs by reducing printed catalogues, and a potential energy saving cost of €10,939 at one of their exhibitions.

The role of standards, therefore, should not be underestimated in finding a prac-tical means to embed sustainability. However, the use of standards is conceptually very new to the sporting industry where *sustainability* and *corporate social responsibility* are more familiar. There is also the drawback of standards being treated as tick box exercises which inhibit progress; they are treated as a ceiling rather than a starting point in moving towards best practice.

The principal driver for participating organizations in the pilot study shown in Case Study 13.8 was achieving cost reductions, with measures that could produce a more demonstrable ROI or translate easily to financial gains (e.g. energy manage-ment). Some participants noted for other measures (e.g. stakeholder engagement) that not being able to predict ROI was a barrier to implementation. However, once implemented, all participants noted, when prompted, that the process of implementing these measures provided a wider range of benefits (e.g. improved stakeholder relationships). Thus, translating intangible benefits into more tangible data will assist in the selection of, and allocation of resources for, a wider range of beneficial sustainability measures.

This process will require organization personnel to gather data to reduce the risk of litigation due to enhanced understanding of legal compliance issues and improve productivity between an organization and its employees, suppliers and other stakeholders. Some of the participants in the pilot study (CLT envirolaw 2014b) noted that this data could be time-consuming to gather. Being able to pro-duce a projected ROI figure for measures is widely seen as conducive to acquiring management buy-in and securing a sufficient budget for measures.

Areas for future research

The pilot study provided up-to-date information on the view of sustainability strategies in the sporting sector and identified patterns worthy of further explora-tion (CLT envirolaw 2014b). Additional respondents should help develop further insights on these patterns. However, in order to produce more financial data on the benefits attested by participants, a few alterations need to be made to the existing method. Potential improvements might be:

- requesting more detailed information on the cost of implementing various sustainability measures, in terms of time, money and other resources invested;
- ranking of the different drivers, barriers and benefits by each participant to assign a weight to the different points raised;
- more questions around growing legal compliance risks which organizations are facing;
- focusing more in the interviews on the potential for gathering ROI for each measure – for example, by:
  - gathering information through employee, sponsor/investor and/or sup-plier surveys; or

- considering the potential litigation costs or fines as a result of non-compliance with legal obligations.

References

ASTM. (2014) 'Home'. Available online at www.astm.org/ABOUT/overview.html (accessed 23 May 2014).

Balch, O. (2013) 'Sustainability and aports: A winning behaviour change combination?' *The Guardian*, 2 December.

Carbon Disclosure Project. (2014) 'Home'. Available online at https://www.cdp.net/en-US/Pages/HomePage.aspx (accessed 23 May 2014).

Casper, J. M., Pfahl, M. E., and McSherry, M. (2012) 'Athletics department awareness and action regarding the environment: A study of NCAA athletics department sustainability practices'. *Journal of Sport Management*, 26: 11–29.

Casper, J. M., Pfahl, M. E., and McCullough, B. (2014) 'Intercollegiate sport and the environment: Examining fan engagement based on athletics department sustainability efforts'. *Journal of Issues in Intercollegiate Athletics*, 7: 65–91.

Chartered Institute of Personnel and Development. (2013) 'The role of HR in corporate responsibility'. Available online at www.cipd.co.uk/hr-resources/research/role-hr-corporate-responsibility.aspx (accessed 23 May 2014).

CLT envirolaw. (2014a) 'Introductory guide on ISO 20121'. Available online at http://clt-envirolaw.com/introductory-guides-research-and-reports (accessed 23 May 2014).

CLT envirolaw. (2014b) 'A pilot study on the sports sector's views on sustainable strategies and their return on investment'. Available online at http://clt-envirolaw.com/introductory-guides-research-and-reports (accessed 23 May 2014).

Doppelt, B. (2009) *Leading Change Toward Sustainability*. Sheffield, United Kingdom: Greenleaf Publishing.

Dow Jones Sustainability Indices. (2014) 'Dow Jones Sustainability Indices'. Available online at www.sustainability-indices.com (accessed 23 May 2014).

Earthshift. (2011) 'Sustainability return on investment (S-ROI)'. Available online at www.earthshift.com/start/sustainability-return-on-investment-sroi (accessed 23 May 2014).

Elkington, J. (1998) 'Partnerships from cannibals with forks: The triple bottom line of 21st-century business'. *Environmental Quality Management*, 8: 37–51.

Ernst & Young. (2010) 'The sustainability journey: From compliance, to opportunity, to integration'. Available online at www.tapestrynetworks.com/documents/Tapestry_EY_ACLN_InSights_Aug10.pdf (accessed 23 May 2014).

FTSE4Good. (2014) 'FTSE4Good ESG ratings'. Available online at www.ftse.com/products/indices/FTSE4Good (accessed 23 May 2014).

Galbraith, J. (1995) *Designing Organizations: An Executive Briefing on Strategy, Structure, and Process*. San Francisco, CA: Jossey-Bass.

Galbraith, J. (2014) 'Star Model'. Available online at www.jaygalbraith.com/images/pdfs/StarModel.pdf (accessed 23 May 2014).

Global Action Plan. (2014) 'Pump it up: The sustainable travel plan with a difference'. Available online at http://managingpartnergap.co.uk/Attachments/journey_march_11_a3 (accessed 23 May 2014).

Global Reporting. (2011) 'Starting points: GRI sustainability reporting: How valuable is the journey?' Available online at https://www.globalreporting.org/resourcelibrary/Starting-Points-2-G3.1.pdf (accessed 23 May 2014).

Globescan. (2004) 'Guess what? People do read CSR reports'. Available online at www.globescan.com/news_archives/csr04_gri_PR.html (accessed 23 May 2014).

Institute for Business and Human Rights. (2013) 'Striving for excellence: Mega sporting events and human rights'. Available online at www.ihrb.org/pdf/2013-10-21_IHRB_Mega-Sporting-Events-Paper_Web.pdf (accessed 11 October 2014).

International Organization for Standardization. (2014) 'Home'. Available online at www.iso.org/iso/home.html (accessed 23 May 2014).

Lambert, G. (2013) 'International Standards Organization, 9 January'. Available online at www.iso.org/iso/home/news_index/news_archive/news.htm?Refid=Ref1690 (accessed 1 May 2014).

Larrinaga-Gonzalez, C. and Bebbington, J. (2001) 'Accounting change or institutional appropriation? A case study of the implementation of environmental accounting'. *Critical Perspectives on Accounting*, 12: 269–92.

Kirwan, P. (2013) 'The business case for sustainability: The Aviva Stadium'. Available online at www.ecocem.ie/uploads/news/1357570027.pdf (accessed 23 May 2014).

Mathews, M. R. (1997) 'Twenty-five years of social and environmental accounting research: Is there a silver jubilee to celebrate?' *Accounting, Auditing & Accountability Journal*, 10: 481–531.

Network for Business Sustainability. (n.d.) 'Embedding sustainability into organizational culture: Framework and best practices'. Available online at http://nbs.net/wp-content/uploads/CultureReport_v4_F2.pdf (accessed 23 May 2014).

Queen Elizabeth Olympic Park. (2014) 'The park'. Available online at http://queenelizabetholympicpark.co.uk/the-park (accessed 23 May 2014).

Savitz, A. (2013) *The Triple Bottom Line: How Today's Best-run Companies are Achieving Economic, Social and Environmental Success – and How You Can Too*. San Francisco, CA: John Wiley & Sons.

Theron, C. and McKenzie, S. (2012) 'Exploring the nexus between sustainability standards and sustainability legislation as drivers to improved sustainability in business'. Available online at http://clt-envirolaw.com (accessed 11 October 2014).

Whistler 2020. (2011) 'Does sustainability cost more?' Available online at www.whistler2020.ca/whistler/site/genericPage.acds?instanceid=1967867&context=1967866 (accessed 23 May 2014).

Willard, B. (2012) *The New Sustainability Advantage*. British Columbia, Canada: New Society Publishers.

World Health Organization. (2014) 'Universal access'. Available online at www.who.int/hiv/universalaccess2010/worldsummit.pdf (accessed 23 May 2014).

14

SUSTAINABILITY AND SPORT SPONSORSHIPS

Izabel Loinaz and Ryan Cabinte

Overview

This chapter outlines the basic structure of sponsorships associated with sport organization-led sustainability initiatives. The reader is first given a general overview of the sponsorship market and activities. Then the chapter covers objectives, metrics, activations, and key success factors of this category of sponsorships. Throughout the chapter, case studies are highlighted to help the reader further understand the application of sustainability partnerships between sponsors and sports organizations.

Introduction

We are in an era of unprecedented opportunity for brands to participate in sponsorship relationships with sports organizations through more activations and platforms than previous decades. There is more opportunity for value alignment and true partnerships in boosting brand affinity, creating impactful programs, supporting shared value initiatives, and improving the overall performance of both the sports organizations and corporate business practices. Sustainability platforms have opened up yet another avenue for engaging in partnerships, garnering new revenue opportunities for rights holders and communication channels for brands.

The defining characteristic of the connection between sustainability, sports, and sponsorships is innovation, giving both parties a platform for a meaningful storytelling. This platform can be leveraged for an impactful and lasting win–win relationship that meets the objectives set forth by both the sponsor and the sports organization.

Sponsorship market

Before examining sustainability-related sports sponsorship, it is useful to understand the sports sponsorship market in general. Companies generally engage in sponsorship activities to create promotional opportunities, improve community relations, improve brand awareness, foster favorable company and brand associations, and create entertainment opportunities. Companies seek *sports* sponsorship as a way to obtain more value than traditional marketing channels. Sports fans are thought to be more receptive to marketing messages due to a sense of loyalty to the team, region, athletes, or sports. Moreover, sports-related sponsorships offer an enhanced ability to identify the brand within a geographical region, or highlight particular products or brand attributes associated with the sports rights holder, such as health and wellness, competitiveness, excitement, excellence, tradition, fair play, inclusiveness, or dependability.

According to IEG (a sponsorship firm in Chicago), in North America alone sponsorship spending totaled $20.6 billion for 2014 and is projected to grow to $21.4 billion in 2015 (IEG, 2015). To put this in perspective, sponsorship spending is equal to one-third of US television advertising spending. Of the $20.6 billion, 70 percent represents sports sponsorship spending, totaling $14.35 billion. Sponsorship spending has been growing steadily between 3.9 and 5.9 percent annually in a post-2008 economy (IEG, 2015).

On a global level, North American sponsorships represent the largest percentage of spending at 37 percent of a total $55.3 billion in 2014 and a projected $57.5 billion in 2015. Europe and Asia Pacific comprise the bulk of the remaining market at 26 percent and 23 percent respectively. Although Central and South America held 7 percent for 2014, these markets are rapidly growing, in large part due to the major sporting events of the 2014 FIFA World Cup and 2016 Summer Olympics, both held in Brazil. FIFA raised $1.4 billion in sponsorship revenue for the 2014 World Cup, a 10 percent increase from the previous tournament in South Africa (Montesinos, 2014).

Defining the sustainability sponsorship market

While there is little quantitative study of the market for sustainability-related sports marketing, the general contours and players are nevertheless well defined: *sponsors* partner with *rights holders* to convey messages about sustainability to *consumer audiences* aggregated by the rights holders. Key classes of rights holders in this market include teams, venues, leagues, individual athletes, jewel events, and collegiate athletics departments. Both sponsors and rights holders seek to convey sustainability messages in response to prevailing trends in consumer interest in sustainability and corporate social responsibility.

In the overall consumer market, sustainability is increasingly important to consumers. In a report produced by WBCSD (2008), an international business leadership and sustainability consortium, 65 percent of consumers say they feel "a sense of responsibility to purchase products that are good for the environment and society." This is a trend reflected in the target market of sports entities and sponsors as well. In an attempt to track fan attitudes around the environmentally branded NASCAR Green, Michael Lynch (NASCAR's Managing Director of Green Innovation) said, "Four years ago, NASCAR fans tracked with the baseline of the U.S. population," when it came to being green. "Today, NASCAR fans are 50% more likely than non-fans to consider themselves green…and avid NASCAR fans are 100% more likely" (Crespin, 2012).

In a survey conducted by Turnkey Sports & Entertainment in 2014, 81 percent of sports fans said they cared about the environment and 73 percent said they worry for younger generations in respect to the state of the environment (Broughton, 2014). This is compared to the national average in a poll conducted by the Harris Poll in 2013, finding 62 percent stated they cared about the environment (19 percent below sports fans) and 63 percent were concerned for future generations (10 percent below sports fans). Furthermore, in this same survey, 43 percent of fans reported they were more likely to support a sponsor of a property that engages in green practices.

For universities, a competitive advantage for attracting and recruiting perspective students now includes the students' perception of the university's commitment to sustainability. According to the Princeton Review's Guide to 322 Green Colleges, among the 9,955 college applicants surveyed in 2013, 62 percent said information regarding a college's commitment to the environment had an impact on the student's decision to apply to or attend the school (Princeton Review, 2013). As one of the largest vehicles for broadcasting its brand and values, a university's athletic program can be key in communicating a commitment to sustainable practices and an attractive activation platform for corporate sponsors.

Lastly, there is a rise in corporations integrating sustainability into the brand identity, with 80 percent of the largest 250 global corporations publishing a Corporate Social Responsibility (CSR) report (KPMG, 2013). Some are going as far as publishing integrated financial reports. Of the S&P 500 companies, 65 percent publish a sustainability-related monetary estimate in a Form 10-K, and 7 of the companies are publishing a true integrated financial and sustainability report (Investor Responsibility Research Center Institute, 2013). Historically, the first integrated report was published in 2011 by the sports apparel giant Puma, one of the most active sponsors of world sports, from national teams to clubs and individual athletes (Puma, 2011). These are the types of corporations with a sustainability story to tell and are looking to partnerships with sports organizations as a platform for amplifying the message.

Objectives, metrics, and activations

Because sponsorship messages typically seek to affect consumer attitude, as opposed to generate direct sales, detecting and quantifying return on investment (ROI) is perhaps one of the more complicated and difficult aspects of sponsorship.

Measurement of success can be further complicated by the integration sustainability objectives and metrics, such as with a Green Sports Score Card or CSR goals.

Therefore, participants in the market for sustainability-related sports sponsorship must establish clear *objectives* of the sponsorship, and definable *metrics* that will be used to measure those objectives. Without such clarity, practitioners will find it difficult selecting appropriate *activations* to generate these outcomes and, in the worst cases, be subject to consumer perceptions of greenwashing. This section outlines some commonly pursued objectives and metrics, with activations used to obtain these goals.

Objectives

The relationship between corporate sponsors and rights holders can be characterized as one of symbiotic objectives. At its most basic, corporations are seeking visibility and brand lift by association with a favorable rights holder, and rights holders are seeking revenue opportunities and community involvement partners.

Sponsors

Sponsors are typically divided into two major categories:

- corporations, generally characterized as for-profit entities; and
- organizations, such as government agencies and non-profits.

For the corporations, a sponsorship engagement is part of the company's marketing mix, on average about 18 percent of the marketing budget (IEG, 2013). The main objectives of corporate sponsorship deals are to (IEG, 2013):

- increase brand loyalty (80 percent);
- create awareness/visibility (77 percent);
- change or reinforce image (65 percent);
- showcase community/CSR (51 percent).

Rights holders

The top objective of rights holders universally can be characterized as revenue generating. Sponsorship revenue is a significant percentage of a sport entity's revenue budget. For example, the National Football League garnered $1.07 billion in sponsorship revenue during the 2013 season, constituting approximately 17 percent of the overall revenue (IEG, 2014a). The National Basketball Association's sponsorship revenue was at 14 percent for the 2013 season (IEG, 2014b). However, revenue from sponsorships can be far more sustaining for an organization such as the International Olympic Committee, which relies on 45 percent revenue from sponsorship deals (International Olympic Committee, 2014). Leveraging multiple platforms for sponsorship activations, such as adding sustainability partnerships to the mix, is a bottom-line imperative.

As with any sponsorship engagement, the alignment of objectives between the sponsor and rights holder with a sustainability platform is paramount for a successful partnership. Many of these objectives are implemented to fund programs or initiatives not fully allocated in the operating budget.

An example of this alignment is the prevalence of renewable energy installations such as solar arrays and wind turbines (see Case Study 14.1). In this type of partnership model, the company gains exposure, brand lift, and engagement while, quite often, the rights holder receives free or discounted products and services, offsetting the capital investment and reducing the cost risk barrier.

CASE STUDY 14.1: SOLAR ENERGY

Arizona Public Service (APS), in partnership with the Arizona Diamondbacks (Chase Field) and the Phoenix Suns (US Airways), has maintained ownership of a collective 1,302 solar panels between the two sports facilities, producing approximately 420,000 kWh annually (NRDC, 2014). The sports facilities serve as the host site for the solar installations, as well as co-branded activation platforms for communicating the sustainability values of each partner. The solar power feeds into the grid, and the sports facility operators purchase the solar energy through a Power Purchase Agreement with APS.

In many cases, the ability to achieve sustainability goals is dependent on influencing the behaviors of employees, concessionaires, and fans, such as waste diversion (recycling, compost, and excess material donations), water use, and energy efficiency. In partnership with a sponsor, a sports organization can leverage brand awareness to strengthen education and behavior change campaigns aimed at achieving goals such as zero waste (see Case Study 14.2).

Metrics

Once the objectives of potential partnerships are identified, setting appropriate metrics to gauge the performance of sponsorship activity in meeting those objectives is necessary. As mentioned above, because the direct effects of sponsorship tend to be based in consumer attitude, detecting and quantifying return on investment is one of the more complicated aspects of sponsorships.

Generally, the top three most valuable metrics favored by sponsors are:

- awareness of the overall brand;
- awareness of a specific product or program;
- attitude towards the brand or program.

(IEG, 2013)

CASE STUDY 14.2: WASTE DIVERSION

Coca-Cola and the Atlanta Braves partnered to help the Braves improve the recycling rate in Turner Field. The campaign leveraged the brand visibility of Coca-Cola, with Coca-Cola-shaped recycling bins placed around the stadium. The PET bottles collected were then recycled into a post-consumer fabric to produce 2,000 stadium staff uniforms. Embroidered on each of the shirts, next to the logos of the Braves and Coca-Cola, is the number of bottles used to manufacture each garment (Little, 2010). The shirts attracted great attention from the fans and provided an education opportunity for the Braves to communicate how the fans can be a part of the organization's sustainability goals.

BASF, the largest global chemical company, has activated several partnerships in college athletics and pro sports to demonstrate how the company "creates chemistry for a sustainable future" (BASF, 2014). In pursuit of a common goal, BASF is the official Zero Waste partner of both the Seattle Mariners and University of Colorado Athletics. BASF provides not only the materials necessary to achieve a goal of zero waste (featuring compostable bags made from the company's branded ecovio®) but also promotes fan engagement campaigns aimed at educating and inspiring the public to adopt more sustainable practices beyond the stadium. Sustainable Saturdays at Safeco Field (Seattle Mariners) and Sustainable Games at the Coors Event Center (University of Colorado) occur at regular intervals throughout the season, with activations of media centers and promotional contests, to energize the fans to participate in the waste diversion efforts.

These metrics hold true for sustainability sponsorships as well. The ROI is dependent on the ability of both parties to stimulate the interest of the fans enough to create a lasting impression of the message of environmental value and stewardship.

When evaluating sponsorship performance, rights holders must consider the following:

- Sponsor satisfaction – Are there sufficient activation opportunities to serve current sponsors and attract new sponsors? Are the sponsors reaching their goals through the activations?
- Sponsorship revenue – Are the partnerships satisfying revenue goals?
- Sponsorship contribution to goals of the rights holder – How are the sponsorship activations contributing to the sustainability goals of the sports organization?

The majority of the data for these metrics are collected from surveys, headcounts, and digital tracking.

Activations

When the top objectives and metrics are brand awareness and attitude, the more the sponsor can interface with the fans while the fans have a positive overall feeling, the more successful the activation. Providing multiple platforms for visibility and engagement improves results and attracts high-quality sponsors. Some of the highest ticket partnerships involve naming rights and business-to-business (B2B) exclusivity.

Traditionally, the top leveraged activations or channels are:

- naming rights;
- public relations;
- social media;
- internal communications;
- hospitality;
- merchandising.

(IEG, 2013; IMR Sports Marketing, 2010)

Activations around sustainability partnerships are part of the multi-platform offering, providing additional opportunities for existing sponsors to diversify messaging and fan engagement. This diversification opportunity further strengthens the relationship between the sponsor and rights holder.

Since much of the sustainability messaging in sponsorships involves an educational component, many of the sustainability platform activations lend themselves to a more immediate experience of the products or programs for the fans. This creates an opportunity for a deeper emotional imprint, eliciting the positive feeling of participating in a solution for the greater good, and therefore elevating the attitude associated with the brand (see Case Study 14.3).

CASE STUDY 14.3: PARTNERSHIP IN INNOVATION

BASF has partnered with University of Michigan Athletics and University of Texas Athletics to sponsor activations called Team Chemistry Challenge. For the top prize of $25,000, each school hosts competitions between student teams with the challenge of devising solutions to reducing the environmental impacts of game-day events. Team Chemistry Challenge is one of a handful of activations BASF and the universities have implemented to highlight the role of chemistry, innovation, and athletics in sustainable development (BASF, 2014).

Key success factors in sustainability sponsorships

Three key factors commonly characterize a successful sports sponsorship with a sustainability platform:

- authentic alignment in the partnership;
- creating a green brand or identity;
- effectively communicating the story.

Each of these success factors should not be considered in isolation, but as components that build upon each other to optimize the success of the partnership. The foundation of a successful sponsorship should assure all aspects of the sponsorship have integrity and authenticity to all of the partners. Communicating a consistent story across all platforms supports the authentic connection of the partners and their intended outcomes. The most successful stories will often create a *green* brand or identity and ultimately be directly linked to the partners' core business strategy.

Authenticity of alignment

The foundation of any successful partnership is an authenticity of alignment between the partnering organizations. If a sponsorship activation is not believable to a consumer, both brands are at risk of losing credibility. This is particularly true with sustainability-related sponsorships, which inherently evoke the value of transparency and which consumers increasingly scrutinize for greenwashing.

This alignment is both an opportunity and a risk. For those companies searching for a platform to tell its own story and are authentically integrating sustainability as part of their brand, aligning with a sports organization with similar values is a tremendous opportunity. Companies not secure in their positioning around the environment and social issues have much to lose if they over-communicate the importance of the sustainability attributes of their sponsorship. This may deter some otherwise worthy partnerships out of fear of consumer backlash.

Creating a green brand or identity

While creating a separate green or sustainability brand is not a necessity for successful sponsorships, doing so provides a succinct tool for communicating a commitment to environmental stewardship. A green brand does not profess achievement of superiority—rather it communicates a commitment to the pursuit of improvement through evaluation, performance, and innovation. A stand-alone green brand creates its own visibility and recognition, making it easier to leverage and scale. Lastly, in order to maintain integrity of commitment, the green brand must be directly linked to the core business strategy and values (see Case Study 14.4).

CASE STUDY 14.4: NASCAR GREEN

NASCAR Green was created in 2008. Today the brand has grown to secure 22 official NASCAR Green partners, from Coca-Cola Recycling to Liberty Tire (the Official Tire Recycler), and nearly 60 additional corporate sponsorships. With over 100 sanctioned tracks, there are numerous opportunities for sponsorship activations—for example, 3M's solar installation of 40,000 panels at the Poconos Raceway, the largest of its kind in the world housed in a sports facility. The NASCAR Green brand allows for consistent communication and guidance for its 13 NASCAR-owned tracks as well as enhancing initiatives implemented by individual tracks (NASCAR, 2014).

Effectively communicating the story

A sponsor partnership is largely about communicating stories that enhance brand awareness and perception, and authentically aligning values, culture, and product with that brand. As mentioned earlier, authenticity is the guiding principle in communicating sustainability messaging. In some successful partnerships, it is not strictly about sustainability as it is about telling a story of innovation and performance. Clarity in the storyline and the understanding of the audience are the fundamentals of crafting an effective sustainability story.

The primary storyline can be about environmental stewardship, social benefit, performance, and efficiency, or any other host of categories. Alignment and consistency of the storyline between the partners improves the viability of the story. A compelling sustainability story can be told based on the shared values between stewardship and sports such as: fair play, inclusivity, transparency, opportunities to succeed, and good community relations. Once the storyline is clarified, understanding the behaviors and mindset of the audience will strengthen the context of the story and amplify the effects.

Additional opportunities and challenges

The practice of sustainability-related sports sponsorships carries with it idiosyncratic opportunities and challenges, some of which we have discussed in earlier sections of this chapter. The following are further factors to consider when engaging in sponsorship activities with a sustainability platform.

Opportunities

We previously talked about the opportunity gained by diversification through sustainability sponsorship activations and the benefits of strengthening existing partnerships. An additional benefit to diversification is in opening up the field of sponsorship to previously untapped partner categories. Companies in industries such as waste management and energy, and even corporations with smaller marketing budgets, are now able to compete for partnerships through the sustainability platform of a sports rights holder. "Being environmentally conscious improves our brand's image so that we now talk with companies that never would have approached us before, such as Johnson & Johnson and Georgia Pacific" (Jackie Ventura, operations coordinator for the HEAT Group (Miami Heat); NRDC, 2013: 44).

Sustainability provides a platform for innovation and co-branded product production, as we saw with BASF and Team Chemistry Challenge. The mobile technology market is emerging as an additional co-branding opportunity for innovation. Coupling sustainability and corporate-sponsored mobile apps is a highly evolved opportunity for engagement, education, and data tracking on a mass scale.

Through sponsorships anchored in sustainability, individual athletes, who have previously relegated their environmentalism issues to philanthropy, now have the opportunity to align those values with their sponsors by seeking out partners' values of environmental stewardship and CSR. Nowhere do you see that more than in winter adventure sports due to the profound impact of climate change. Athletes such as pro snowboarder Kimmy Fasani and world champion freeskier Alison Gannett are partnering with corporate sponsors such as Cliff Bar to help promote both their sport and their environmental values.

Challenges

Introducing new initiatives with specific sustainability criteria can potentially cause friction with existing sponsors if there is a resulting conflict of alignment. Collaboration and sensitivity to preserving the endurance of the relationship must be part of the process.

When pursuing sponsorships for sustainability platforms, sports organizations can potentially find it challenging to communicate the value to the various stakeholders in the sponsorship process. The intricate network of marketing, sales, brokers, finance, legal, and sustainability departments can be a challenging web to navigate. Each sports organization and corporate sponsor has its own processes to consider. Again, patience and sensitivity to the nature of these relationships must be employed for the improved chance of a successful partnership.

Conclusion

The new arena of fostering sustainability sponsorship engagements offers great opportunity for innovation, fan engagement, and diversification of partnership activations. With an eye on maintaining authentic alignment, as the story of integrating sustainability is woven through the various channels and platforms of the partnership, implementation of successful sponsorship engagements can be as varied as the brand cultures they represent.

References

BASF (2014) 'News and media relations'. Available online at www.basf.com/group/news-and-media-relations/index (accessed October 15, 2014).

Broughton, D. (2014) 'Study: Green fans willing to spend'. *Sports Business Daily*. Available online at www.sportsbusinessdaily.com/Journal/Issues/2014/07/21/Research-and-Ratings/Green-survey.aspx (accessed July 28, 2014).

Crespin, R. (2012) 'NASCAR Green is Really Purple'. *Forbes*. Available online at www.forbes.com/sites/csr/2012/09/05/nascar-green-is-really-purple (accessed October 12, 2013).

IEG (2013) 'Survey: Sponsors require more agency support, spend less on activation'. Available online at www.sponsorship.com/iegsr/2013/04/22/Survey--Sponsors-Require-More-Agency-Support,-Spen.aspx (accessed October 15, 2013).

IEG (2014a) 'NFL sponsorship revenue totals $1.07 billion in 2013 season'. Available online at www.sponsorship.com/IEGSR/2014/01/27/NFL-Sponsorship-Revenue-Totals-$1-07-Billion-In-20.aspx (accessed October 10, 2014).

IEG (2014b) 'NBA sponsorship revenue totals $679 million in 2013–2014 season'. Available online at www.sponsorship.com/iegsr/2014/08/11/NBA-Sponsorship-Revenue-Totals-$679-Million-In-201.aspx (accessed October 10, 2014).

IEG (2015) 'New Year to be One of Growth and Challenges for Sponsorship Industry'. Available online at www.sponsorship.com/iegsr/2015/01/06/New-Year-To-Be-One-Of-Growth-And-Challenges-for-Sp.aspx (accessed March 11, 2015).

IMR Sports Marketing (2010) 'Sponsorships lead in digital activation'. Available online at www.imrpublications.com/newsdetails.aspx?nid=29 (accessed October 20, 2013).

International Olympic Committee (2014) 'Revenue sources and distribution'. Available online at www.olympic.org/ioc-financing-revenue-sources-distribution?tab=sources (accessed October 10, 2014).

Investor Responsibility Research Center Institute (2013) 'Integrated financial and sustainability reporting in the United States'. Available online at http://irrcinstitute.org/pdf/FINAL_Integrated_Financial_Sustain_Reporting_April_2013.pdf (accessed October 22, 2013).

KPMG (2013) 'The KPMG survey of corporate responsibility reporting'. Available online at www.kpmg.com/Global/en/IssuesAndInsights/ArticlesPublications/corporate-responsibility/Documents/corporate-responsibility-reporting-survey-2013.pdf (accessed October 18, 2013).

Little, A. (2010) 'Can professional sports do more than politics to save the planet?' *Forbes*. Available online at http://blogs.forbes.com/amandalittle/2010/11/15/can-professional-sports-do-more-than-politics-to-save-the-planet (accessed April 12, 2011).

Montesinos, D. (2014) 'FIFA to reap US $1.4 billion in sponsorship revenues from Brazil 2014'. Available online at http://latam.portada-online.com/2014/01/27/fifa-to-reap-1-4-billion-in-sponsorship-revenues-from-brazil-2014 (accessed October 14, 2014).

NASCAR Green (2014) 'Home'. Available online at http://green.nascar.com (accessed October 10, 2014).

Natural Resources Defense Council (NRDC) (2013) 'Game changer: How the sports industry is saving the environment'. Available online at www.nrdc.org/greenbusiness/guides/sports/game-changer.asp (accessed October 18, 2013).

Natural Resources Defense Council (NRDC) (2014) 'Solar electric guide for your stadium or arena'. Available online at www.b-e-f.org/solarguide (accessed October 18, 2013).

Princeton Review (2013) 'Guide to 322 green colleges'. Available online at www.princetonreview.com/uploadedFiles/Sitemap/Home_Page/Campaign/2013/GreenGuide/_MEDIA/2013_green-guide.pdf (accessed November 10, 2013).

Puma (2011) '2011 annual report'. Available online at www.puma-annual-report.com/GB/IndexGBEN.jsp?chapter=06&slide=2 (accessed October 18, 2013).

World Business Council for Sustainable Development (WBCSD) (2008) 'Sustainable consumption facts and trends'. Available online at www.wbcsd.org/pages/edocument/edocumentdetails.aspx?id=142 (accessed October 10, 2013).

SECTION V

Facility and event management

15

PREPARING ENVIRONMENTALLY FRIENDLY EVENTS

*Cheryl Mallen, Chris Chard, Courtney Keogh,
and Adel Mansurov*

Overview

This chapter discusses environmentally friendly sport events, including the concepts of conscious capitalism, Sport-ES², perspicacity, and resilience. The discussion then moves to *sport event environmental managerial performance*, including sport event environmental policy, targets, and considerations for successfully meeting targets. Next, the discussion shifts to *sport event environmental operational performance*, including tracking/monitoring and an environmental audit. Key issues are integrated into the discussion to illustrate the difficulties in activating excellence in environmental safeguards and the need for advanced understandings to ensure the preparations for environmentally friendly sport events are successful.

Introduction

Sport is critically linked to our natural environment and is not immune from the environmental situation. Sports link to nature stems from the utilization of the natural environment as a competition area or venue site. Further, nature also impacts sport. This is shown as extreme weather conditions are playing havoc on winter sport events. For instance, the 2010 Vancouver Olympic Winter Games struggled with an unusual lack of snow (CBC News, 2010) and the preparations for the 2014 Sochi Olympic Winter Games were plagued with flooding in the months prior to the Games (The Associated Press, 2013). Moreover, the 2013 Pure Silk-Bahamas Ladies Professional Golf Association Classic in Nassau, Bahamas, saw a 12-inch (30.5 cm) rain storm that forced officials to shorten the course layout to 12 from 18 holes after six holes were deemed unplayable due to the excessive water collecting on the course (Case, 2013). A conclusion, according to Haigh and Griffiths, is that "when increasingly abnormal extreme weather events…are considered, moral and ethical arguments are overshadowed by the powerful, legitimate, urgent and proximate properties of the natural environment...to be a primary stakeholder" (Haigh and Griffiths, 2009: 356).

There is a growing awareness and concern for the natural environment as a stakeholder in sport (Schmidt, 2006). Literature on the detrimental environmental consequences of sport is mounting, and sport has sought to advance some safeguards. The literature that examines the issue is limited, however, and is based on *the impact of the Olympic Games* (Kearins and Pavlovich, 2002; May, 1995; Paquette et al., 2011), *the production of major championships in rugby* (Collins et al., 2007), *European football* (Dolles and Soderman, 2010), *extreme sports* (Brymer et al., 2009), *motorsport* (Dingle, 2009), and *debating environmentalism in sport* (Mallen and Chard, 2011). Additionally, one of the best sport event environmental action reports to date is the *Olympic Games Impact (OGI) Study for the 2010 Olympic and Paralympic Winter Games Post-Games Report* released in October 2013 (OGI, 2013).

Conscious capitalism in Sport-ES

In this chapter, sport is presented as being able to generate a profit while, simultaneously, acting to safeguard the natural environment through "conscious capitalism" (Mackey and Sisodia, 2013). A mindset for conscious capitalism involves a concern for the natural environment that is integrated within daily activities and, in particular, as an integral part of all decision-making processes. Conscious capitalism can be promoted by any member or organization in sport, such as event managers, athletes, facility managers, spectators, and members of the media. Importantly, a movement to conscious capitalism is growing, despite what is considered a general lack of financial commitment to fully fund environmental activities (Mallen et al., 2011). Evidence illustrates that sport events, and their associated sport facilities, are adapting to incorporate *sport environmental sustainability (Sport-ES)* through a mindset of conscious capitalism by confronting environmental challenges without losing the concept of a profit business model.

Sport events—their unique role in Sport-ES²

Sport events, and their associated sport facilities, are in a unique position as test sites for environmentally sustainable strategies that can then be extended into social life. The ability to try strategies and then communicate successful opportunities associated with sport events incorporating environmental sustainability can aid in educating, promoting, and leading our broader society onto a more sustainable pathway—in a profit-based world. This positions sport to be capable of *sport environmental sustainability²* or *Sport-ES²*; the squared portion represents the role of (1) advancing sport events, and their associated facilities, to be environmentally sustainable, while also (2) leading society in the pursuit of conscious capitalism. This dual-purpose role for sport events is supported through perspicacity and resilience.

Perspicacity

Perspicacity involves an intelligence that offers quick, advanced insights and understandings, and in this instance these elements are noted as key to the successful implementation of sport event environmental sustainability (Mallen and Adams, 2013). This definition implies that, first, if sport events are to truly become environmentally sustainable then the event leadership needs to advance their consciousness for Sport-ES, including being trained to perceive the natural environment as a primary stakeholder of the event. Second, the leadership requires experience that can lead to a synergy of best practices that support Sport-ES².

Resilience

Resilience is a key concept that involves our mental "capacity for renewal, re-organization and development" (Folke, 2006: 253). Importantly, resilience implies that, as we adapt for Sport-ES², we need a mindset that is open for renewing sport event processes, for re-organizing and instituting sport event environmentally friendly options. This resilience mindset understands that there is no requirement to go back to the past status quo in how activities were completed. Sport events can be hardy or robust and can succeed in tandem with environmental pursuits.

Preparing for sport event environmental managerial performance

This chapter now focuses on key elements in sport event environmental managerial performance. Elements within this performance include areas such as policy, targets, committees, and relationships, and implementing strategies for success, stakeholder disclosure, and funding. Key issues and their management will be integrated within the discussion.

Sport event environmental policy

An excellent sport event environmental plan begins with a *policy statement* that promotes environmental sustainability as a priority. An example is found in the International Olympic Committee (IOC) Olympic Charter (2013) that states they will "encourage and support a reasonable concern for environmental issues, to promote sustainable development in sport and to require that the Olympic Games be held accordingly" (p. 17). A further example is the Fédération Internationale de Football Association's (FIFA) (2013: n.p.) statement:

> FIFA is dedicated to taking its environmental responsibility seriously. Issues such as global warming, environmental conservation and sustainable management are a concern for FIFA, not only in regards to FIFA World Cups™, but also in relation to FIFA as an organisation. That is why FIFA has been

engaging with its stakeholders and other institutions to find sensible ways of addressing environmental issues and mitigate the negative environmental impacts linked to its activities.

What do these current policy statements really indicate? Typically, they promote, but do not require, a level of environmental sustainability for a sport event. Although the IOC Charter uses the word *require* in their policy, as do others, there is no penalty for failing to comply. Paquette et al.'s (2011) research found that the Olympic Games *bid committee* promises were not legally based implementation requirements by the *hosting committee*, as they were separate legal entities. Further, the authors of this chapter suggest that the IOC's use of the phrase "a reasonable concern" is open to multiple interpretations. Does this mean do only what is convenient? The Olympic Games Global Impact Study (OGGI), however, is now standard practice and promotes a large number of environmental safeguards to be instituted at the Games, where possible. Current sport event environmental policy statements, thus, generally do not indicate a focus on a required full spectrum of environmental activity, such as safeguarding our water resources, energy resources, the air supply, and land/waste management, or mandate that the safeguards promised in event bids must be instituted.

The authors of this chapter, thus, recommend that a policy statement needs to avoid multiple descriptor statements and be one overarching sentence indicating that the sport event will promote environmental sustainability as a priority. Then, sport event managers should be encouraged to systematically build a standard for sport event environmental sustainability that can be advanced over time. Further, and importantly, the standard environmental targets should have the same value as sport technical requirements at sport events and be mandated for implementation. Soon, the event environmental standards can be incorporated into sanctioning body requirements for hosting particular sports events. The best practices in Sport-ES can be shared and, over time, the events can raise the minimum environmental target requirements, keeping the concept of conscious capitalism as a priority.

Sport event environmental targets

A first step when establishing sport event environmental targets requires visioning an appropriate standardized level of Sport-ES. *If you do not have a vision of how you want to advance sport events so they are environmentally sustainable...then how can you work towards that vision?* Two key resources to aid in the visioning process—or seeing in your mind what level of environmental sustainability that should be pursued—include (1) the Mallen and Chard (2011) framework for *debating the future of environmental sustainability in the sport academy* and (2) the Mallen and Chard (2012) manuscript on *what could be in sport facility environmental sustainability.*

Next, specific sport event environmental targets need to be set that include safeguarding all aspects, including that of land management, water stewardship, energy resources, and air quality management. It is important to work directly with the internal and external stakeholders in developing these targets. The synergy of environmental targets and the activities to safeguard these aspects makes a substantial contribution to Sport-ES. Glavič and Lukman (2007: 1884) provided a list of environmental activities that were arranged on the principles to prevent and control degradation to "form an interconnected system" between organizational activities and the natural environment. An adaptation of their list has been integrated within the bullet points in the targets below. As you read the target information, keep in mind the following:

- *Are we sophisticated enough in sport to move forward for a full spectrum environmental plan (incorporating all target areas: land management, water stewardship, energy resources, and air quality management)? If not, what needs to be done to gain this sophistication?*
- *What is the basic level of Sport-ES that should be enacted at every major sport event (and what is the level for local sport events)?*

Target—land/waste management

Land/waste management involves three key areas, including:

- renewable resources to reduce/mitigate the use of land-based resources and waste;
- regeneration and recovery of resources (recycling, reuse, and repair);
- resource reduction dematerialization (a redesign and remanufacturing of products to ensure the reduction of waste).

A common strategy in waste management involves diverting waste through recycling/composting. The Vancouver Olympic Games reported a waste diversion rate of up to 98 percent (OGI, 2013). Getting proper disposal by patrons at events is, however, generally problematic. Strategies are needed to aid in ensuring disposal is made in the correct bin, including clear signage with pictorial directions and verbiage, in multiple languages if applicable, and having people stationed at every site during the event to guide individuals to complete the task correctly.

Another common strategy in waste management is the reduction/elimination of plastic water bottle use. This strategy has been integrated into multiple events from road races to multi-sport games, albeit not always with a high level of success. It is, thus, important to generate well-conceived implementation compliance-based strategies to aid success. For instance, ensuring all food/beverage contractors follow the no disposable water bottles plan, otherwise some event participants simply bring bottled water from their meal areas to the competition venue; others quickly follow suit. Also, ensuring the use of distributed refillable water bottles is very difficult as participants *forgetting* their bottle cannot be left to get dehydrated. The provision of small disposable cups until event participants retrieve their refillable bottles is a typical response that can prove problematic as the cups can blow onto competition areas and generate spilled water throughout the event areas.

Further, all officials must also be required to use refillable bottles or participants see no reason for their compliance. Signage in residences indicating a need to bring the refillable bottle is necessary, including in all stairwells and elevators, in multiple languages, if applicable; also, reminders at meetings, and buy-in from coaches and administrators, is a necessity for success. Remember, different cultural norms impact personal compliance, and ensuring easy access to low-priced refillable bottles aids in compliance should they forget the bottle they were given initially.

Creative waste management strategies are being generated as well. For instance, all events at the Air Canada Centre, home to professional basketball and hockey events in Toronto, Canada, use a freezer-type chest to dispose of their compost; then bacteria is added and the pile is churned until it becomes a vegetable liquid that flows down a tube directly into the sewer drain. This eliminates the need for 8 dump trucks to haul the material away weekly—the equivalent of 32 full-sized dump truck trips per month hauling approximately 500 metric tons of organic waste offsite annually, saving thousands of dollars in haulage fees per year (Mallen et al., 2013). Additional creative strategies for waste management and compliance are needed.

Target—energy management

Energy management involves three key areas of focus, including:

- minimizing energy demand;
- reclamation of energy for reuse;
- reducing one's carbon footprint to become carbon neutral.

Sport events have been working to reduce their energy demand with better-designed light bulbs and sensors. Additionally, transportation has been a target to reduce energy and the associated greenhouse gases. It was noted that 87.5 percent of the greenhouse gases at the Vancouver Olympic Games was generated from transportation (OGI, 2013), and the public transportation system aided to reduce this patron and athlete impact. Also, the 2006 FIFA World Cup held in Germany reduced energy consumption through an effective management strategy in public transportation (FIFA, 2006).

Some events have calculated their *carbon footprint* and then have worked to become carbon neutral. A carbon footprint comprises "the total set of greenhouse gas emissions caused directly and indirectly by an individual, organization, event, or product" (The Carbon Trust, 2007: 1). To determine the carbon footprint, the emissions produced are calculated, and then reductions can be identified, tracked, monitored, and managed. Numerous carbon calculators can be found online, such as: www.planetair.ca; www.carbonzero.ca; www.terrapass.com; and www.clearwater.org. Once calculated, sport events can become carbon neutral by reducing their impact and/or purchasing carbon offsets.

Carbon offsets can be purchased to make an event carbon neutral. This involves investing in a project, such as a bioenergy project being instituted anywhere in the world. Many of the carbon calculators guide you to bioenergy projects. One easy carbon offset involves "Tree Canada" (https://treecanada.ca/en) that calculates the number of trees needed to offset carbon emissions. You pay then for the trees, and they plant and nurture tree saplings through to maturity for as low as $4.00 CDN per tree.

Additionally, according to Li et al. (2012: 76), renewable energy is currently at 10 percent of our (world) energy options, but "is expected to increase to 60% by 2070." Sport events have been held at sport facilities that use renewable energy source procurers, such as solar and wind energy sources. Interestingly, inventive alternative energy options are on the rise at key facilities hosting major sport events. For instance, Rexall Place, in Edmonton, Canada, recovers the heat released from the ammonia in the cooling compressors to heat water that is then used to melt snow scraped off the ice by the "Zamboni-type" machine in the process of making ice. Also, the Air Canada Centre in Toronto has a "Deep Lake Water Cooling" system that uses a kilometer-long pipe laid deep into Lake Ontario that draws cold water, which is then pushed past large fans to cool air that is pumped into the building for air conditioning; the system eliminates the need for air conditioning compressors (Enwave Energy Corporation, 2014). Further joint sport event and sport facility actions that aid in energy management can advance Sport-ES.

Target—water stewardship

Water stewardship involves three key areas, including:

* minimizing water demand through water conservation;
* reclaiming and reusing water;
* purification and end-of-pipe requirements (ensuring the purification prior to discharge into the water).

Typically, water demand is reduced with the application of products that restrict flow on taps and showers at sport facilities where events are held. Additionally, reclamation strategies involve collecting water as it is being utilized and repurposing it, generally for lawn and flower bed watering. Purification involves purchasing green products and ensuring sourcing/procurement includes products with environmental marks or labels. End-of-pipe involves reducing/eliminating the use of chemicals and ensuring disposal safeguards against pollutants getting into the drinking water and surface water, including items such as: aluminum, arsenic, cadmium, chromium, copper, iron, lead, magnesium, manganese, mercury, zinc, bacteria, viruses, protozoa, ammonia, sodium, Ph, and sulphates (Gunton and Joseph, 2007: 27–8). For instance, the 2013 World Junior Canoe/Kayak Championships in Welland, Canada, tried a novel strategy whereby they stationed the motor boats at sites down the race course. This meant that the boats did not follow each race and, thus, greatly reduced the gasoline and oil discharged into the water source.

Target—air quality stewardship

Air quality stewardship involves two key areas, including:

- reduce emissions;
- end-of-pipe requirements (ensuring the purification prior to discharge into the air).

In air stewardship, the emphasis is on reducing emissions that are typically greenhouse gases or pollutants, including sulphur, nitrogen, carbon monoxide, and particulates. Sport events can manage their transportation activities to reduce emissions in a number of ways, such as following the requirement enforced in the city of San Francisco (USA) to shut vehicles off if they are idling for more than two minutes. Sport events that promote public transport are also aiding in emission reductions.

When it comes to purification of the air, it is suggested that sport events offer air quality testing so athletes, especially those with asthma, understand the air quality environment in which they will compete. The 2015 Pan Am Games in Toronto, Canada, utilized portable air quality testing apparatus developed at the University of Toronto for this purpose. Air testing statements offered proof of air quality and can ensure patrons and athletes are provided with a high level of air quality events. This new equipment may make this testing a standard practice at future sport events.

Air quality levels also provide important information for those managing facilities hosting sport events. For instance, golf industry course superintendents have noted that air quality management is imperative to growing and maintaining healthy grass, particularly on golf greens. This seems applicable to all pitches as well. Adequate air flow allows grass to grow easily, without unnecessary fertilizers and excessive watering. Increased air flow not only allows for more natural grass growth, but also reduces the maintenance required, thereby decreasing the pollution caused by turf equipment (Keogh, 2013). Overall, strategies that reduce emissions by sport event activities to ensure excellent air quality for all event participants is at the primary level and needs to be advanced.

Preparing for sport event environmental operational performance

This chapter now focuses on sport event environmental operational performance based on tracking/monitoring and managing environmental activities for the resulting inputs and outputs expressed within an environmental audit.

Tracking/monitoring and managing environmental activities for success

Setting an environmental target is not enough; sport events need strategies to ensure the success of target safeguards for the natural environment. A key to ensuring success involves tracking/monitoring and the management of each environmental target. This means an event must establish a feedback process that engages with related stakeholders and includes designated timelines in order to continuously develop understandings on the progress towards each target, including if the generated strategies for compliance are being implemented and their success. This is a time-consuming task, but a necessity to ensure results. Otherwise, *greenwashing* can occur. Greenwashing is the act of an event making environmental promises, and gaining pre-event publicity for the environmental plans, that are then not fulfilled. To offset this typical practice of greenwashing, events must develop a standard whereby tracking/monitoring and managing is instituted as best practice and the final environmental outcome reports are the priority.

A sport event environmental audit of the resulting inputs/outputs

One of the hardest activities to complete in safeguarding the natural environment at sport events is to calculate the overall event environmental impact based on the inputs or savings with respect to oil, gas, electrical, water, chemical, paper, etc. usage, as well as the outputs with respect to general waste per ton and emissions, such as carbon dioxide. This can be difficult because strategies for making these calculations at sport events are not generally part of the standard operations and they are time consuming.

It is strongly advised that each sport event manager begin to address this and to complete event environmental audits. These audits are not necessarily for general public distribution; they are for sport events to learn best practices in environmental sustainability and to advance their abilities in this area. Thus, the scope and strategy for reporting must be designed.

Standard reporting frameworks are needed for each sport and their events to make the data comparable between events. A timeframe is needed, along with an overview concerning the distribution of the audit information. The *Olympic Games Impact (OGI) Study for the 2010 Olympic and Paralympic Winter Games Post-Games Report* released in October 2013 is an excellent example, but is an unrealistically high standard for most sport events to complete. Thus, the question arises: *What should a template for an environmental audit and report include for a major sport event?*

It is recommended that you study a number of sport events in order to learn more concerning successful environmental performance. Table 15.1 outlines a framework for the examination, with an aim of enhancing learning about successful event environmental performance.

TABLE 15.1 Considerations for enhancing learning about successful event environmental performance

1. Examine the environmental *policies* established for sport events in your region.	Consider the examination of: • the environmental policy statements; • the associated environmental laws and regulations; • the integration of the environmental safeguards into event contracts.
2. Examine the environmental *targets* established at sport events.	Consider the examination of: • the environmental strategies instituted; • the compliance strategies used to improve the success of the environmental strategies; • the tracking/monitoring of the success of the environmental strategies and the management of arising issues.
3. Examine sport event environmental *best practices*.	Consider the examination of: • what is working well and can be shared as a best practice for use by other sport events instituting environmental practices.
4. Examine stakeholder environmental *buy-in*.	Consider the examination of: • the environmental buy-in that has been achieved from the multiple stakeholders, including the event administrative board of directors, staff/volunteers, coaches, participants, sponsors, host city representatives, and other groups such as interpreters.
5. Examine sport event environmental *documentation disclosure*.	Consider the examination of: • the type of environmental information being disclosed; • the range of quantification and comparability within the disclosed information; • the disclosure method and timing; • what changes in environmental reporting you would like to see that could aid in advancing sport environmental sustainability.

Source: authors.

Finally, certification or standards programs play a part in sport environmental sustainability, although they can be cost prohibitive. Examples of certification programs include the United States Green Building Council's third-party Leadership in Energy and Environmental Design (LEED) certification program for green building construction; and the International Organization for Standardization ISO 20121 Environment Management System. Despite the number of standard organizations and programs, there continues to be issues concerning their use in guiding transformations for environmental safeguards. These standards programs can guide efforts in environmental sustainability; however, they allow each participant to interpret their environmental activities to meet the standard. Also, events can submit what they are planning to complete; fulfillment is not always achieved.

Currently, there are no standard environmental activities that an event must institute, and it is proposed that devising these standards and implementing them can ensure sport events are moving forward in environmental sustainability. Also, importantly, a key issue was outlined on the ISO website whereby environmental sustainability is industry specific, and to meet this need the certification programs "would have to be specific to each business activity and this would require a specific EMS standard for each business" (ISO 14004, 2004, n.p.). Standards, thus, have now been generated specifically for the sport event industry; two such standards for reference include the British Standard for Sustainable Event Management (BS 8901) (www.bsi-global.com/bs8901) and the Canadian Standard Association (CSA) Z2010-10 Requirements and Guidance for Organizers of Sustainable Event (shop.csa.ca).

Finally, there are a number of strategies that have been presented to aid in the advancement of environmental sustainability. For instance, the Life Cycle Assessment (LCA) strategy "measures the impact of products and services 'cradle to grave,' covering the phases of resource extraction, manufacture, distribution, use and disposal" (Dolf, 2011: 8). A recent LCA study by Dolf (2011) offers an excellent example of an examination of a higher education institution, including the environmental impact of the teams, events, and venues. Triple Bottom Line (TBL) focuses on managing all of the costs associated with its activities including social, environmental, and financial (McDonough and Braungart, 2002). Meanwhile, the Triple Top Line (TTL) promotes the integration of sustainability with "accountability [from] the beginning of the design process" (McDonough and Braungart, 2002: 252). Finally, the Balanced Scorecard (BSC) is a reporting tool used to clearly outline all organizational aspects and frame the actions (Braam and Nijssen, 2004).

It is important to note that no matter what strategy is considered, the majority of sport organizations and events operate their environmental plan with limited funding—and this is not expected to change in the near future. Yet, conscious capitalism indicates that events can be operated with an environmental focus and still be profit-driven. Creative and innovative event managers are, thus, succeeding despite the lack of funding.

Conclusions

This chapter defined sustainability, conscious capitalism, Sport-ES^2, perspicacity, and resilience. Further, the discussion outlined key areas in both *sport event environmental managerial performance* and *sport event environmental operational performance*. Importantly, the chapter promoted that you must devise your vision concerning the level of environmental sustainability for an event, set the targets, and then, importantly, track/monitor the activities and be ready to institute implementation strategies to ensure the sport event environmentally friendly strategies are implemented and are successful. Overall, the management team of each event is responsible for the safeguarding of the natural environment for future sporting generations.

References

Braam, G. and Nijssen, E. (2004). Performance effects of using the balanced scorecard: A note on the Dutch experience. *Long Range Planning, 37*, 335–49.

Brymer, E., Downey, G., and Gray, T. (2009). Extreme sports as a precursor to environmental sustainability. *Journal of Sport and Tourism, 14*, 1–12.

Case, R. (2013, May 23). Severe weather forces LPGA to shorten course layout. Available online at www.parstars.com/Golf-News/Story/ArticleId/190.aspx (accessed March 2015).

CBC News. (2010). No snow at Olympic site leaves VANOC scrambling. Available online at www.cbc.ca/news/canada/british-columbia/no-snow-at-olympic-site-leaves-vanoc-scrambling-1.918004 (accessed June 2013).

Collins, A., Flynn, A., Munday, M., and Roberts, A. (2007). Assessing the environmental consequences of major sport events: The 2003/04 FA Cup Final. *Urban Studies, 44*, 457–76.

Dingle, G. (2009). Sustaining the race: A review of literature pertaining to the environmental sustainability of motorsport. *International Journal of Sport Marketing and Sponsorship, 11*, 80–96.

Dolf, M. (2011). Life cycle assessment of the UBC Thunderbirds teams, events, and venues, Vancouver, UBC Centre for Sport and Sustainability. Available online at http://circle.ubc.ca/handle/2429/42332 (accessed June 2013).

Dolles, H. and Soderman, S. (2010). Addressing ecology and sustainability in mega-sporting events: The 2006 Football World Cup in Germany. *Journal of Management and Organization, 16*, 603–16.

Enwave Energy Corporation. (2014). Downtown Toronto is chilling with Enwave. Available online at www.enwave.com/district_cooling_system.html (accessed June 2013).

Fédération Internationale de Football Association (FIFA). (2006). *Green goal: The environmental concept for the 2006 FIFA World Cup.* Report published by the Organizing Committee, 2006 FIFA World Cup.

Fédération Internationale de Football Association (FIFA). (2013). FIFA and the environment. Available online at www.fifa.com/aboutfifa/socialresponsibility/environmental.html (accessed June 2013).

Folke, C. (2006). Resilience: The emergence of a perspective for social-ecological systems analyses. *Global Environmental Change, 16*, 253–67.

Glavič, P. and Lukman, R. (2007). Review of sustainability terms and their definitions. *Journal of Cleaner Production, 15*, 1875–85.

Gunton, T. and Joseph, C. (2007). *Toward a national sustainable development strategy for Canada: Putting Canada on the path to sustainability within a generation.* Report to the David Suzuki Foundation, Vancouver, British Columbia, 4(4), 401–18.

Haigh, N.L. and Griffiths, A. (2009). The natural environment as primary stakeholder: The case of climate change. *Business Strategy and the Environment, 18*, 347–59.

International Olympic Committee (IOC) Olympic Charter (2013). Mission and role of the IOC. Available online at www.olympic.org/Documents/olympic_charter_en.pdf (accessed June 2013).

International Standards Organization (ISO) 14004. (2004). Environmental management systems: General guidelines on principles, systems and support techniques. Available online at www.iso.org/iso/catalogue_detail?csnumber=31808 (accessed June 2013).

Kearins, K. and Pavlovich, K. (2002). The role of stakeholders in Sydney's Green Games. *Corporate Social Responsibility and Environmental Management, 9*(3), 157–69.

Keogh, C. (2013). Greener golf operations: A comparative case study of Ontario golf courses engaged in environmental sustainability initiatives. Unpublished Master's thesis, Faculty of Applied Health Sciences, Brock University.

Li, Y., Wang, X., Jin, Y., and Ding, Y. (2012). An integrated solar-cryogen hybrid power system. *Renewable Energy*, *37*, 76–81.

Mackey, J. and Sisodia, R. (2013). *Conscious capitalism*. Boston, USA: Harvard Business Review Press.

Mallen, C. and Adams, L. (eds). (2013). *Event management in sport, recreation and tourism: Theoretical and practical dimensions* (2nd ed.). New York, USA: Routledge.

Mallen, C., Adams, L., Stevens, J., and Thompson, L. (2011). Environmental sustainability in sport facility management: A Delphi study. *European Sport Management Quarterly*, *10*, 367–89.

Mallen, C. and Chard, C. (2011). A framework for debating the future of environmental sustainability in the Sport Academy. *Sport Management Review*, *14*, 424–33.

Mallen, C. and Chard, C. (2012). What could be in Canadian sport facility environmental sustainability. *Sport Management Review*, *15*, 230–43.

Mallen, C., Chard, C., and Adams, L. (2013). A water resource sustainability best practice at a sport facility: A case study. *EYQEW*, *1*, 1–10. Available online at eyqew.com (accessed June 2013).

May, V. (1995). Environmental implications of the 1992 winter Olympic Games. *Tourism management*, *16*(4), 269–75.

McDonough, W. and Braungart, M. (2002). Design for the triple top line: New tools for sustainable commerce. *Corporate Environmental Strategy*, *9*, 251–8.

Olympic Global Impact (OGI). (2013, October). *Olympic Games Impact (OGI) Study for the 2010 Olympic and Paralympic Winter Games: Post-Games Report*. VANOC: Vancouver, British Columbia. Available online at http://css.ubc.ca/projects/olympic-games-impact-study/ogi-links (accessed June 2013).

Paquette, J., Stevens, J., and Mallen, C. (2011). The IOC: An interpretation of environmental sustainability, 1994–2008. *Sport in Society*, *14*, 355–69.

Schmidt, C. (2006). Putting the Earth to play: Environmental awareness and sports. *Environmental Health Perspectives*, *114*, A286–A295.

The Associated Press. (2013). Floods, mudslides prompt state of emergency in Sochi. Available online at www.cbc.ca/sports/2.722/floods-mudslides-prompt-state-of-emergency-in-sochi-1.1867554 (accessed June 2013).

The Carbon Trust. (2007). Calculate your carbon footprint. Available online at www.carbontrust.com (accessed June 2013).

16

BUILDING SPORT'S GREEN HOUSES

Issues in sustainable facility management

Timothy B. Kellison

Overview

In this chapter, a review of green building in sport is provided. The chapter begins with a discussion of the current trends in sustainable sport facility design, with a focus on sustainable sites, water efficiency, energy and atmosphere, materials and resources, indoor environmental quality, and innovation in design and operations. Next, the most prominent certification systems for sustainable design are summarized. Current issues and challenges to sustainable projects in sport are then highlighted. In the chapter's conclusion, the future of pro-environmental design in arenas, ballparks, and stadiums is considered.

Introduction

There is little doubt that sport arenas, ballparks, and stadiums are deeply tied to their cities. The allocation of millions, and sometimes billions, of public dollars toward the construction or renovation of sport facilities implies that policymakers, local residents, and athletic teams attribute significant value to these venues (Long 2013). Much of this supposed worth is financial: the sport facility provides a home for a high-profile professional team or event, which may consequently produce greater tax revenues, create jobs, and stimulate urban renewal (Kellison & Mondello 2012). However, other perceived benefits of mega sport facilities are largely symbolic. As one of the most recognizable structures in a cityscape, a stadium may induce civic pride or invoke positive feelings of nostalgia among local residents (Horne 2011; Seifried & Meyer 2010). Furthermore, in a business in which teams' star players can be traded in an instant, the facility is a stable and familiar face of the sport organization.

Given the symbolism ascribed to sport facilities by fans, elected officials, ordinary citizens, historians, urban planners, and sportswriters, it should come as no surprise that sport organizations have begun using their facilities as symbols in their broad strategic communications. These messages are delivered in unique ways across all levels of sport: a small town might finance new green spaces to signal its pledge to curbing childhood obesity; a local park might institute a public smoking ban to encourage healthier living; and—central to this chapter—a team might incorporate pro-environmental elements into the design of a new facility in order to demonstrate its commitment to environmental stewardship.

This chapter explores the integration of pro-environmental design in the planning, construction, operation, and maintenance of sport facilities. In the first section, I highlight recent technological advances and strategic initiatives in sport facility management. One of the most popular trends—third-party accreditation—is further detailed in the second section. Third, I identify the key concerns of those contemplating sustainable design. This chapter concludes with a discussion of future directions in sustainable facility management.

Trends in facility design

In the U.S., buildings are responsible for 14 percent of the nation's potable water consumption, 30 percent of waste output, 40 percent of raw materials use, 38 percent of carbon dioxide emissions, 24–50 percent of energy use, and 72 percent of electricity consumption (U.S. Green Building Council 2011). Given their expansive designs and the vast number of spectators they serve, sport facilities are expected to account for a significant portion of natural resource consumption. For instance, it was widely reported in 2013 that AT&T Stadium, home of the Dallas Cowboys, consumed more electricity on game days than the entire country of Liberia (Lefebvre 2013). Due in part to mounting pressure to operate their businesses in more environmentally conscientious ways, many sport organizations have begun looking at innovative means to manage their facilities in order to showcase their staunch support of pro-environmental initiatives.

The U.S. Green Building Council (USGBC), the organization responsible for the popular Leadership in Energy and Environmental Design rating system (LEED, discussed later in this chapter), outlines six broad categories in which organizations can reduce their environmental impacts. As summarized in Table 16.1 and discussed further below, these categories represent building and design considerations as well as operations and maintenance. Furthermore, they can be applied to both new constructions and existing facilities.

Sustainable sites

A key consideration of sustainable design is made before the first foundations are poured. During the site-selection process, designers, planners, and team officials

TABLE 16.1 Strategies in sustainable sport facility design and operations

Strategy	Example
Sustainable sites	
Brownfield location	Nationwide Arena (Columbus, OH)
Accessibility of public transportation	London Olympic Park (U.K.)
Carpooling incentives	Dodger Stadium (Los Angeles, CA)
Water efficiency	
Water conservation in restrooms	Sanford Stadium (Athens, GA)
Greywater reuse	Dakota Community Centre (Winnipeg, MB)
Rainwater harvesting	Suncorp Stadium (Queensland, Australia)
Energy and atmosphere	
Passive ventilation	ANZ Stadium (Sydney, Australia)
Neighborhood planning	Oriole Park at Camden Yards (Baltimore, MD)
Installation of wind turbines	Lincoln Financial Field (Philadelphia, PA)
Installation of solar panels	National Stadium (Kaohsiung, Taiwan)
Materials and resources	
Recycled building materials	Nike Reuse-a-Shoe
Recycling programs	Ohio Stadium (Columbus, OH)
Indoor environmental quality	
LED lighting/reduced spill light	Bell Centre (Montreal, QC)
Innovation in design and operations	
Compostable cups	Jobing.com Arena (Phoenix, AZ)
Temporary facilities and seating	London Olympic Park (U.K.)
Shared or dual-purpose facilities	MetLife Stadium (East Rutherford, NJ)
Repurposing existing venues	2020 Olympic Games (Tokyo, Japan)
Green building certification	LEED, BREEAM

Source: author.

must think about myriad environmental factors, including location and linkages, neighborhood patterns and design, access to transportation, stormwater management, and the heat island effect (USGBC 2011). Ideal development sites should encourage *smart growth* ("an approach that protects open space and farmland by emphasizing development with housing and transportation choices near jobs, shops, and schools" (USGBC 2011: 51)), sufficiently respond to stormwater management without compromising the quality of surface and ground water, and minimize the increased air temperature that often accompanies urban spaces.

Historically, owners of big-time sport teams have not always been amenable to thinking seriously about the environmental impact of their site selections. Particularly during the "cookie-cutter" period of the 1960s and 1970s, the suburbs were a popular choice for a new stadium because of their proximity to the city's highway system and the abundance of space to build parking lots (Chapin 2000). In the past 20 years, however, many big-time sport facility constructions have returned to urban centers with the hopes of catalyzing economic activity, repopulating downtown residences, and revitalizing city centers (Santo 2010). Still, given the sprawling footprints of arenas, ballparks, and stadiums, selecting a sustainable site can be incredibly challenging for facility designers. In other words, landlocked urban cores afford few site choices for huge sport facilities.

Interestingly, the fact that many city building sites are landlocked has actually encouraged pro-environmental design in sport venues. For example, a number of new facilities have been built on *brownfields*, or land "which may be complicated by the presence or potential presence of a hazardous substance, pollutant, or contaminant" (Environmental Protection Agency 2011). In these cases, the land must be decontaminated before it can be developed, and thus projects built on brownfields "go beyond just reducing their effects on the environment and enhance the community" (USGBC 2011: 51). Brownfield redevelopments have been choices for sport developments of all types. With dramatic views of the Manhattan skyline, a golf course was built over once-abandoned and polluted land in Bayonne, New Jersey, providing a new recreational space for local residents (Holusha 2000). Similarly, Nationwide Arena in Columbus, Ohio, and Nationals Park in Washington, DC, were both constructed on brownfields (John Glenn School of Public Affairs 2008; Lambert 2008), as was London's Olympic Stadium and much of the surrounding park (International Olympic Committee (IOC) 2013).

Another challenge in sustainable site selection is responding to transportation needs. This problem is especially pronounced when designing large public assembly facilities like arenas, ballparks, and stadiums. The environmental impact of traffic can be tempered by locating the facility near public transportation hubs, encouraging the use of other forms of transportation like bicycling, and incentivizing travel by alternative-fuel and high-occupancy vehicles (e.g., by offering preferred or no-fee parking). Given the enormous amount of traffic large sporting events can generate, transportation planning is of central importance to facility and event planners. For example, in preparation for the 2012 Olympic and Paralympic Games, the city of London spent an estimated £6.5 billion upgrading its transportation infrastructure (Hervey & Chennaoui 2012). Elsewhere, during the 2013 World Series, Dodger Stadium officials waived parking fees for vehicles with four or more passengers, while Los Angeles' transit authority provided free stadium shuttles to anyone with game tickets (Nelson & Dilbeck 2013).

Water efficiency

In many cities, sport facilities have been at the center of water-management controversies. Faulty water pipes at Lucas Oil Stadium in Indianapolis resulted in an increase in monthly water usage from 2.5 million gallons to nearly 14 million gallons; this increase subsequently raised the facility's water bill by 240 percent, which the city was responsible for paying (Milz 2011). All across the globe, water-shortage crises have had wide-ranging implications for facility managers. For example, in Zimbabwe, football matches were canceled when the under-watered field was deemed too dangerous for play (Zililo 2013). Furthermore, questions were raised regarding Rio de Janeiro's readiness to host the 2014 FIFA World Cup and 2016 Olympic and Paralympic Games amid major water shortages in the city (Barchfield 2013).

Given the wide array of amenities offered in major sport facilities, managers face unique challenges due to the high demand for water and other resources. As part of a comprehensive water-conservation strategy, facility managers must consider ways to reduce both indoor and outdoor water use. Restaurants and food-preparation areas, public restrooms, locker room and shower facilities, heating and cooling systems, the maintenance of playing surfaces (e.g., irrigating fields or resurfacing ice), and landscaping not only place large demands on municipal water supplies, but they also produce significant amounts of wastewater that require proper processing by the city. In regions where water conservation is such a priority that field irrigation is restricted, artificial field turf can be installed (Clarey 2010). For existing facilities, outdated or inefficient systems have led some managers to devise creative ways to reduce water consumption: for instance, a 2007 drought in the southeastern United States led University of Georgia facility managers to post signs in the public restrooms requesting that patrons avoid flushing the toilets "if it's yellow" (Associated Press 2007). Other pro-environmental strategies for improving water efficiency have existed for some time, including the use of water-flow restrictors and automatic sensors on sinks, the installation of waterless urinals, landscaping with plants that require little watering, and harvesting stormwater to meet irrigation needs.

A number of sport facilities have adopted innovative techniques to improve water efficiency. In Manitoba, ice rink managers piloted a program in which greywater—spent water from sinks and showers—was reused in their ice resurfacing machines (Canadian Press 2011). At Target Field in Minneapolis, the Twins partnered with water-management company Pentair to install an advanced underground water collection, filtration, storage, and recycling system capable of irrigating the field for four hours at a rate of 125 gallons per minute (Pentair n.d.). Water collection is also a priority for large facilities such as Suncorp Stadium in Queensland, where managers take advantage of their oversized roof to capture rainwater for reuse (Suncorp Stadium 2010).

Energy and atmosphere

Along with concerns about water use, much of the attention on green stadium buildings has focused on ways to reduce reliance on nonrenewable resources and eliminate the emission of harmful pollutants into the earth's atmosphere. Systems that harness energy from renewable sources such as sunlight and wind are most recognizable, but facility designers and operators may also minimize their environmental impact in other ways. For example, a team might adopt a policy to purchase only appliances with satisfactory efficiency ratings, such as those meeting ENERGY STAR standards. Additionally, facilities with passive designs can benefit from so-called free energy, such as natural light and wind. ANZ Stadium, constructed for the 2000 Olympics and Paralympics in Sydney, utilized a passive ventilation system that cooled the facility by drawing "air out from the grandstand through thermal stacks" (BHP Steel 2003: 2). Routine equipment maintenance and regular energy audits are also important elements of energy efficiency; regardless of how well a system is designed, unmaintained or improperly operated equipment can negate pro-environmental effects.

The return of professional sport stadiums to their cities' downtown areas has also provided opportunities for city planners to build more sustainable urban communities. A host of cities have sought to use new arenas, ballparks, or stadiums as anchors of downtown revitalization projects or sports district developments, including Baltimore (Hamilton & Kahn 1997), Cleveland (Austrian & Rosentraub 1997), and San Diego (Chapin 2002). As noted by the USGBC (2011), "Community planning can support building configurations that minimize solar gain in summer and maximize it in winter" (65). When a sport facility is part of a larger master plan, designers can think about issues such as building orientation and transportation accessibility in order to exploit free energy and compel visitors to arrive using means other than single-occupant vehicles.

Perhaps the most visible cue that a sport organization is committed to reducing its environmental impact is the display of renewable energy systems such as solar panels and wind turbines. Smaller-scale projects—such as the single wind turbine erected above Cleveland's Progressive Field—serve as much to raise fan awareness as they do to reduce nonrenewable energy consumption (Kellison & Kim 2014). The three wind turbines built outside Apogee Stadium at the University of North Texas (UNT) are estimated to reduce energy consumption at the school's athletic facilities by a mere 6 percent (Figure 16.1). Yet, they serve as symbols of the university's environmental commitment and reminders of Apogee Stadium's status as one of the most eco-friendly sport facilities in the world (North Texas Athletics 2012). More sophisticated projects include:

- Lincoln Financial Field (home of the National Football League's Philadelphia Eagles), where wind turbines and solar panels are capable of producing six times the amount of energy consumed during Eagles games (Bauers 2013);

- the National Football League's San Francisco 49ers' partnership with NRG Energy to create the NRG Solar Terrace at Levi's Stadium (Levi's Stadium 2013); and
- the National Stadium in Kaohsiung, Taiwan (Figure 16.2), a 55,000-seat facility covered in 8,844 photovoltaic panels capable of generating enough energy to power almost 80 percent of the stadium's surrounding neighborhoods (Jordana 2013).

FIGURE 16.1 Apogee Stadium, located on the campus of the University of North Texas, was the first college or professional sports stadium to receive LEED Platinum certification

Source: Brandon Cooper.

FIGURE 16.2 The National Stadium in Taiwan, where over 8,000 solar panels make up its shell

Source: Peellden.

Materials and resources

Facility managers must be cognizant of the environmental impacts of their decisions at all stages of the building process. Beginning at the design phase, contractors should consider using green building materials when possible. Construction materials should be sourced locally, thereby reducing the need to transport materials over long distances. These materials should also be durable; made from *rapidly renewable materials* (which "can naturally be replenished in a short period of time"; USGBC 2011: 73) or from recycled material; and be capable of being repurposed at the end of the building's life cycle. Since 1990, the Nike Reuse-a-Shoe program has processed worn shoes into scrap material used to construct courts, tracks, and field turf in over 450,000 locations worldwide (Nike 2013). For London's Olympic Stadium, recycled aggregate was used in almost 40 percent of the concrete used; additionally, some of the 50 million tons of guns, ammunition, and knives collected by Scotland Yard were melted into scrap and used for the stadium's steel supports (IOC 2012; Meinhold 2010).

Waste management is another important component of sustainable facility planning and operations. During the construction stage, planners should develop strategies to repurpose building equipment and surplus materials no longer needed at the site. At many existing facilities, teams have begun instituting comprehensive recycling programs in order to manage the waste created during events. For example, officials at The Ohio State University recently launched their Zero Waste at Ohio Stadium initiative, endeavoring to divert more than 90 percent of the waste created on Saturday game-days through recycling and composting (The Ohio State University 2012).

Many teams have also been able to capitalize on fan appeal and the reverence often given to arenas, ballparks, and stadiums at the end of a facility's life span (Trumpbour 2006). Prior to facility demolition, teams often hold public sales for memorabilia and equipment, auctioning off a wide variety of keepsakes, including stadium seats; corridor signage; basketball nets and hockey goals; photographs; locker room doors; trainers' tables; lockers; benches; kitchen appliances; athletic equipment; flooring and field turf; dirt and sod; lawnmowers and other maintenance vehicles; medical equipment; trash cans; hot dog rollers and popcorn makers; and ceiling banners. In addition to the pro-environmental impact of diverting these items away from landfills, teams can benefit by avoiding the costs associated with equipment removal and by earning extra capital from the sale of obsolete—yet historic and sentimental—items.

Indoor environmental quality

The places where individuals work and patronize are worthy of facility managers' attention, as issues related to air quality, lighting, thermal conditions, and ergonomics can impact the health and well-being of building occupants (USGBC 2011). Managers for buildings of all types employ a number of strategies to improve indoor environmental quality, including improving air movement, installing entryway floor coverings, prohibiting smoking, using eco-friendly cleaning and pest-control products, and investing in ergonomic office furniture.

The complicated designs of sport facilities—enormous public-assembly centers with hundreds of supporting and auxiliary spaces—and the wide range of events that a sport facility might host demand a holistic approach to managing indoor environmental quality. For indoor sport facilities, an efficient ventilation system is especially important given the fumes created by the use of pyrotechnics at concerts, shows, and games. For outdoor facilities situated in mixed-use neighborhoods, designers have been charged with curbing the light and noise pollution accompanying evening sporting events.

Efforts to address some of these challenges have simultaneously improved occupant comfort, provided facility owners with utility savings, and produced environmental benefits. For instance, improved lighting technology has not only decreased the amounts of wattage and bulbs needed to light an outdoor field, but also has reduced spill light in adjacent neighborhoods. After switching to LED lighting in 2012, Montreal's Bell Centre realized an estimated C$125,000 in annual savings (Belson 2013). Additionally, to improve air quality, some ice-rink managers have sought to eliminate exhaust fumes caused by propane-powered ice resurfacers by switching to electric-powered alternatives (Caldwell 2009).

Innovation in design and operations

Many teams have devised creative design and operations strategies that do not fall under any of the aforementioned categories. These innovations range in cost and scope. For instance, a sophisticated solar array at Kauffman Stadium in Kansas City is being used to power the stadium's refrigeration system, thereby producing sun-cooled beer (Kaegel 2012). At many stadiums, that beer is being poured into compostable cups made from corn-based materials (e.g., Phoenix Coyotes n.d.).

On a larger scale, some sport-facility architects have begun rethinking the design process altogether:

• The London Olympic and Paralympic Games were hailed for building temporary facilities to house sports like basketball (Figure 16.3) and for its post-Games plan to downsize the Olympic Stadium (Oliver et al. 2012).

FIGURE 16.3 The Basketball Arena, a 12,000-seat stadium used for the 2012 Summer Olympic and Paralympic Games in London. The facility's design allowed for easy dismantling upon the conclusion of the games

Source: Matt Brown.

- The recent partnership between the National Football League's New York Jets and New York Giants to share MetLife Stadium not only saved money for the teams and government, but it also eliminated the harmful environmental impact of constructing two new stadiums (Bagli 2005).
- Of the 37 athletic venues proposed for the 2020 Olympic and Paralympic Games in Tokyo, 15 will be existing facilities (Martin 2013).

As discussed in previous chapters, sport organizations are increasingly engaging in marketing campaigns designed to raise awareness of the teams' own corporate pro-environmental strategies and to grow public interest in environmental issues. As part of their educational outreach, teams have highlighted their facilities' eco-friendly designs to captive audiences at sporting events and during stadium tours. As a reflection of their comprehensive commitment to green planning and operations, many teams have pursued and attained third-party certification of their facilities' pro-environmental designs. This accreditation process is discussed in further detail in the following section.

Green building certification

Managers of new or existing eco-friendly facilities may seek further validation of their sustainable initiatives after the construction or renovation process has been completed. A small—but growing—number of collegiate and professional sport facilities have met the design and operations standards of third-party organizations like the USGBC. Not originally designed with mega sport facilities in mind, these certification systems have challenged facility managers to think about innovative ways to meet tough environmental metrics.

Leadership in energy and environmental design

In North America, the USGBC's Leadership in Energy and Environmental Design (LEED) rating system is the most recognized third-party accreditor of green building (Chamberlain 2008). Worldwide, over 50,000 projects have received some form of LEED certification, with nearly 45,000 of these in North America (USGBC 2013). The LEED rating system consists of prerequisites and credits—or points—awarded for meeting standards in the following general categories: Sustainable Sites, Water Efficiency, Energy and Atmosphere, Materials and Resources, Indoor Environmental Quality, Innovation in Design, and Regional Priority (USGBC 2009). Based on the total number of credits received, a project may qualify for one of four classifications: Certified, Silver, Gold, or Platinum (in order of least number of credits required to greatest number of credits required).

While the LEED rating system can be applied to a number of project types including schools, healthcare, and neighborhood development, sport facilities typically fall into one of two rating categories: (1) New Construction and Major Renovations or (2) Existing Buildings (EB). In 2008, Nationals Park, home to

Major League Baseball's Washington Nationals, became the first LEED-certified sport facility across the major American sporting leagues: Major League Baseball, Major League Soccer, the National Basketball Association, the National Football League, the National Hockey League, and the Women's National Basketball Association. Since then, over 15 facilities in those leagues have received various levels of LEED certification, ranging from EB certification of Chicago's Soldier Field (built in 1924) to Gold certification of major-league facilities in Pittsburgh, Orlando, and Miami. College athletic facilities have also actively pursued LEED certification, including UNT's Apogee Stadium, which was designated LEED Platinum in 2011 (North Texas Athletics 2012).

International variants

Rating systems similar to LEED exist outside North America. The most recognized, the British-based Building Research Establishment Environmental Assessment Methodology (BREEAM), was developed in 1990 and has certified over 250,000 buildings worldwide (BREEAM 2013). Smaller-scale rating schemes exist in a number of other countries, including Germany (i.e., the German Sustainable Building Council's *Deutsche Gesellschaft für Nachhaltiges Bauen e.V.*) and Japan (i.e., Comprehensive Assessment System for Built Environment Efficiency). Like LEED, these rating systems have been used to designate sport facilities as green. In April 2013, Thyagaraj Stadium (Delhi) received a gold rating by the Indian Green Building Council (*Economic Times* 2013). Additionally, Aviva Stadium (Dublin) and the Millennium Stadium (Cardiff) both met the British Standard for Sustainability Management Systems for Events (BS 8901; British Standards Institution 2013).

While not an accreditation system, the International Organization for Standardization (ISO) provides a number of benchmarks intended to improve efficiency and minimize environmental impacts. Several of these standards have direct relevance to sport organizations, including ISO 14001 for environmental management and ISO 20121:2012 for event sustainability management. Metrics from both ISO 14001 and ISO 20121:2012 have been met by several professional teams (e.g., Manchester United's Old Trafford) and events (e.g., 2012 Olympic and Paralympic Games) (Lambert 2013).

Governance

As early adopters of the pro-environmental movement, many of the sport organizations highlighted in this chapter introduced their sustainable initiatives without pressure from league-wide guidelines or government mandates. Furthermore, the establishment of partnerships between like-minded organizations has provided a vehicle through which leaders in sport and environmental design can engage in meaningful discourse about trends, technology, and challenges to green building. For example, the Green Sports Alliance launched in 2011 "to help sports teams, venues and leagues enhance their environmental performance" (Green Sports

Alliance 2013a). What began as a small grassroots organization of six professional teams and five sport venues has since grown into an international network of over 190 professional and collegiate teams and venues (Green Sports Alliance 2013b). Each year, the organization holds an international summit at which members can learn about environmental best practices, engage in roundtable discussions, collaborate with other industry leaders, and tour eco-friendly facilities. The overnight growth of the Green Sports Alliance illustrates the current trendiness of sustainable practices in sport.

Of course, there are big differences between starting a recycling program and constructing a LEED-certified facility. As momentum for the green movement in sport continues to strengthen, governing bodies may elect to adopt formal environmental policies catering specifically to issues of sport-facility design. Already, some American counties and cities have offered tax breaks to facility owners for their inclusion of green stadium elements. Further, some policymakers have introduced legislation requiring that stadium proposals include plans for pro-environmental features before being considered for taxpayer support (Pfahl 2013). On the other hand, over 60 percent of new professional sport stadiums from 2006 to 2013 were constructed without the integration of major sustainable designs, and some lawmakers have pursued statewide bans on certain forms of pro-environmental certifications for government construction projects (Badger 2013). Clearly, consensus has yet to be achieved among civic leaders regarding the cost-effectiveness of sustainable arenas, ballparks, and stadiums.

Among governing bodies and sport leagues, environmental agendas are on the rise. Both FIFA and the IOC have insisted that cities bidding to host the organizations' flagship events make environmental-impact minimization a focus in their facility proposals (FIFA n.d.; Swan 2012). Due to their authority over selecting sites for their mega events, both FIFA and the IOC have substantial influence on whether World Cup and Olympic facilities are designed with sustainability in mind. Conversely, while broad initiatives like the NHL's Gallons for Goals and MLB's Greening Program may signal league-wide support of environmental causes, professional sport leagues have decidedly less control over their clubs' facility designs. Thus, given that teams are highly autonomous during the facility planning process, decisions to incorporate green designs into new venues are likely to rest on ownership and local government. So, what leads some facility owners to implement wholesale sustainable practices while others decline to invest in green technology? When deciding whether to pursue a sustainable facility design, a number of incentives and barriers are considered, as discussed in further detail below.

Challenges to sustainable design

The environmental, economic, and social benefits of sustainable design represent compelling reasons to engage in pro-environmental behavior. Owners of green sport facilities may realize positive publicity, new sponsorship opportunities, tax credits, reduced utility costs, longer facility lifecycles, and long-term savings

(Nyikos et al. 2012). Colleges and universities can expect to realize these benefits with greater confidence since there is no possibility that their teams will be sold. Short-term owners might also benefit when selling a team because of the value associated with a green building's technology and anticipated long-term savings. Despite these incentives, some decision-makers have been reluctant to adopt large-scale sustainable designs.

Upfront costs—both perceived and actual—are likely the top concern for decision-makers. In numerous studies, researchers have found *perceived cost premiums* in excess of 10 percent to be the biggest deterrent to green building (cf. Mapp et al. 2011). A recent analysis of LEED vs. non-LEED buildings by Nyikos et al. (2012) found actual cost premiums for LEED buildings averaged 4.1 percent. Despite the added cost of LEED-certified facilities, that same study found the long-term savings of green buildings to be significant: energy costs in LEED-certified buildings were 31 percent lower, while operating costs were US$.70 per square foot less than their non-LEED equivalents. While much of the higher cost is related to equipment, construction, and operations, a portion of the premium cost is related to obtaining formal accreditation. For example, the cost of LEED certification is calculated by the building's gross square footage, which can be quite high for sport arenas, ballparks, and stadiums. Mapp et al. (2011) estimated the direct cost for LEED certification to be less than 2 percent of the total project cost. Based on the average costs of MLB, NBA, NFL, and NHL venues from 2000 to 2013, this cost amounts to nearly $8 million per facility (Long 2013).

A second complication of embracing environmental measures is the historic lack of technological systems designed specifically for sport facilities. The sheer expansiveness of arenas, ballparks, and stadiums somewhat contradicts many sustainable design principles like utilizing smaller spaces with smaller footprints, limiting field irrigation, and repurposing and retrofitting existing facilities. As the growing number of pro-environmental sport facilities indicates, however, engineers have developed increasingly sophisticated ways to accommodate both environmental and guest-amenity needs. In fact, both AEG and Populous—two of the most well-known international sport-facility-design firms—have pledged commitments to environmental stewardship (AEG 2012; Populous 2013).

In addition to the historical engineering challenges, those sport facilities designed with the intent of receiving third-party accreditation have faced issues when trying to meet criteria of certification systems that were not specifically written for arenas, ballparks, and stadiums. For example, in order to receive certain LEED credits for Site Selection, the USGBC advises facility planners to *limit* parking (e.g., adding no new parking) so as to "spark interest in alternative transportation issues" (USGBC 2011: 54). While this strategy might be effective for smaller-scale projects, discouraging travel to a sport facility might have several drawbacks for collegiate and professional teams. First, teams would have to develop unconventional alternatives to handle the large volume of out-of-town guests arriving just for the event. Second, teams and cities would lose a large portion of parking revenue. Third, a loss of surface parking would threaten traditions like tailgating parties, possibly resulting in disenchanted fans (Holden 2013; La Gorce 2013). None of these factors negates the positive environmental impact of encouraging spectators to utilize public transit and seek other transportation alternatives, but each does raise economic and logistic questions for event planners.

Each of the three challenges discussed above is directly related to the relative newness of sustainable design in sport. Early adopters of green building have limited experience and information to deal with uncertainty about the construction and operating costs, sluggish technological innovation, and the complexity of applying conventional accreditation standards. Yet, interest and action in sustainable sport facility design continues to spread around the globe, with little sign of slowing.

Future directions

In many ways, large sport facilities are antithetical to green building. On game days, they create huge strains on local resources. They often draw tens of thousands of people to a single site, thereby increasing traffic that contributes significantly to air pollution. Facilities like football stadiums are used infrequently, while others constructed for international mega events like the Olympic and Paralympic Games may be abandoned altogether (cf. Pack & Hustwit 2013). But recent technological advances and the commitment to environmental stewardship by a growing number of sport organizations are highlighting the belief that sustainable sport is a worthwhile endeavor.

Looking forward, a number of facility planners have created ambitious designs for future sustainable stadiums. When it was announced that the 2022 FIFA World Cup bid was awarded to Qatar, some critics called into question the conventional wisdom of hosting an outdoor sport in such a dry and hot climate. In response to this concern, several architecture firms have released conceptual plans to keep the facilities cool. For instance, building designer Tangram Gulf proposed an innovative air-conditioning system for the stadium in Doha; instead of an electric-powered system, the stadium would be cooled by channeling desert winds (Grozdanic 2013). Another proposed solution to the Qatar heat is the use of artificial clouds, floating carbon structures that would shade spectators from the sun (BBC 2011); a similar system is part of a new proposed stadium in Croatia (Schwartz 2010). Plans for China's Dalian Shide Stadium call for green walls made of living plants that change color with the seasons, a feature unseen in any stadium before:

> [The design] represents a new direction in sports architecture by moving away from the creation of a building based on pure form. The organic architecture of the building challenges the typical stadium typology to become more than an impressive skin wrapped around an ordinary seating bowl.
>
> (Jordana 2009)

Like the other innovations discussed, Dalian Shide Stadium's planned living walls challenge traditional elements of building design by blurring the divide between steel-and-concrete sport venues and the natural environment.

Long a drain on their natural surroundings, today's mega sport facilities are being built with the environment in mind. Sustainable site selection, water efficiency, energy use, materials sourcing, and indoor environmental quality each challenge facility planners to think about new ways to positively contribute to the ecosystem. Due in part to the success of rating systems like LEED and BREEAM, sport-venue designers are answering calls to be more environmentally sensitive. Additionally, through engineering marvels like passive air-conditioning systems, artificial clouds, and living walls, sport facility planners are demonstrating the possibility of arenas, ballparks, and stadiums in new frontiers once thought of as unsuitable for big-time spectator sports.

Perhaps most important to keep in mind is that sustainable design in sport is still in its infancy. The addition of solar panels on stadium roofs, the adoption of LEED standards by college and professional teams, the sudden growth of the Green Sports Alliance, and the support of green initiatives by professional leagues are all developments of the past 10 years. There remains considerable uncertainty about some aspects of sustainable sport facilities, including their actual costs and benefits, the effectiveness of their green technology, and the public goodwill they generate. Despite these concerns, the exponential growth of green building in sport suggests that managers will continue to think about ways to temper their facilities' environmental impacts.

References

AEG (2012) 'AEG's 2012 environmental sustainability report'. Available online at www.aegworldwide.com/media/swf/2012_sustainability_report/index.html (accessed 20 November 2013).

Associated Press (2007) 'Georgia football fans told not to flush', *Associated Press*, 4 November. Available online at https://prev.dailyherald.com/story/?id=70575 (accessed 11 March 2015).

Austrian, Z. and Rosentraub, M.S. (1997) 'Cleveland's gateway to the future', in R.G. Noll and A. Zimbalist (eds) *Sports, jobs and taxes: The economic impact of sports teams and stadiums*, Washington, DC: The Brookings Institution Press.

Badger, E. (2013) 'Why are some states trying to ban LEED green building standards?', *The Atlantic Cities*, 28 August. Available online at www.theatlanticcities.com/design/2013/08/why-are-some-states-trying-ban-leed-green-building-standards/6691 (accessed 19 November 2013).

Bagli, C.V. (2005) 'Three winners in stadium deal: Giants, Jets and governor', *The New York Times*, 01 October. Available online at www.nytimes.com/2005/10/01/nyregion/01stadium.html (accessed 18 November 2013).

Barchfield, J. (2013) 'Brazil: Water shortage dries Rio de Janeiro taps', *Associated Press*, 29 October. Available online at http://bigstory.ap.org/article/brazil-water-shortage-dries-rio-de-janeiro-taps (accessed 16 November 2013).

Bauers, S. (2013) 'Philadelphia Eagles green: Lincoln Financial Field generating energy with solar panels, turbines', *Philadelphia Inquirer*, 16 April. Available online at http://articles. philly.com/2013-04-16/entertainment/38558948_1_don-smolenski-turbines-desean-jackson (accessed 17 November 2013).

BBC (2011) 'Artificial clouds could help cool 2022 Qatar World Cup', 24 March. Available online at http://news.bbc.co.uk/sport2/hi/football/9435035.stm (accessed 20 November 2013).

Belson, K. (2013) 'Sports beginning to see the energy-efficient light', *The New York Times*, 08 October. Available online at www.nytimes.com/2013/10/09/business/energy-environment/sports-beginning-to-see-the-energy-efficient-light.html?_r=0 (accessed 17 November 2013).

BHP Steel (2003) 'Olympic case study: Stadium Australia'. Available online at www. bluescopesteel.com.au/files/Stadium_Australia.pdf (accessed 17 November 2013).

BREEAM (2013) 'What is BREEAM?'. Available online at www.breeam.org/about. jsp?id=66 (accessed 11 March 2015).

British Standards Institution (2013) 'Standards'. Available online at www.bsigroup.com/ en-GB/standards (accessed 18 November 2013).

Caldwell, D. (2009) 'At 2010 Games, the ice rinks will be greener', *The New York Times*, 29 January. Available online at www.nytimes.com/2009/02/01/automobiles/01ICE. html?em (accessed 17 November 2013).

Canadian Press (2011) 'Recycled shower water eyed for ice rinks', *Canadian Press*, 07 July. Available online at www.cbc.ca/news/canada/manitoba/recycled-shower-water-eyed-for-ice-rinks-1.1029082 (accessed 16 November 2013).

Chamberlain, L. (2008) 'Serving architects, consultants in everything green become mainstays', *The New York Times*, 26 August. Available online at www.nytimes. com/2008/08/27/business/27green.html?pagewanted=all&gwh=FD4BEC722440FA7 ADD471BEBC488760E (accessed 18 November 2013).

Chapin, T. (2000) 'The political economy of sports facility location: An end-of-the-century review and assessment', *Marquette Sports Law Review*, 10: 361–82.

—— (2002) 'Beyond the entrepreneurial city: Municipal capital in San Diego', *Journal of Urban Affairs*, 24: 565–81.

Clarey, C. (2010) 'A surge in artificial turf', *The New York Times*, 21 October. Available online at www.nytimes.com/2010/10/22/sports/soccer/22iht-ARENA.html?pagewanted=all (accessed 16 November 2013).

Economic Times (2013) 'Delhi's Thyagaraj Stadium is country's first green stadium', *India Times*, 16 August. Available online at http://articles.economictimes.indiatimes. com/2013-08-16/news/41417815_1_first-green-stadium-thyagaraj-stadium-south-delhi (accessed 18 November 2013).

Environmental Protection Agency (2011) 'Brownfields definition'. Available online at www.epa.gov/brownfields/overview/glossary.htm (accessed 15 November 2013).

FIFA (n.d.) 'FIFA and the environment'. Available online at www.fifa.com/aboutfifa/ socialresponsibility/environmental.html (accessed 19 November 2013).

Green Sports Alliance (2013a) 'About the Green Sports Alliance'. Available online at http:// greensportsalliance.org/about (accessed 19 November 2013).

—— (2013b) 'Members benefits'. Available online at http://greensportsalliance.org/ members-benefits (accessed 19 November 2013).

Grozdanic, L. (2013) 'Tangram's Qatar World Cup stadium sculpts the desert wind to provide passive cooling', *Inhabitat*, 13 May. Available online at http://inhabitat.com/ tangrams-fifa-world-cup-2022-stadium-in-qatar-sculpts-the-desert-wind-to-create-passive-cooling-systems (accessed 16 November 2013).

Hamilton, B.W. and Kahn, P. (1997) 'Baltimore's Camden Yards ballparks', in R.G. Noll and A. Zimbalist (eds) *Sports, jobs and taxes: The economic impact of sports teams and stadiums*, Washington, DC: The Brookings Institution Press.

Hervey, L. and Chennaoui, O. (2012) 'Sky investigation: Olympics bill tops £12bn', *Sky News*, 26 January. Available online at http://news.sky.com/story/920409/sky-investigation-olympics-bill-tops-12bn (accessed 15 November 2013).

Holden, E. (2013) 'Mets fans upset by tailgate beer crackdown at Citi Field', *Yahoo! News*, 02 May. Available online at http://news.yahoo.com/mets-fans-upset-tailgate-beer-crackdown-citi-field-165700488.html (accessed 22 November 2013).

Holusha, J. (2000) 'Commercial property; turning brownfields into fairways and greens', *The New York Times*, 29 October. Available online at www.nytimes.com/2000/10/29/realestate/commercial-property-turning-brownfields-into-fairways-and-greens.html?pagewanted=all&src=pm (accessed 15 November 2013).

Horne, J. (2011) 'Architects, stadia and sport spectacles: Notes on the role of architects in the building of sport stadia and making of world-class cities', *International Journal for the Sociology of Sport*, 46: 205–27.

International Olympic Committee (IOC) (2012) 'Flexible and sustainable: London's Olympic Stadium sets new standards', 08 January. Available online at www.olympic.org/news/flexible-and-sustainable-london-s-olympic-stadium-sets-new-standards/170181 (accessed 17 November 2013).

—— (2013) 'London 2012's sustainable legacy lives on', 31 July. Available online at www.olympic.org/news/london-2012-s-sustainability-legacy-lives-on/205777 (accessed 15 November 2013).

John Glenn School of Public Affairs (2008) 'Assessment of the gross economic impact of the Columbus Blue Jackets and Nationwide Arena on the Greater Columbus Area'. Available online at http://glennschool.osu.edu/faculty/greenbaum_pdf/Phase1_report.pdf (accessed 16 November 2013).

Jordana, S. (2009) 'Dalian Shide Stadium/NBBJ', *Arch Daily*, 15 September. Available online at www.archdaily.com/35207/dalian-shide-stadium-nbbj (accessed 20 November 2013).

—— (2013) 'Taiwan solar powered stadium/Toyo Ito', *Arch Daily*, 17 March. Available online at www.archdaily.com/22520/taiwan-solar-powered-stadium-toyo-ito (accessed 17 November 2013).

Kaegel, D. (2012) 'Solar panels to help power Kauffman Stadium', *MLB.com*, 31 January. Available online at http://kansascity.royals.mlb.com/news/article.jsp?ymd=20120131&content_id=26525142&vkey=news_kc&c_id=kc (accessed 18 November 2013).

Kellison, T.B. and Kim, Y.K. (2014) 'Marketing pro-environmental venues in professional sport: Planting seeds of change among existing and prospective consumers', *Journal of Sport Management*, 28: 34–48.

Kellison, T.B. and Mondello, M.J. (2012) 'Organisational perception management in sport: The use of corporate pro-environmental behaviour for desired facility referenda outcomes', *Sport Management Review*, 15: 500–12.

La Gorce, T. (2013) 'New Jersey: Tailgate parties far beyond burgers and dogs', *The New York Times*, 24 October. Available online at www.nytimes.com/2013/10/27/nyregion/tailgate-parties-far-beyond-burgers-and-dogs.html (accessed 22 November 2013).

Lambert, G. (2013) 'Event sustainability management—ISO 20121 passes 2012 Olympic Games test', *ISO*, 09 January. Available online at www.iso.org/iso/home/news_index/news_archive/news.htm?refid=Ref1690 (accessed 18 November 2013).

Lambert, L. (2008) 'DC turns brownfield into "green" ballpark', *Boston Globe*, 29 March. Available online at www.boston.com/news/nation/articles/2008/03/29/dc_turns_brownfield_into_green_ballpark (accessed 16 November 2013).

Lefebvre, B. (2013) 'What uses more electricity: Liberia, or Cowboys Stadium on game day?', *The Wall Street Journal*, 13 September. Available online at http://blogs.wsj.com/corporate-intelligence/2013/09/13/what-uses-more-electricity-liberia-or-cowboys-stadium-on-game-day (accessed 15 November 2013).

Levi's Stadium (2013) 'NRG Energy installs 49th solar frame to complete Levi Stadium suite tower roof', 29 October. Available online at www.levisstadium.com/2013/10/nrg-energy-installs-49th-solar-frame-complete-levis-stadium-suite-tower-roof (accessed 17 November 2013).

Long, J.G. (2013) *Public/private partnerships for major league sports facilities*, New York: Routledge.

Mapp, C., Nobe, M.C. and Dunbar, B. (2011) 'The cost of LEED—an analysis of the construction costs of LEED and non-LEED banks', *Journal of Sustainable Real Estate*, 3: 254–73.

Martin, A. (2013) 'Tokyo promises to meld technology, tradition with 2020 Olympics', *The Wall Street Journal*, 08 September. Available online at http://online.wsj.com/news/articles/SB10001424127887323623304579062090411749578 (accessed 18 November 2013).

Meinhold, B. (2010) 'London's Olympic Stadium to be made out of recycled guns and knives!', *Inhabitat*, 20 January. Available online at http://inhabitat.com/confiscated-weapons-used-to-build-londons-olympic-stadium (accessed 17 November 2013).

Milz, M. (2011) 'Lucas Oil Stadium's water bills skyrocket', *WTHR*, 15 March. Available online at www.wthr.com/story/14258003/lucas-oil-stadiums-water-bills-skyrocket (accessed 16 November 2013).

Nelson, L.J. and Dilbeck, S. (2013) 'Cardinals game: Carpool incentive for Dodgers Stadium debuts Monday', *Los Angeles Times*, 14 October. Available online at www.latimes.com/local/lanow/la-me-ln-new-carpool-incentive-for-dodger-stadium-debuts-monday-20131014,0,1423637.story (accessed 15 November 2013).

Nike (2013) 'Reuse-a-Shoe'. Available online at www.nike.com/us/en_us/c/better-world/stories/2013/05/reuse-a-shoe (accessed 17 November 2013).

North Texas Athletics (2012) 'Apogee Stadium wind turbines'. Available online at www.meangreenmap.com/turbines.html (accessed 17 November 2013).

Nyikos, D.M., Thal, A.E., Hicks, M.J. and Leach, S.E. (2012) 'To LEED or not to LEED: Analysis of cost premiums associated with sustainable facility design', *Engineering Management Journal*, 24: 50–62.

Oliver, M., O'Mahony, J. and Palmer, D. (2012) 'London 2012 Olympics: Venue guide', *The Telegraph*, 23 July. Available online at www.telegraph.co.uk/sport/olympics/7908313/London-2012-Olympics-venue-guide.html (accessed 18 November 2013).

Pack, J. and Hustwit, G. (2013) *The Olympic city*, sine loco: John Pack and Gary Hustwit.

Pentair (n.d.) 'Helping the Twins hit a "green" grand slam'. Available online at www.pentair.com/case-studies/case-study-2.html (accessed 16 November 2013).

Pfahl, M. (2013) 'The environmental awakening in sport', *Solutions*, 4: 67–76.

Phoenix Coyotes (n.d.) 'Going green'. Available online at http://coyotes.nhl.com/club/page.htm?id=32755 (accessed 18 November 2013).

Populous (2013) 'Sustainability'. Available online at http://populous.com/expertise/sustainability (accessed 20 November 2013).

Santo, C.A. (2010) 'Economic impact of sport stadiums, teams, and events', in C.A. Santo and G.C.S. Mildner (eds) *Sport and public policy: Social, political, and economic perspectives*, Champaign, IL: Human Kinetics.

Schwartz, A. (2010) 'Blue Volcano: A futuristic cloud-covered stadium for Croatia', *Fast Company*, 05 January. Available online at www.fastcompany.com/1506266/blue-volcano-futuristic-cloud-covered-stadium-croatia (accessed 20 November 2013).

Seifried, C.S. and Meyer, K. (2010) 'Nostalgia-related aspects of professional sport facilities: A facility audit of Major League Baseball and National Football League strategies to evoke the past', *International Journal of Sport Management, Recreation & Tourism*, 5: 51–76.

Suncorp Stadium (2010) 'Environment'. Available online at www.suncorpstadium.com.au/The_Stadium/Environment.aspx (accessed 16 November 2013).

Swan, R. (2012) 'Sustainability isn't just management-speak, it's about making the Games happen', *Inside the Games*, 23 July. Available online at www.insidethegames.biz/sustainability/16817-sustainability-isnt-just-management-speak-its-about-making-the-games-happen (accessed 19 November 2013).

The Ohio State University (2012) 'Zero waste at Ohio Stadium: Achieving zero in 2012'. Available online at http://footprint.osu.edu/assets/files/zerowaste/ZeroWaste_2012_Overview_WEB%20full%20quality.pdf (accessed 17 November 2013).

Trumpbour, R.C. (2006) *The new cathedrals: Politics and media in the history of stadium construction*, Syracuse, NY: Syracuse University Press.

U.S. Green Building Council (2009) *Green building design and construction*, Washington, DC: U.S. Green Building Council.

—— (2011) *Green building and LEED core concepts*, 2nd edn, Washington, DC: U.S. Green Building Council.

—— (2013) 'Infographic: LEED in the world'. Available online at www.usgbc.org/articles/infographic-leed-world (accessed 18 November 2013).

Zililo, R. (2013) 'Water shortage hits city stadia', *Chronicle*, 22 October. Available online at www.chronicle.co.zw/water-shortage-hits-city-stadia (accessed 16 November 2013).

INDEX

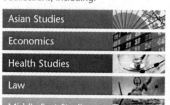